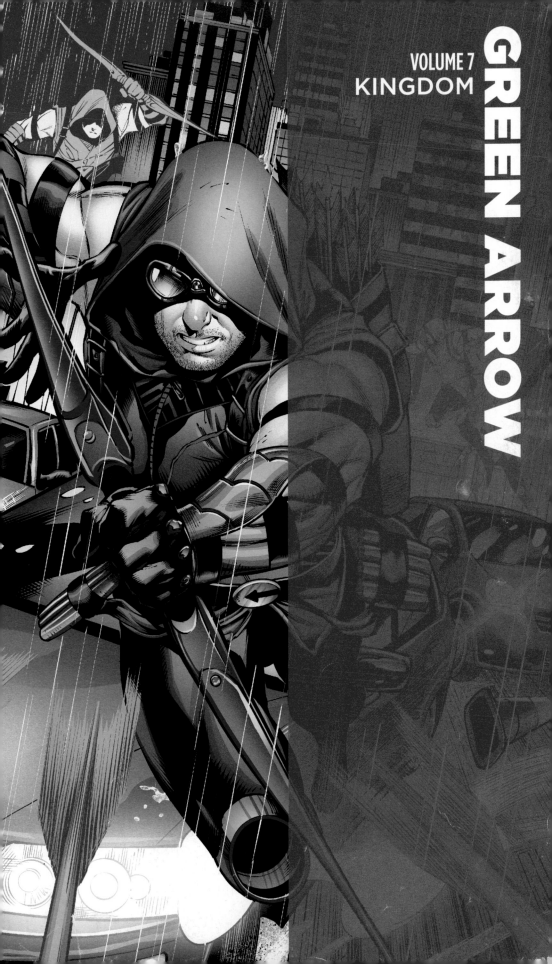

VOLUME 7
KINGDOM

GREEN ARROW

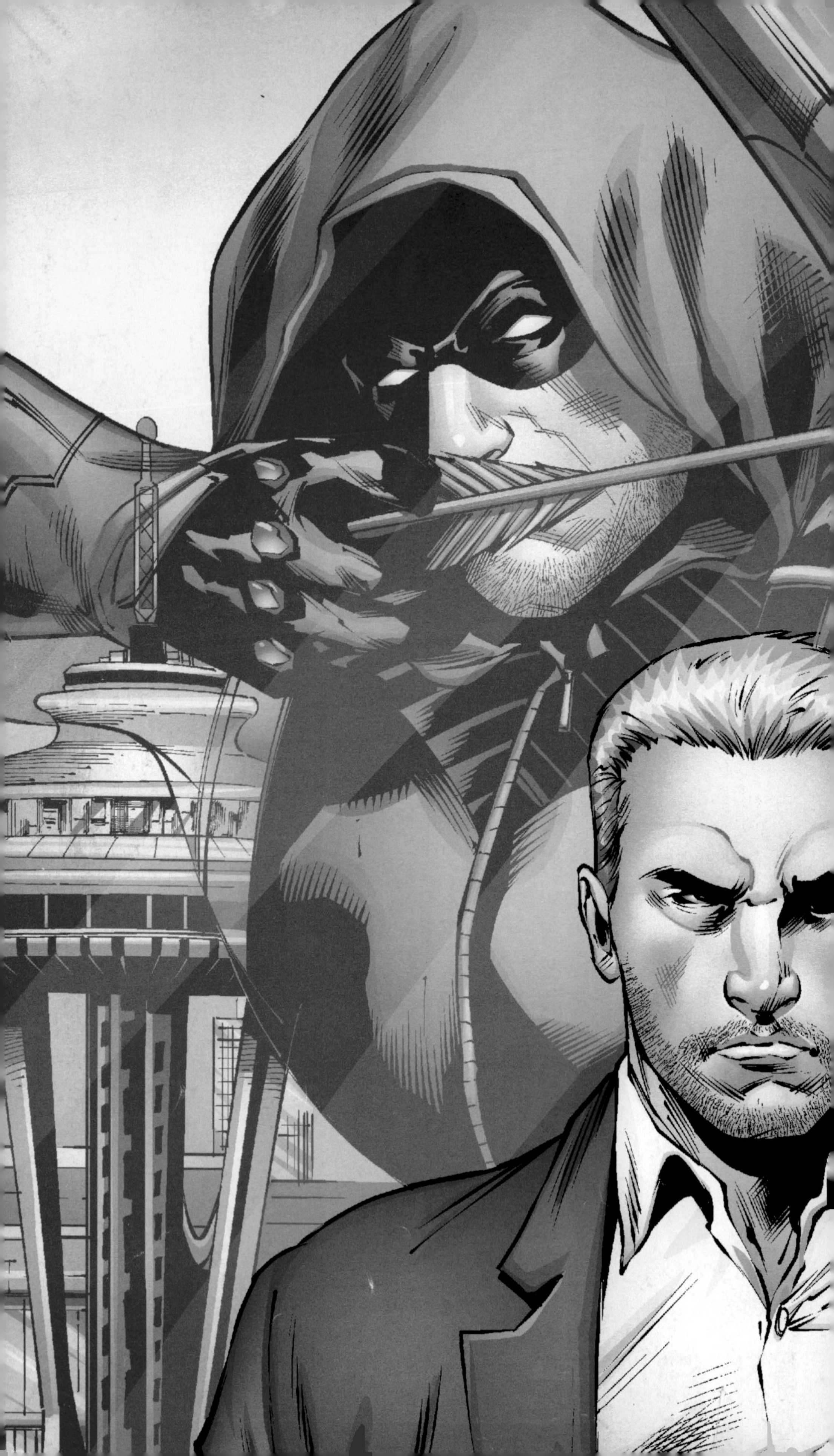

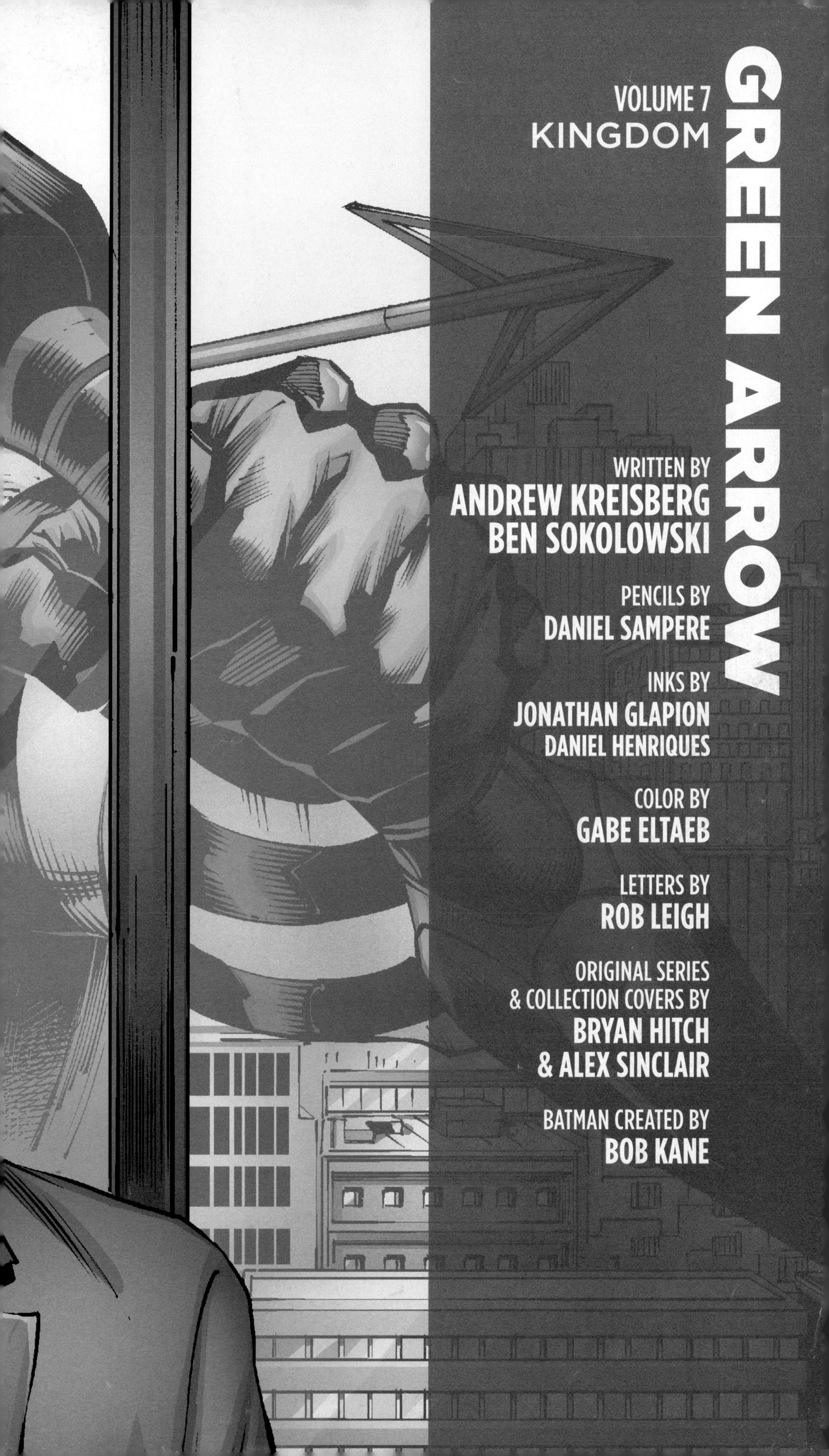

GREEN ARROW

VOLUME 7
KINGDOM

WRITTEN BY
ANDREW KREISBERG
BEN SOKOLOWSKI

PENCILS BY
DANIEL SAMPERE

INKS BY
JONATHAN GLAPION
DANIEL HENRIQUES

COLOR BY
GABE ELTAEB

LETTERS BY
ROB LEIGH

ORIGINAL SERIES
& COLLECTION COVERS BY
BRYAN HITCH
& ALEX SINCLAIR

BATMAN CREATED BY
BOB KANE

BRIAN CUNNINGHAM Editor - Original Series
AMEDEO TURTURRO Assistant Editor - Original Series
JEB WOODARD Group Editor - Collected Editions
LIZ ERICKSON Editor - Collected Editions
DAMIAN RYLAND Publication Design

BOB HARRAS Senior VP - Editor-in-Chief, DC Comics

DIANE NELSON President
DAN DiDIO and JIM LEE Co-Publishers
GEOFF JOHNS Chief Creative Officer
AMIT DESAI Senior VP - Marketing & Global Franchise Management
NAIRI GARDINER Senior VP - Finance
SAM ADES VP - Digital Marketing
BOBBIE CHASE VP - Talent Development
MARK CHIARELLO Senior VP - Art, Design & Collected Editions
JOHN CUNNINGHAM VP - Content Strategy
ANNE DEPIES VP - Strategy Planning & Reporting
DON FALLETTI VP - Manufacturing Operations
LAWRENCE GANEM VP - Editorial Administration & Talent Relations
ALISON GILL Senior VP - Manufacturing & Operations
HANK KANALZ Senior VP - Editorial Strategy & Administration
JAY KOGAN VP - Legal Affairs
DEREK MADDALENA Senior VP - Sales & Business Development
JACK MAHAN VP - Business Affairs
DAN MIRON VP - Sales Planning & Trade Development
NICK NAPOLITANO VP - Manufacturing Administration
CAROL ROEDER VP - Marketing
EDDIE SCANNELL VP - Mass Account & Digital Sales
COURTNEY SIMMONS Senior VP - Publicity & Communications
JIM (SKI) SOKOLOWSKI VP - Comic Book Specialty & Newsstand Sales
SANDY YI Senior VP - Global Franchise Management

GREEN ARROW VOLUME 7: KINGDOM

DC Comics, 4000 Warner Blvd., Burbank, CA 91522
A Warner Bros. Entertainment Company
Printed by RR Donnelley, Salem, VA, USA. 10/9/15.
ISBN: 978-1-4012-5762-0
First Printing.

Library of Congress Cataloging-in-Publication Data

Kreisberg, Andrew, 1971-
Green Arrow. Volume 7, Kingdom / Andrew Kreisberg, Ben Sokolowski, Daniel Sampere.
pages cm — (The New 52!)
ISBN 978-1-4012-5762-0 (paperback)
1. Graphic novels. I. Sokolowski, Ben. II. Sampere, Daniel, 1985- illustrator. III. Title.
PN6728.G725K65 2015
741.5'973—dc23
2015028079

PEFC Certified
Printed on paper from sustainably managed forests and controlled sources
PEFC/29-31-75
www.pefc.org

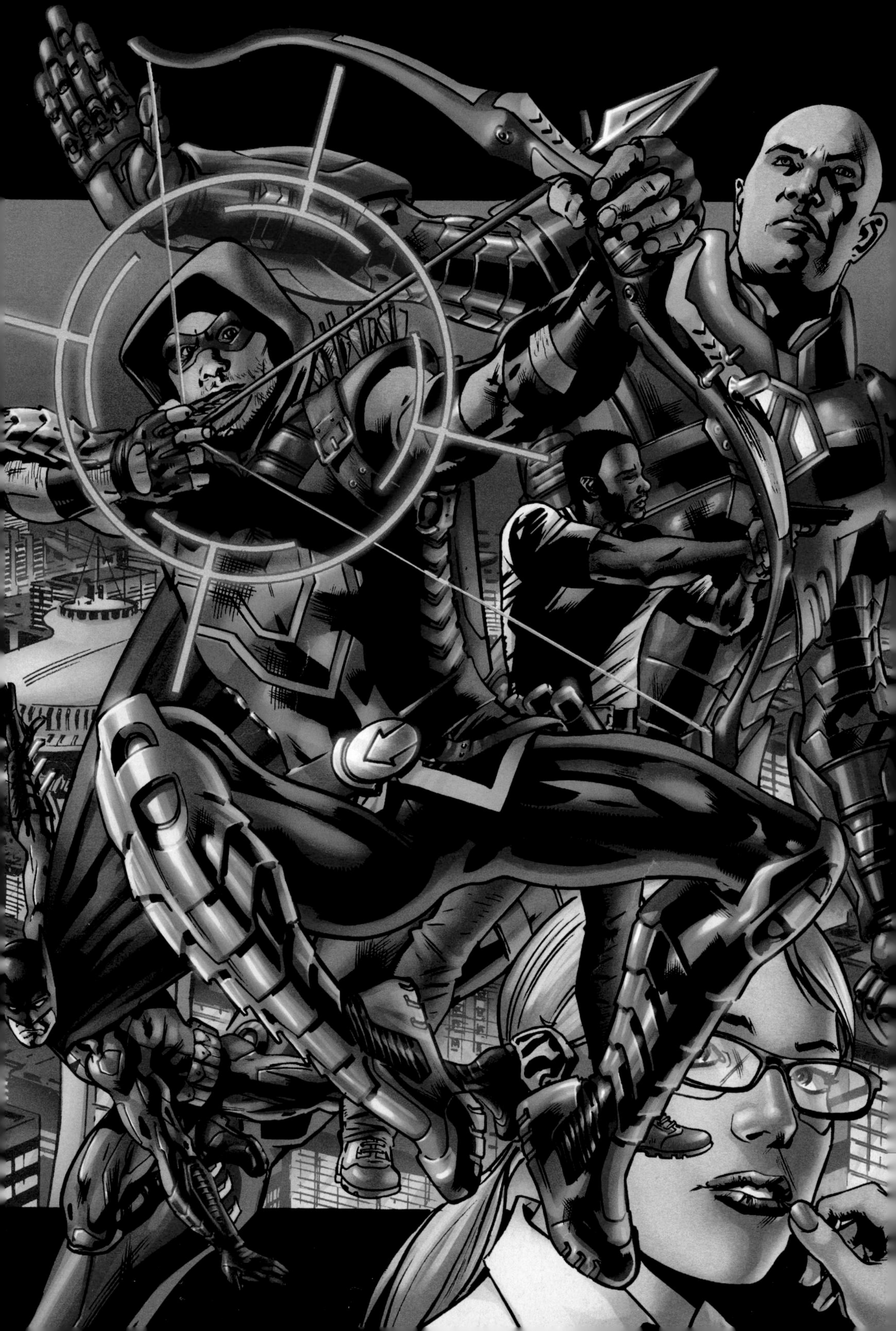

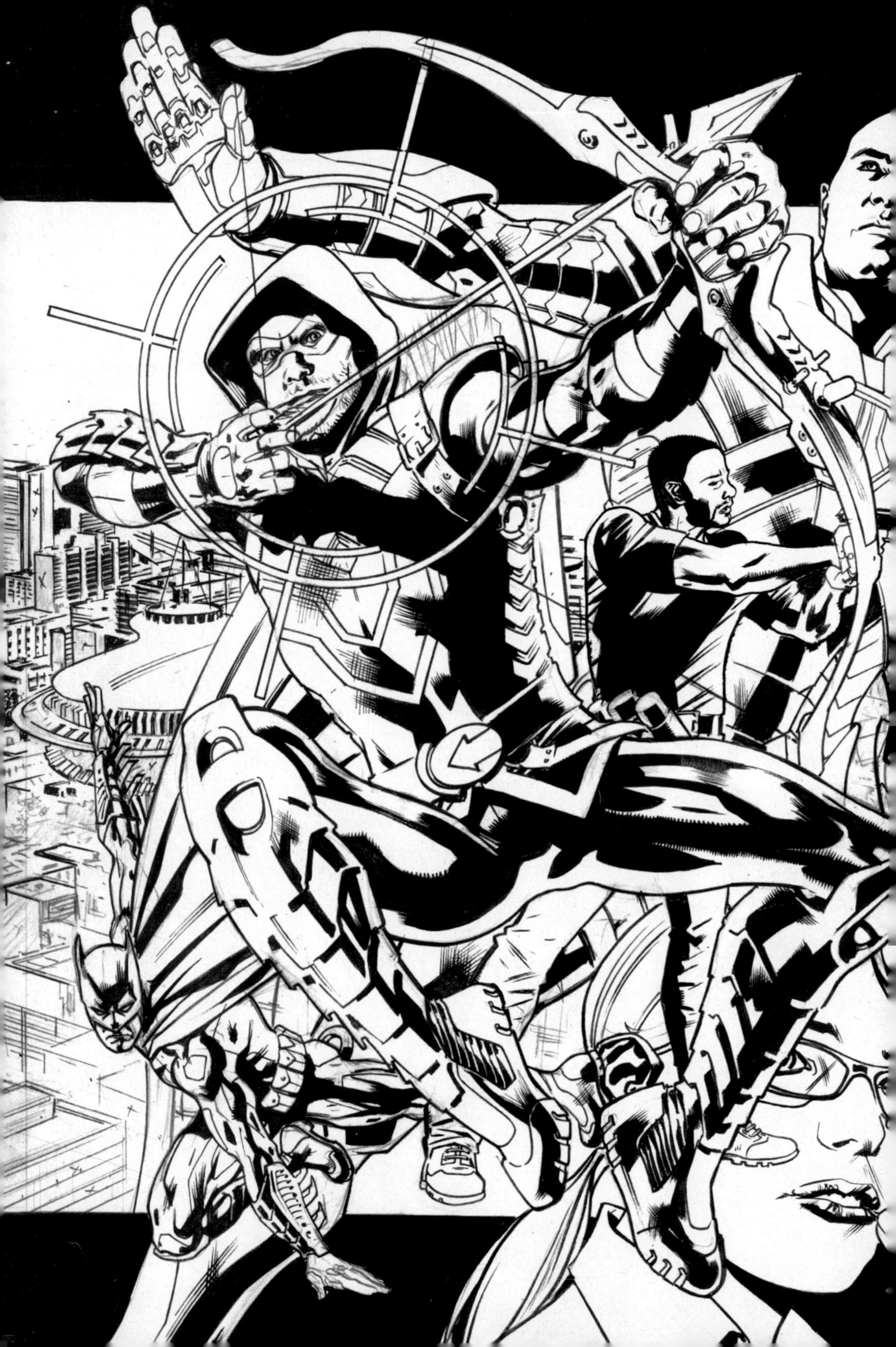

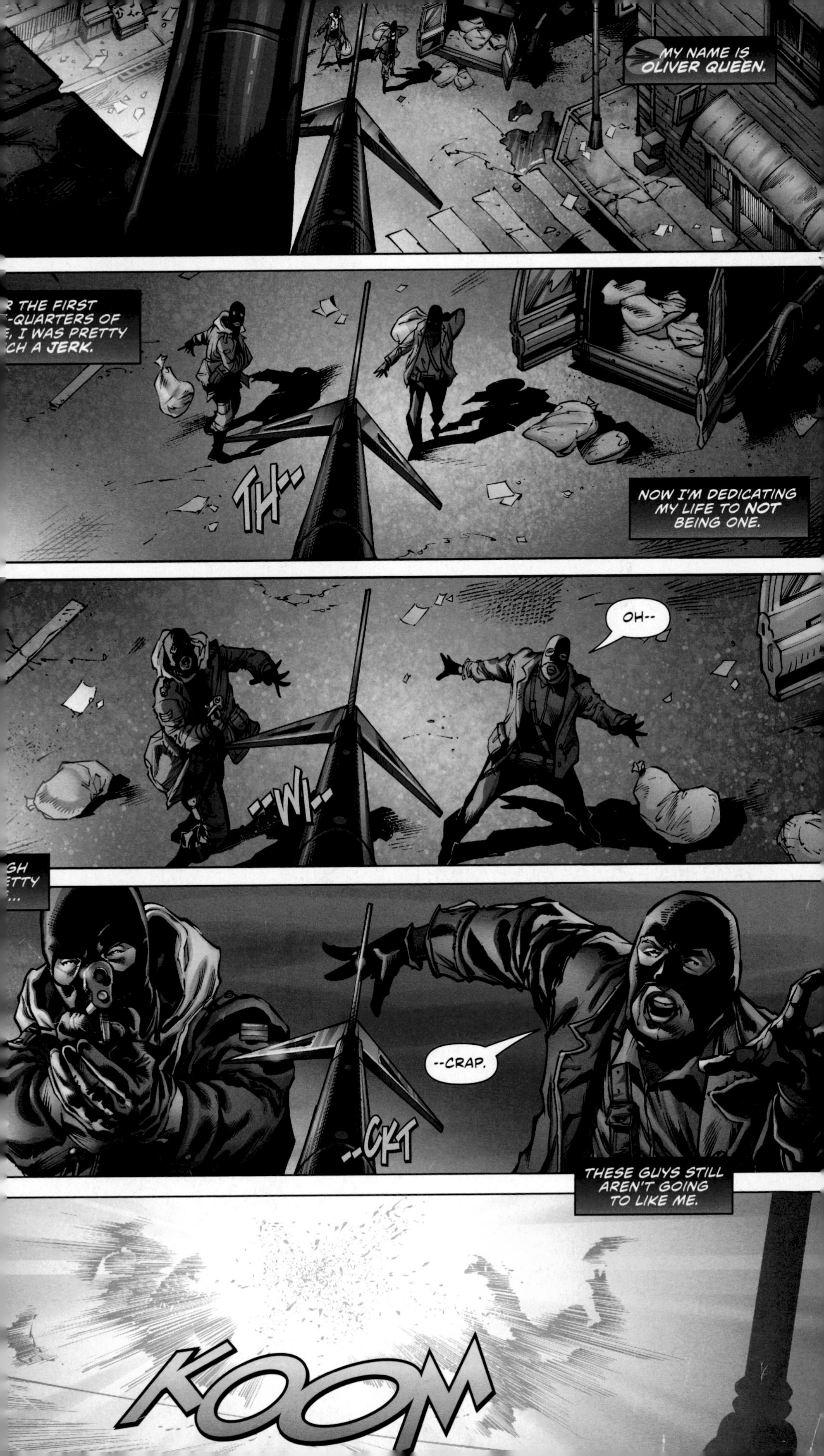
MY NAME IS OLIVER QUEEN.
R THE FIRST -QUARTERS OF E, I WAS PRETTY CH A JERK.
TH--
NOW I'M DEDICATING MY LIFE TO NOT BEING ONE.
OH--
--WI--
GH ETTY
--CRAP.
--CKT
THESE GUYS STILL AREN'T GOING TO LIKE ME.
KOOM

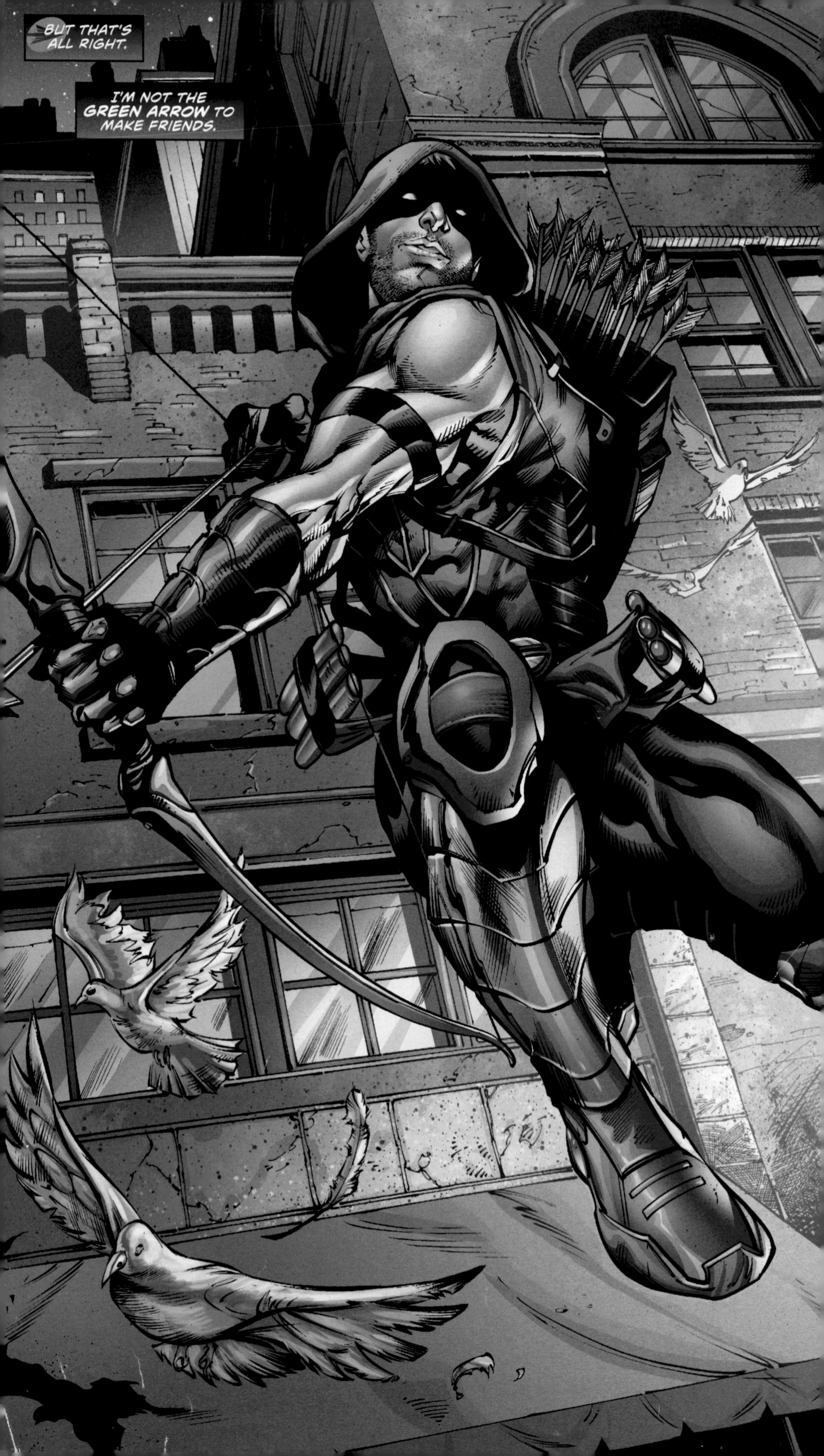
BUT THAT'S ALL RIGHT.
I'M NOT THE GREEN ARROW TO MAKE FRIENDS.

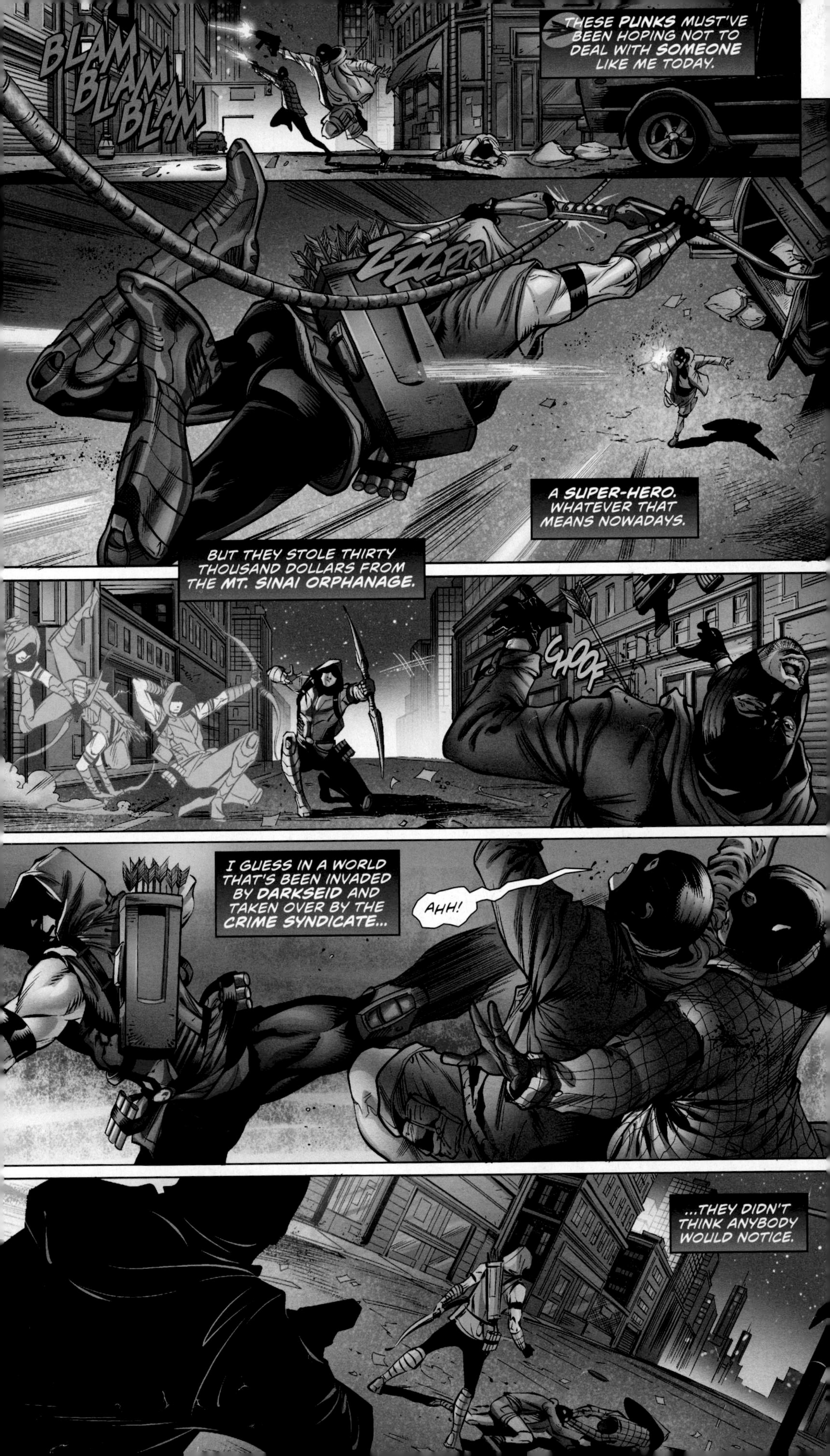

BLAM BLAM BLAM BLAM
THESE PUNKS MUST'VE BEEN HOPING NOT TO DEAL WITH SOMEONE LIKE ME TODAY.
ZZZPP
A SUPER-HERO. WHATEVER THAT MEANS NOWADAYS.
BUT THEY STOLE THIRTY THOUSAND DOLLARS FROM THE MT. SINAI ORPHANAGE.
CHOOF
I GUESS IN A WORLD THAT'S BEEN INVADED BY DARKSEID AND TAKEN OVER BY THE CRIME SYNDICATE...
AHH!
...THEY DIDN'T THINK ANYBODY WOULD NOTICE.

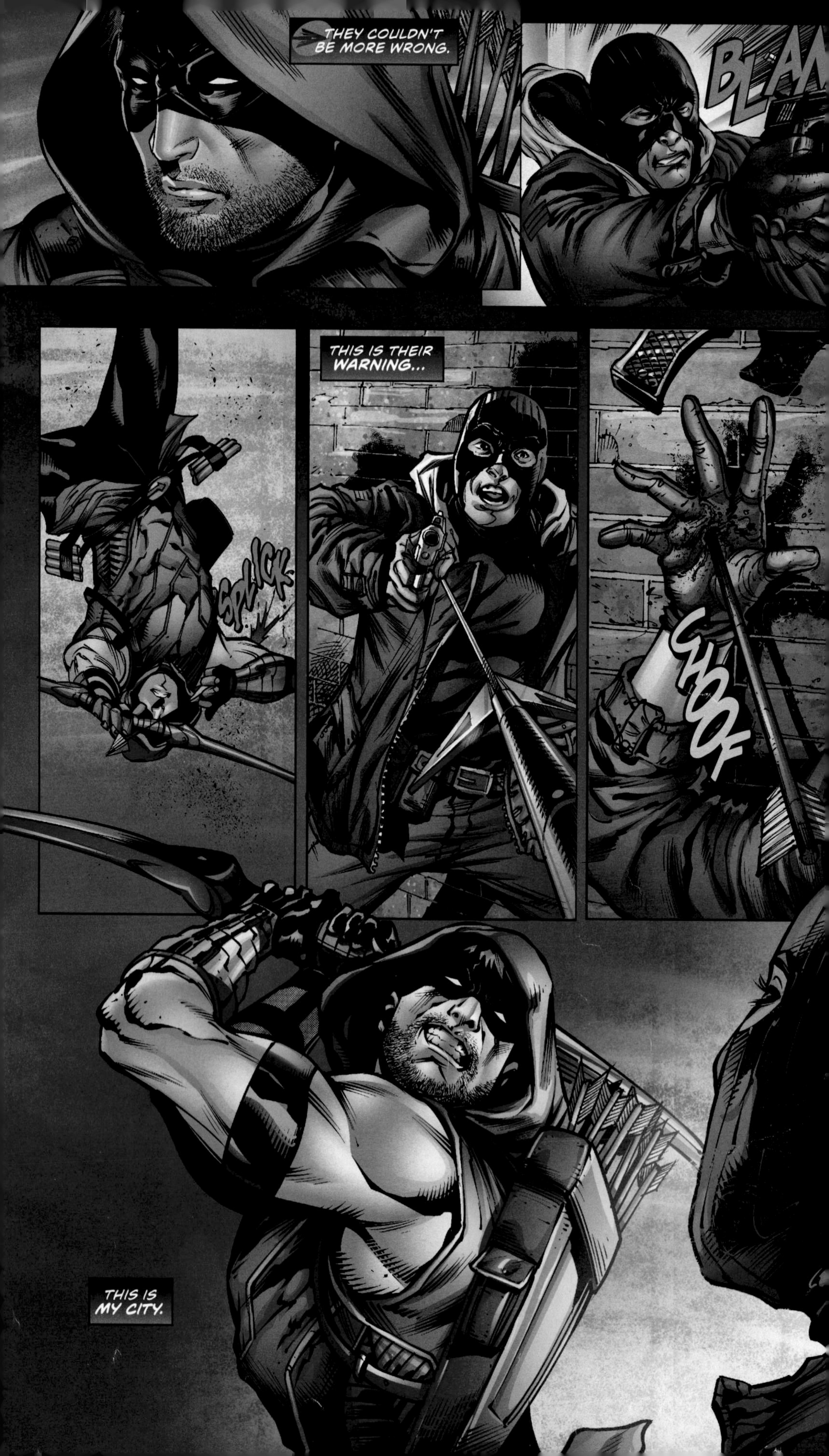
THEY COULDN'T BE MORE WRONG.
BLAM
SPLICK
THIS IS THEIR WARNING...
CHOOK
THIS IS MY CITY.

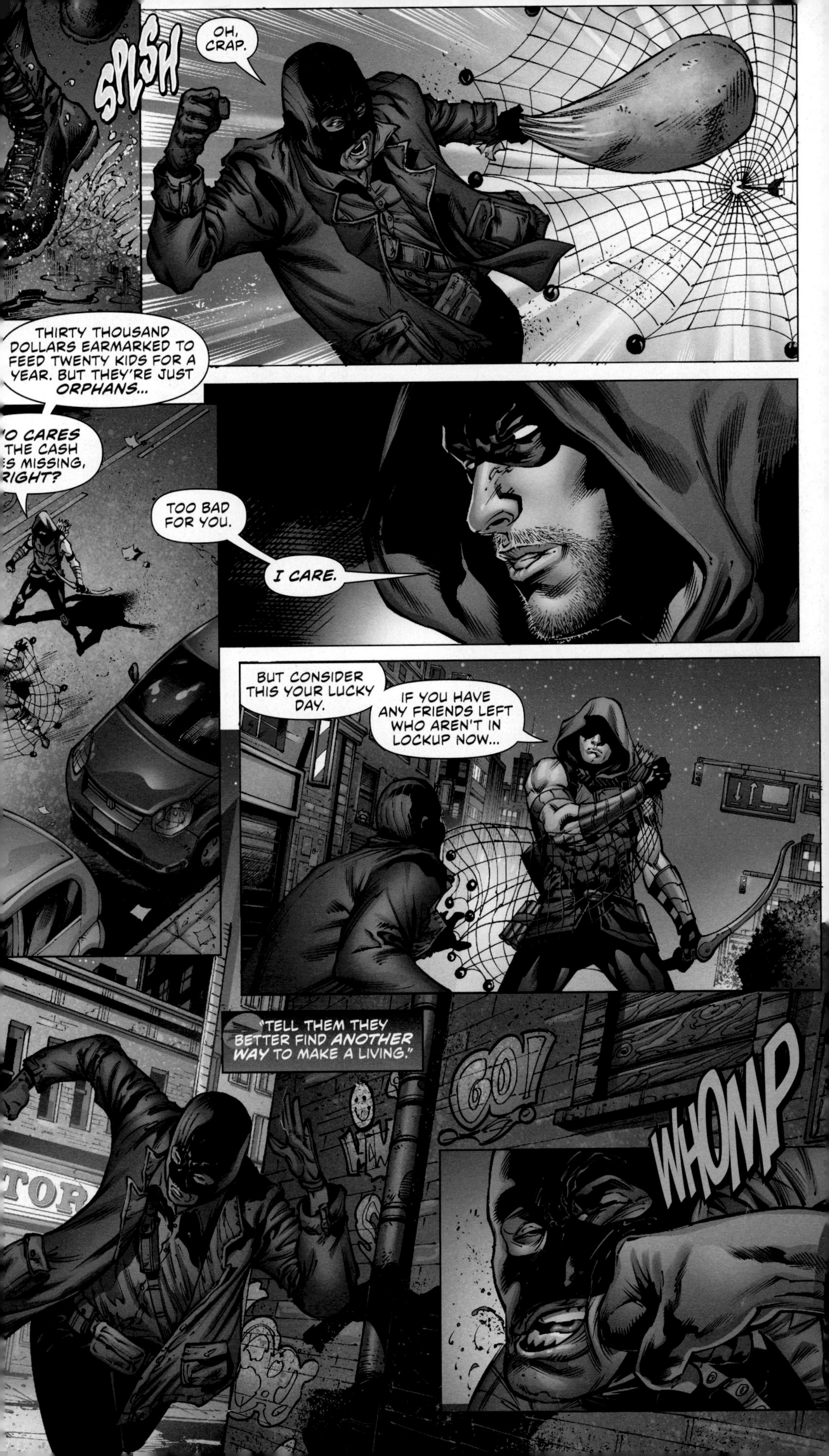
SPLSH
OH, CRAP.
THIRTY THOUSAND DOLLARS EARMARKED TO FEED TWENTY KIDS FOR A YEAR. BUT THEY'RE JUST ORPHANS...
THE CASH
RIGHT?
TOO BAD FOR YOU.
I CARE.
BUT CONSIDER THIS YOUR LUCKY DAY.
IF YOU HAVE ANY FRIENDS LEFT WHO AREN'T IN LOCKUP NOW...
"TELL THEM THEY BETTER FIND ANOTHER WAY TO MAKE A LIVING."
WHOMP

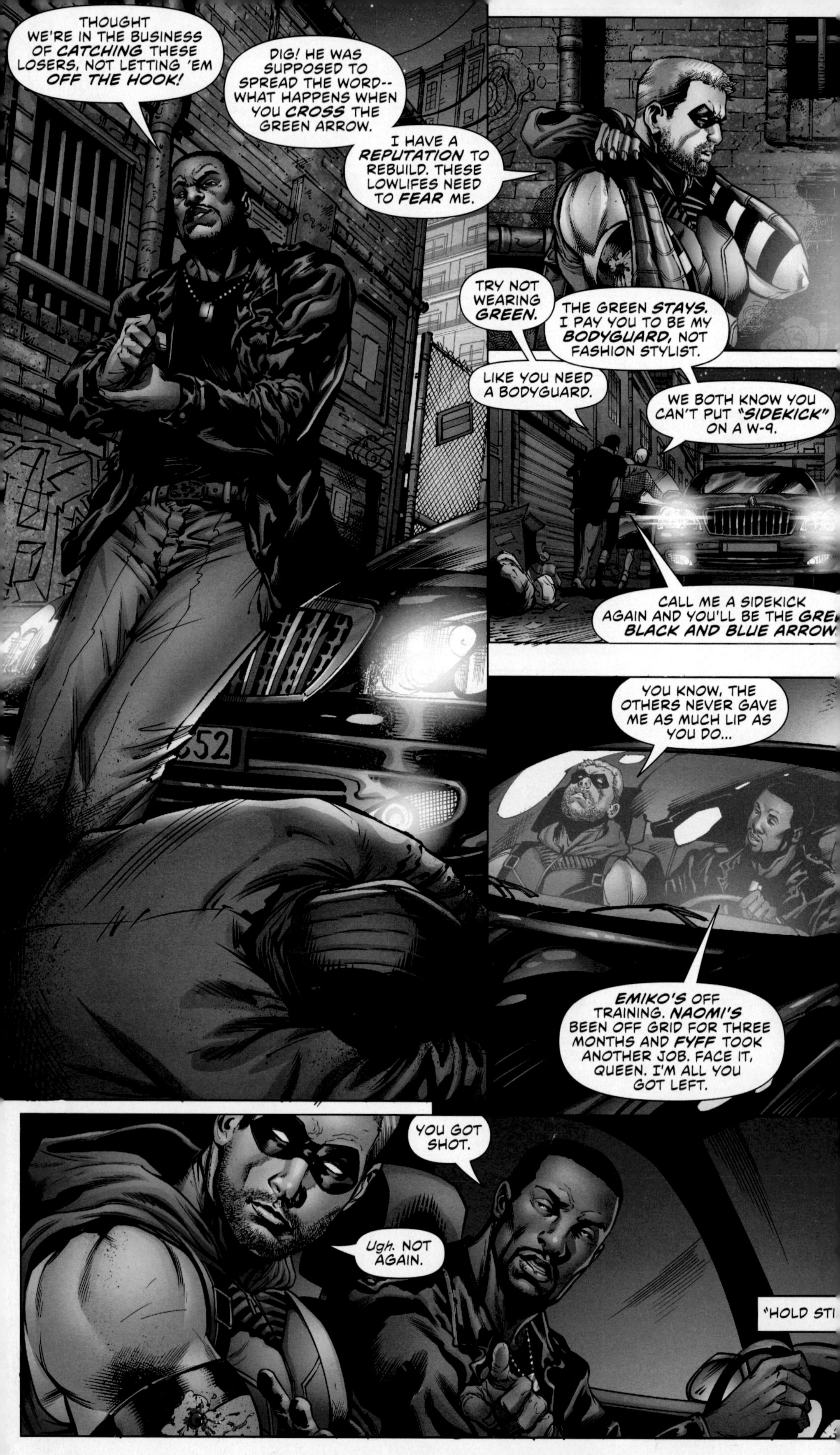
THOUGHT WE'RE IN THE BUSINESS OF CATCHING THESE LOSERS, NOT LETTING 'EM OFF THE HOOK!
DIG! HE WAS SUPPOSED TO SPREAD THE WORD--WHAT HAPPENS WHEN YOU CROSS THE GREEN ARROW.
I HAVE A REPUTATION TO REBUILD. THESE LOWLIFES NEED TO FEAR ME.
TRY NOT WEARING GREEN.
THE GREEN STAYS. I PAY YOU TO BE MY BODYGUARD, NOT FASHION STYLIST.
LIKE YOU NEED A BODYGUARD.
WE BOTH KNOW YOU CAN'T PUT "SIDEKICK" ON A W-9.
CALL ME A SIDEKICK AGAIN AND YOU'LL BE THE GRE
BLACK AND BLUE ARROW
YOU KNOW, THE OTHERS NEVER GAVE ME AS MUCH LIP AS YOU DO...
EMIKO'S OFF TRAINING. NAOMI'S BEEN OFF GRID FOR THREE MONTHS AND FYFF TOOK ANOTHER JOB. FACE IT, QUEEN. I'M ALL YOU GOT LEFT.
YOU GOT SHOT.
Ugh. NOT AGAIN.
"HOLD STI

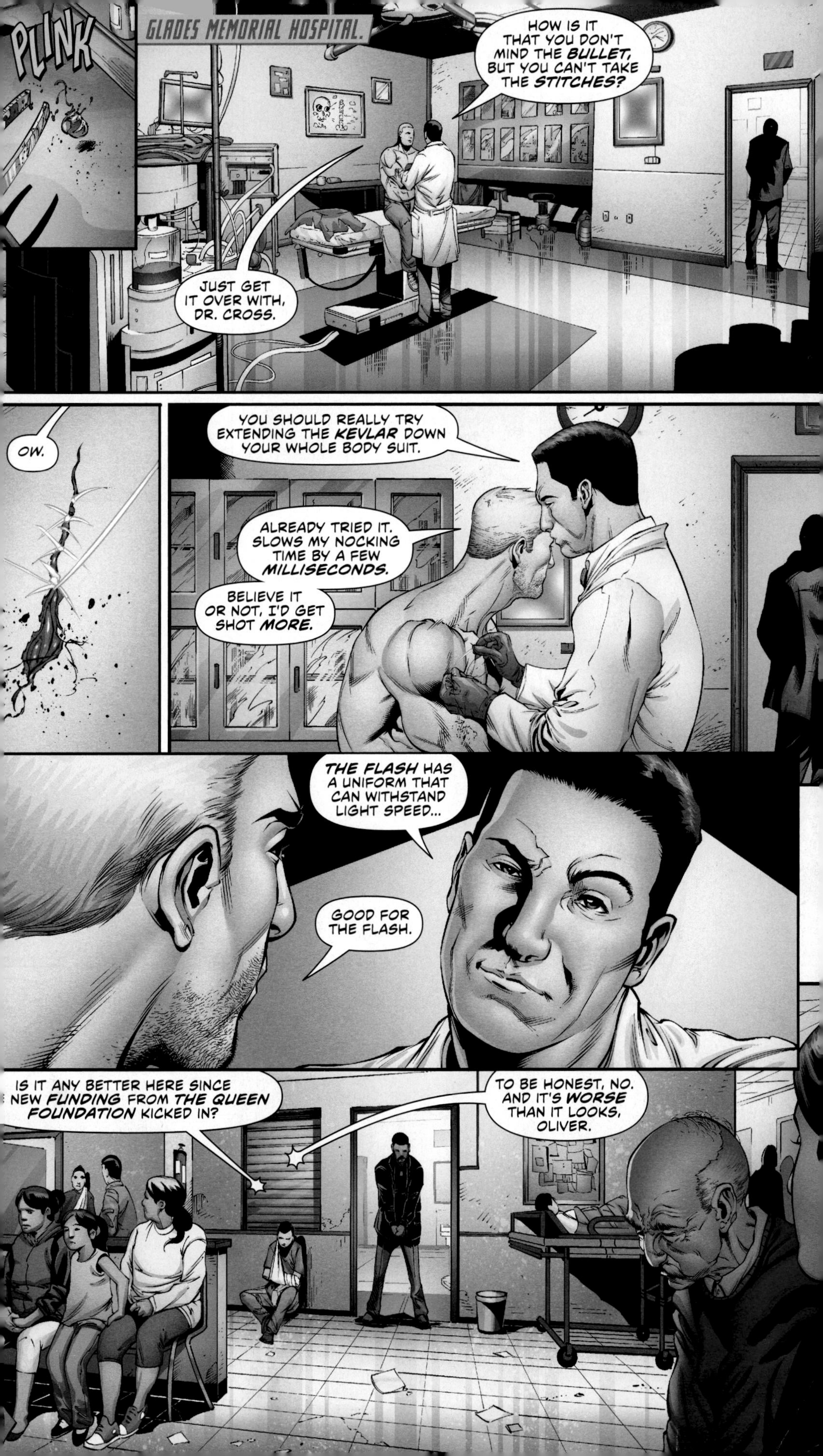
PLINK
GLADES MEMORIAL HOSPITAL.
HOW IS IT THAT YOU DON'T MIND THE BULLET, BUT YOU CAN'T TAKE THE STITCHES?
JUST GET IT OVER WITH, DR. CROSS.
OW.
YOU SHOULD REALLY TRY EXTENDING THE KEVLAR DOWN YOUR WHOLE BODY SUIT.
ALREADY TRIED IT. SLOWS MY NOCKING TIME BY A FEW MILLISECONDS.
BELIEVE IT OR NOT, I'D GET SHOT MORE.
THE FLASH HAS A UNIFORM THAT CAN WITHSTAND LIGHT SPEED...
GOOD FOR THE FLASH.
IS IT ANY BETTER HERE SINCE NEW FUNDING FROM THE QUEEN FOUNDATION KICKED IN?
TO BE HONEST, NO. AND IT'S WORSE THAN IT LOOKS, OLIVER.

MAYOR ALTMAN JUST CUT OUR EMERGENCY RELIEF FUNDING BY 75%. HE SAYS WE'RE NOT IN A STATE OF EMERGENCY.

THIS WHOLE CITY IS AN EMERGENCY.

IF YOU ASK ME, I THINK HE'S SKIMMING THE MILK.

IF ONLY YOU KNEW SOMEONE WHO COULD LOOK INTO THAT.

ON TOP OF THAT, OUR SUPPLY SHIPMENTS WERE INTERCEPTED BY HOOLIGANS, WHICH OUR INSURANCE SUDDENLY WON'T COVER. SO WE'RE PAYING TWICE FOR BASIC ANTIBIOTICS.

I'LL LOOK INTO THAT, TOO.

OLIVER, IF YOU KEEP GOING AFTER THESE PEOPLE, ONE DAY SOON I WON'T BE ABLE TO PATCH YOU UP.

VRRR

ZEHRA:
I'M GOING KILL YOU.

THAT BE SO THAN THI

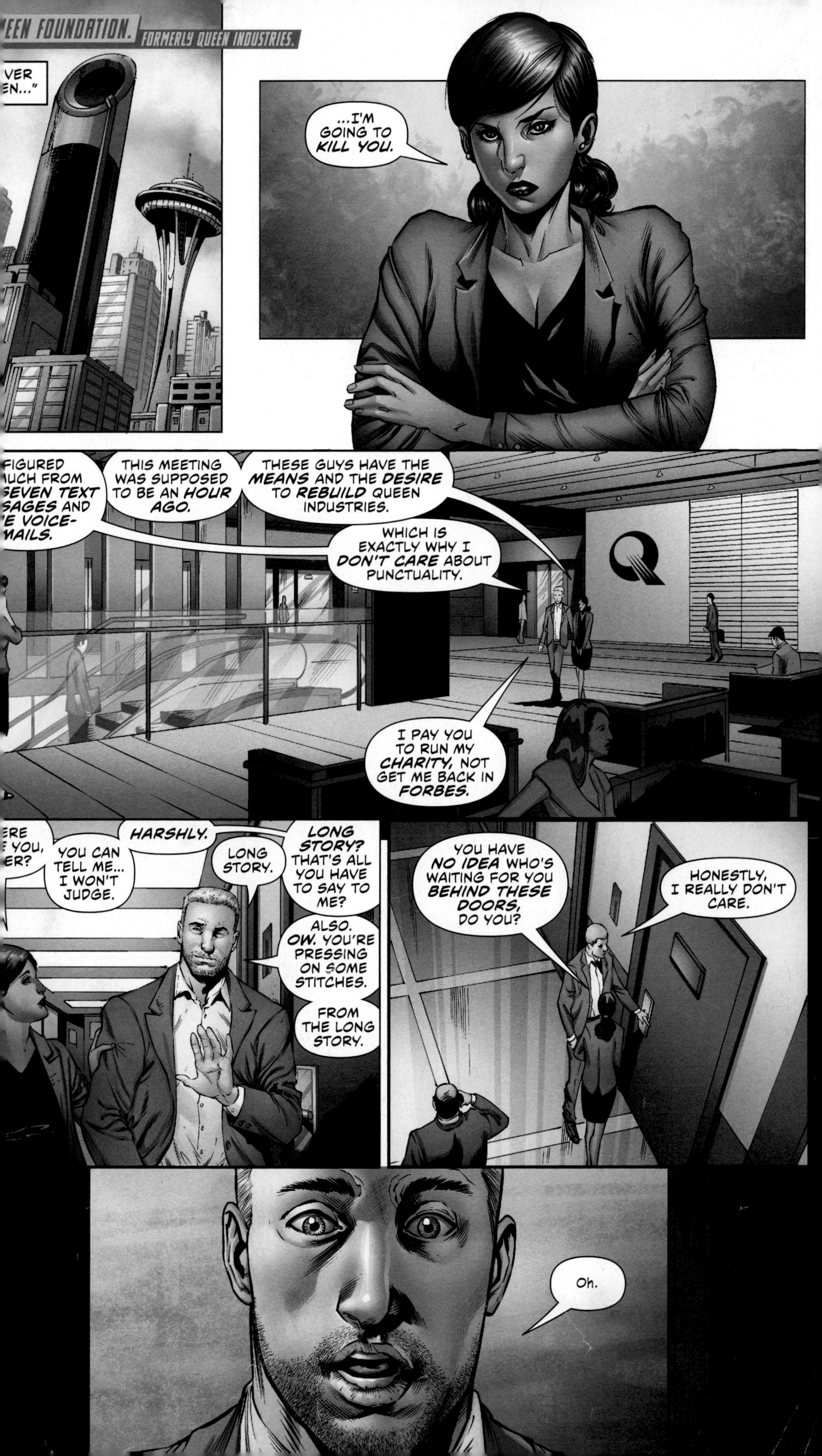

EEN FOUNDATION.
FORMERLY QUEEN INDUSTRIES.
VER
EN..."
...I'M GOING TO KILL YOU.
FIGURED
UCH FROM
SEVEN TEXT
SAGES AND
E VOICE-
MAILS.
THIS MEETING WAS SUPPOSED TO BE AN HOUR AGO.
THESE GUYS HAVE THE MEANS AND THE DESIRE TO REBUILD QUEEN INDUSTRIES.
WHICH IS EXACTLY WHY I DON'T CARE ABOUT PUNCTUALITY.
I PAY YOU TO RUN MY CHARITY, NOT GET ME BACK IN FORBES.
ERE
F YOU,
ER?
YOU CAN TELL ME... I WON'T JUDGE.
HARSHLY.
LONG STORY.
LONG STORY? THAT'S ALL YOU HAVE TO SAY TO ME?
ALSO. OW. YOU'RE PRESSING ON SOME STITCHES.
FROM THE LONG STORY.
YOU HAVE NO IDEA WHO'S WAITING FOR YOU BEHIND THESE DOORS, DO YOU?
HONESTLY, I REALLY DON'T CARE.
Oh.

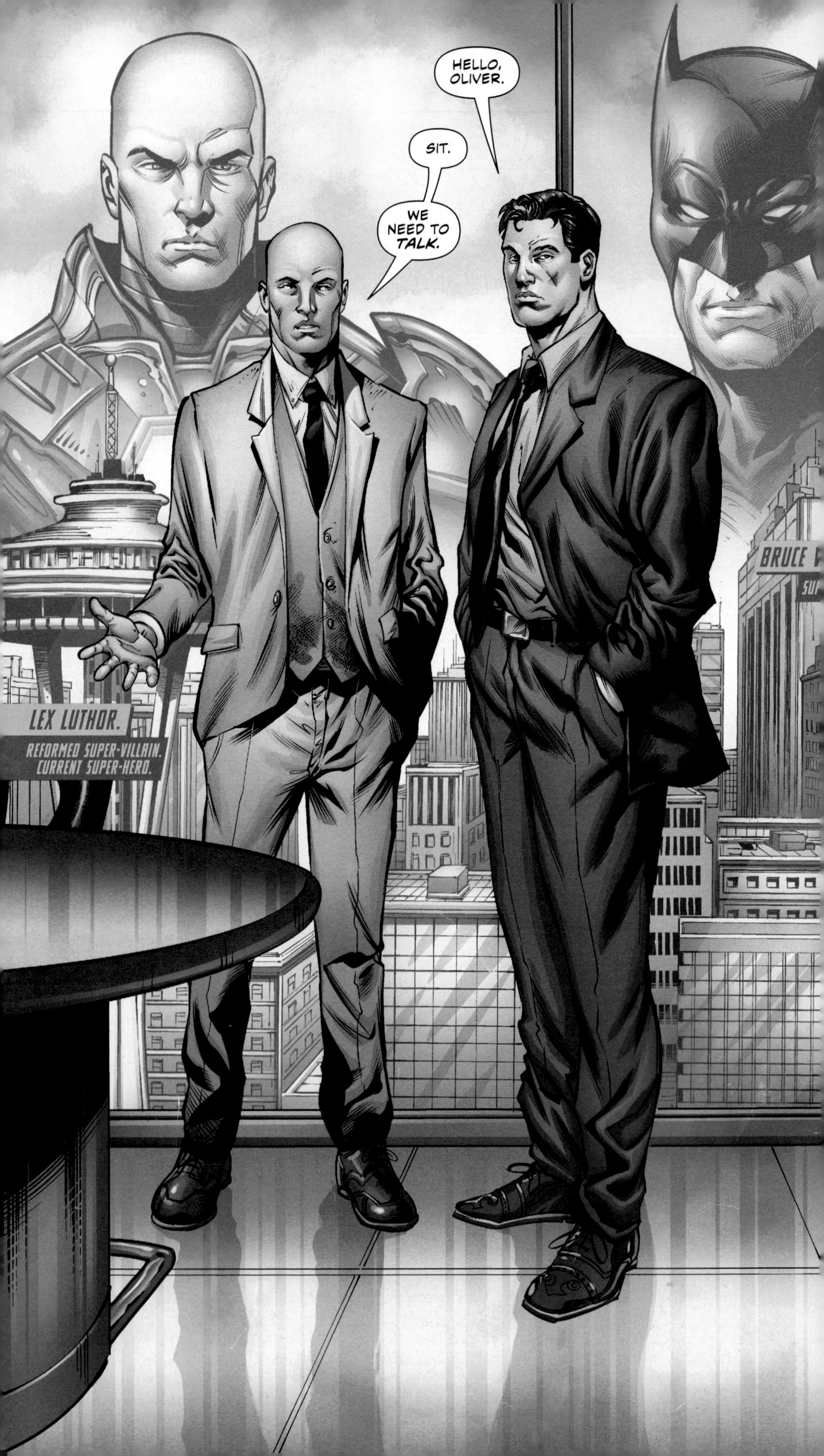
HELLO, OLIVER.
SIT.
WE NEED TO TALK.
LEX LUTHOR.
REFORMED SUPER-VILLAIN. CURRENT SUPER-HERO.

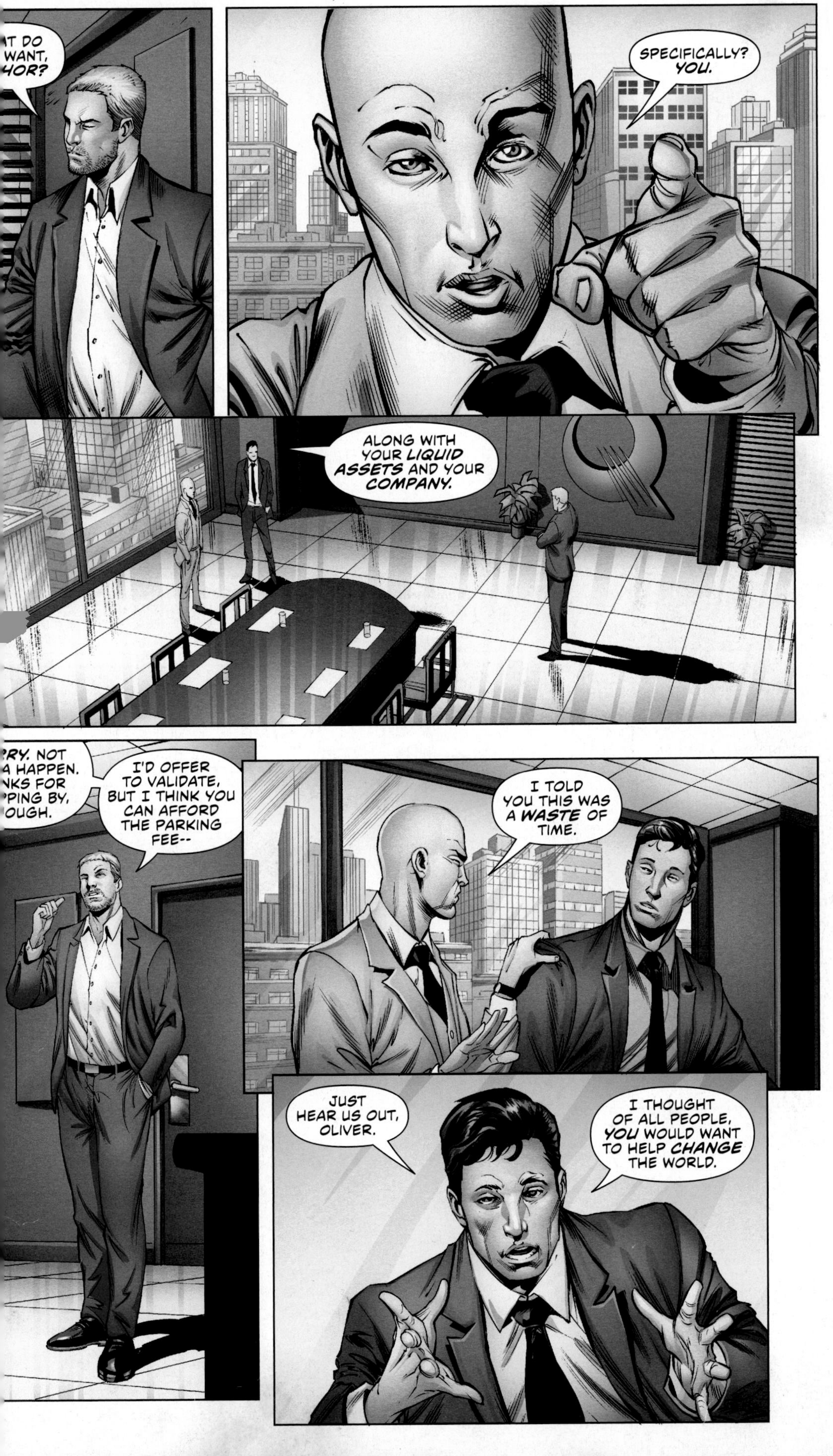
SPECIFICALLY? YOU.
ALONG WITH YOUR LIQUID ASSETS AND YOUR COMPANY.
I'D OFFER TO VALIDATE, BUT I THINK YOU CAN AFFORD THE PARKING FEE--
I TOLD YOU THIS WAS A WASTE OF TIME.
JUST HEAR US OUT, OLIVER.
I THOUGHT OF ALL PEOPLE, YOU WOULD WANT TO HELP CHANGE THE WORLD.

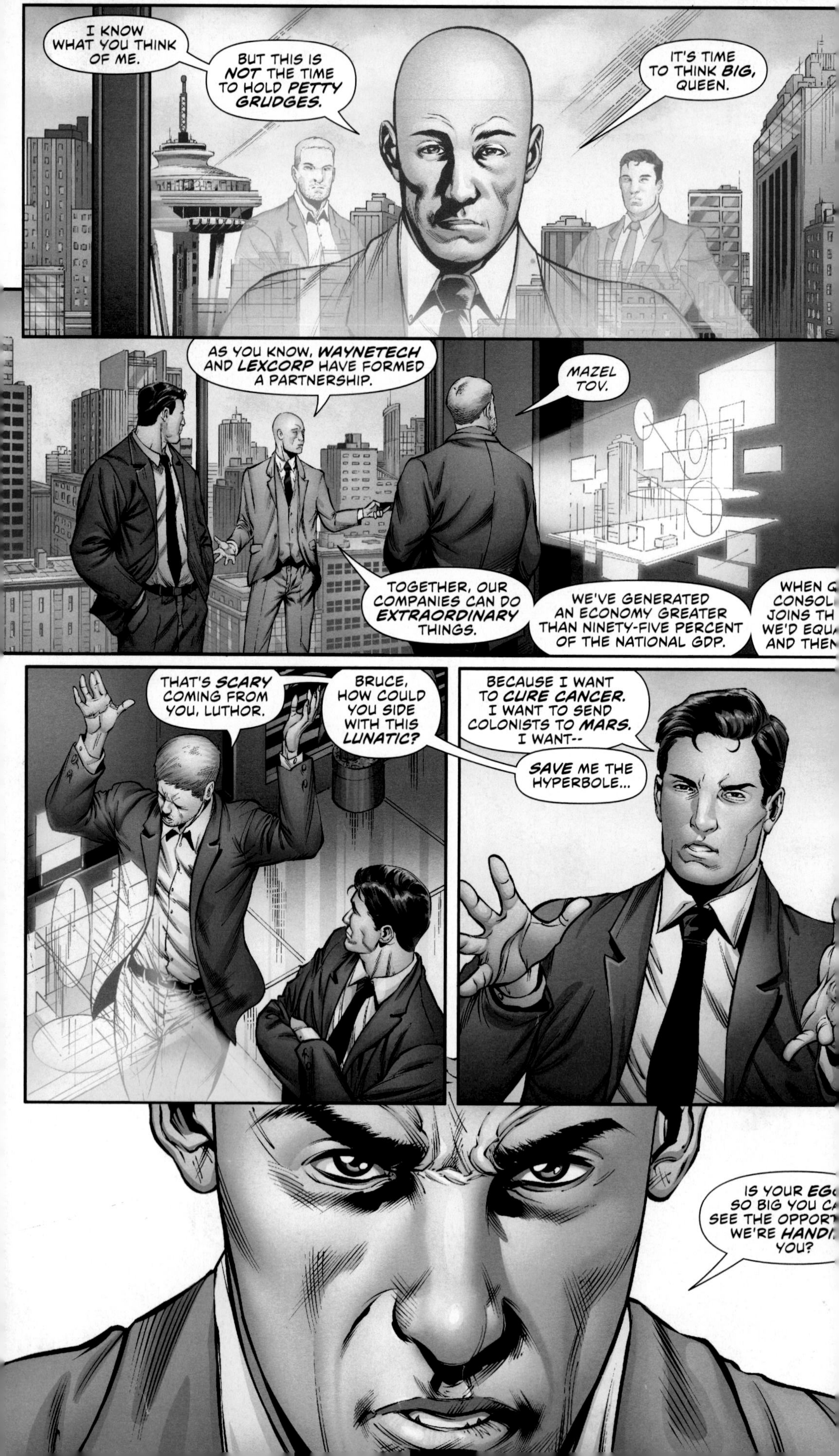
I KNOW WHAT YOU THINK OF ME.
BUT THIS IS NOT THE TIME TO HOLD PETTY GRUDGES.
IT'S TIME TO THINK BIG, QUEEN.
AS YOU KNOW, WAYNETECH AND LEXCORP HAVE FORMED A PARTNERSHIP.
MAZEL TOV.
TOGETHER, OUR COMPANIES CAN DO EXTRAORDINARY THINGS.
WE'VE GENERATED AN ECONOMY GREATER THAN NINETY-FIVE PERCENT OF THE NATIONAL GDP.
THAT'S SCARY COMING FROM YOU, LUTHOR.
BRUCE, HOW COULD YOU SIDE WITH THIS LUNATIC?
BECAUSE I WANT TO CURE CANCER. I WANT TO SEND COLONISTS TO MARS. I WANT--
SAVE ME THE HYPERBOLE...

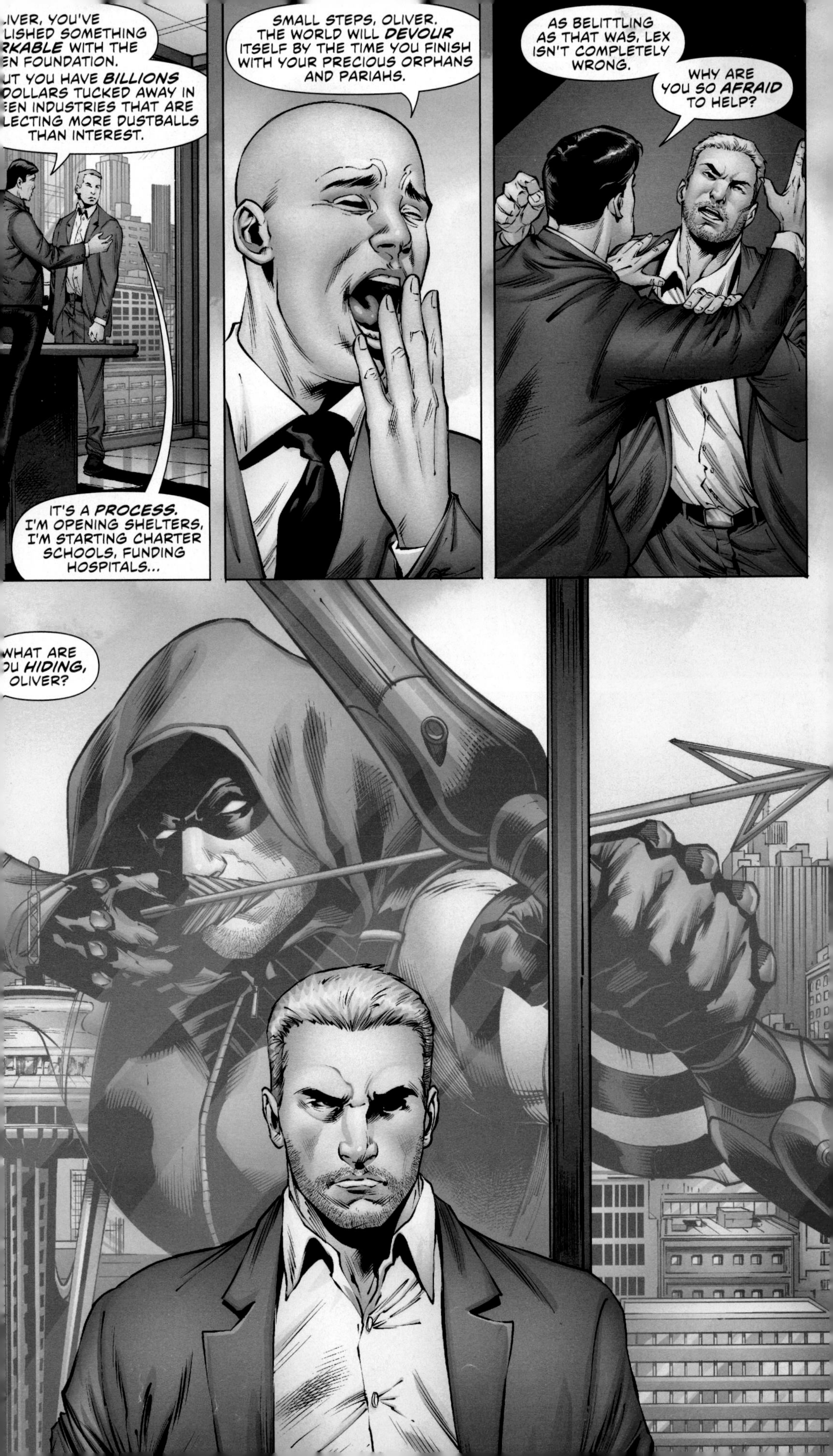

LIVER, YOU'VE
LISHED SOMETHING
RKABLE WITH THE
EN FOUNDATION.
UT YOU HAVE BILLIONS
DOLLARS TUCKED AWAY IN
EEN INDUSTRIES THAT ARE
LECTING MORE DUSTBALLS
THAN INTEREST.
IT'S A PROCESS. I'M OPENING SHELTERS, I'M STARTING CHARTER SCHOOLS, FUNDING HOSPITALS...
SMALL STEPS, OLIVER. THE WORLD WILL DEVOUR ITSELF BY THE TIME YOU FINISH WITH YOUR PRECIOUS ORPHANS AND PARIAHS.
AS BELITTLING AS THAT WAS, LEX ISN'T COMPLETELY WRONG.
WHY ARE YOU SO AFRAID TO HELP?
WHAT ARE
OU HIDING,
OLIVER?

I KNOW *EVERY* EMPLOYEE OF THE QUEEN FOUNDATION. I KNOW THEIR *FAMILIES.* I KNOW THEIR *HOPES* AND *DREAMS.*

BET YOU CAN'T NAME ONE *OTHER* EMPLOYEE AT WAYNETECH.

LUCIUS--

OTHER THAN LUCIUS FOX.

YOU AREN' THE MAN THE PEO YOU SAY ARE.

YOU DON'T GET YOUR *HAND* DIRTY.

"SO WHAT ARE *YOU* HIDING, BRUCE?

"AND *YOU,* LUTHOR...

"...YOU'RE JUST *EVIL.*"

WE'
DO
HER

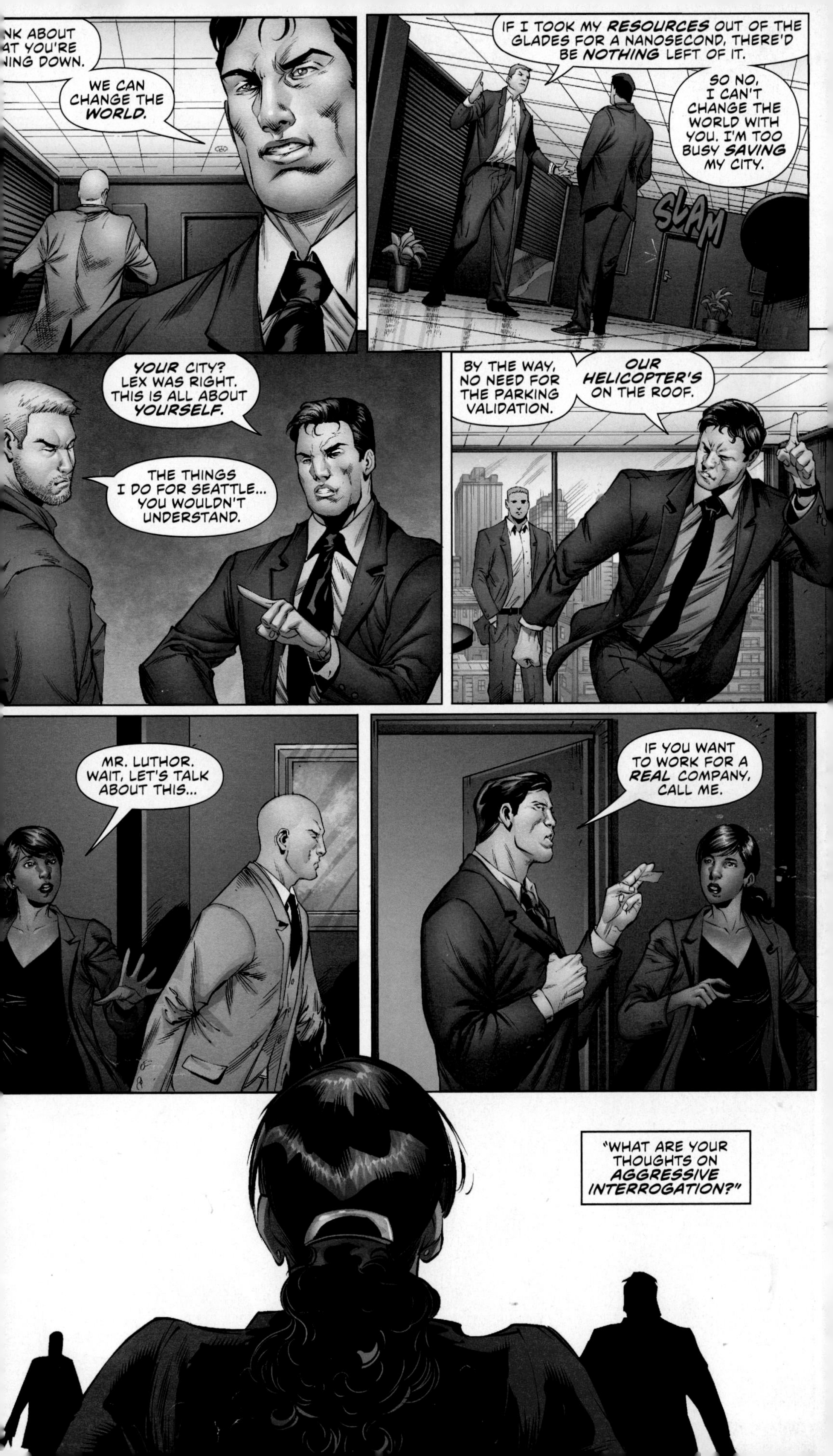
NK ABOUT
AT YOU'RE
NING DOWN.
WE CAN CHANGE THE WORLD.
IF I TOOK MY RESOURCES OUT OF THE GLADES FOR A NANOSECOND, THERE'D BE NOTHING LEFT OF IT.
SO NO, I CAN'T CHANGE THE WORLD WITH YOU. I'M TOO BUSY SAVING MY CITY.
SLAM
YOUR CITY? LEX WAS RIGHT. THIS IS ALL ABOUT YOURSELF.
THE THINGS I DO FOR SEATTLE... YOU WOULDN'T UNDERSTAND.
BY THE WAY, NO NEED FOR THE PARKING VALIDATION.
OUR HELICOPTER'S ON THE ROOF.
MR. LUTHOR. WAIT, LET'S TALK ABOUT THIS...
IF YOU WANT TO WORK FOR A REAL COMPANY, CALL ME.
"WHAT ARE YOUR THOUGHTS ON AGGRESSIVE INTERROGATION?"

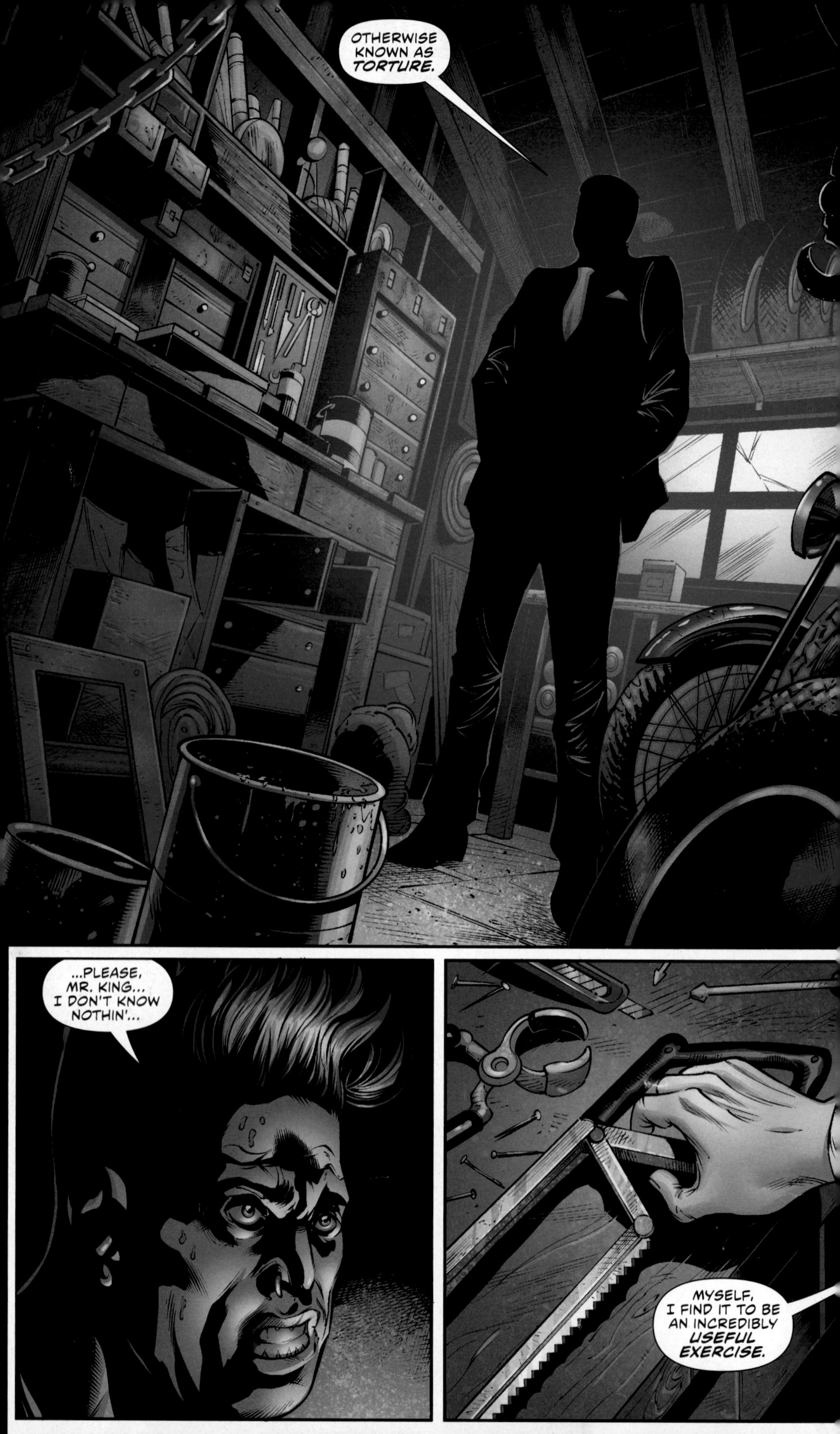
OTHERWISE KNOWN AS TORTURE.
...PLEASE, MR. KING... I DON'T KNOW NOTHIN'...
MYSELF, I FIND IT TO BE AN INCREDIBLY USEFUL EXERCISE.

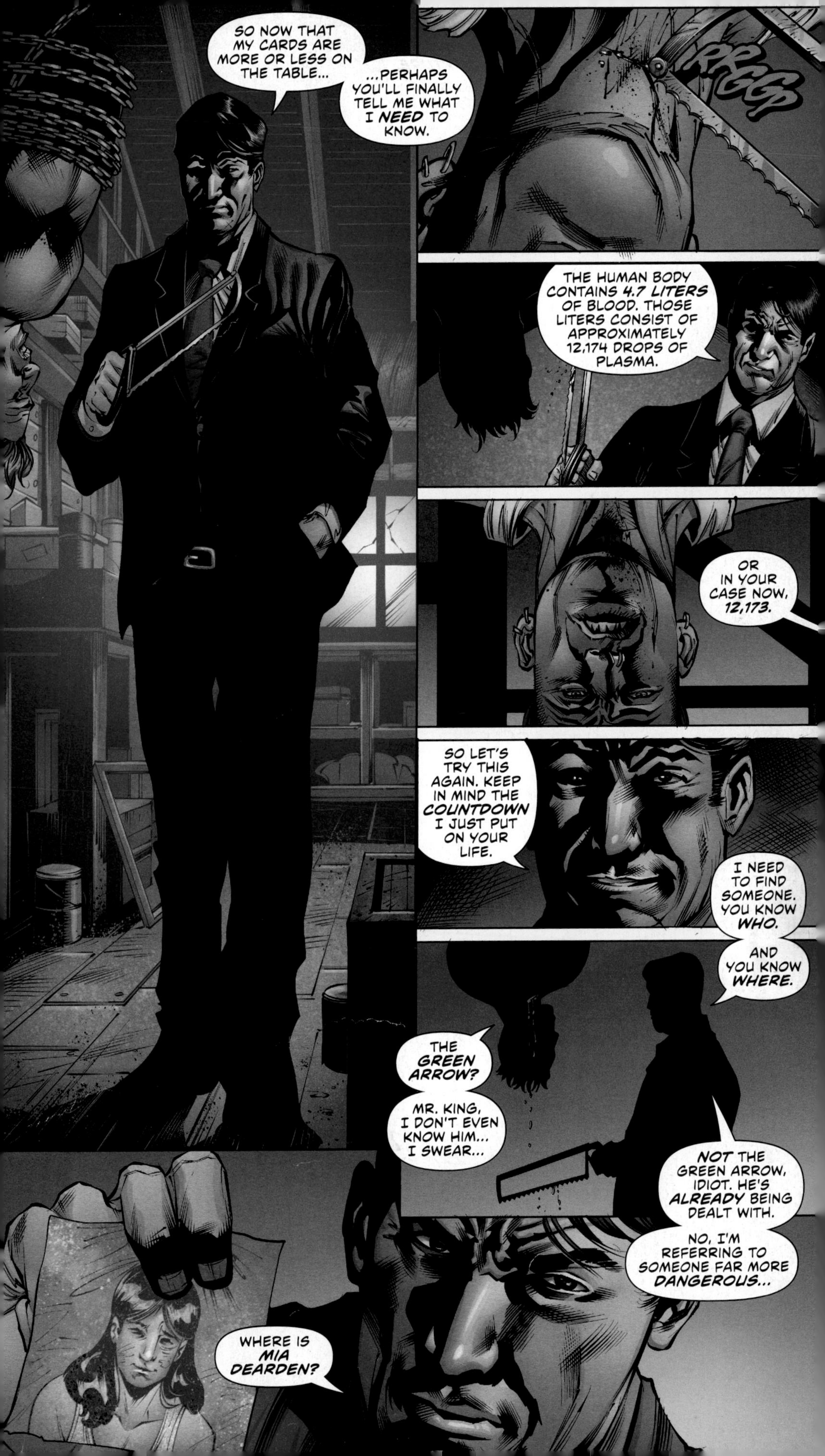
SO NOW THAT MY CARDS ARE MORE OR LESS ON THE TABLE...
...PERHAPS YOU'LL FINALLY TELL ME WHAT I NEED TO KNOW.
RRGGP
THE HUMAN BODY CONTAINS 4.7 LITERS OF BLOOD. THOSE LITERS CONSIST OF APPROXIMATELY 12,174 DROPS OF PLASMA.
OR IN YOUR CASE NOW, 12,173.
SO LET'S TRY THIS AGAIN. KEEP IN MIND THE COUNTDOWN I JUST PUT ON YOUR LIFE.
I NEED TO FIND SOMEONE. YOU KNOW WHO.
AND YOU KNOW WHERE.
THE GREEN ARROW?
MR. KING, I DON'T EVEN KNOW HIM... I SWEAR...
NOT THE GREEN ARROW, IDIOT. HE'S ALREADY BEING DEALT WITH.
NO, I'M REFERRING TO SOMEONE FAR MORE DANGEROUS...
WHERE IS MIA DEARDEN?

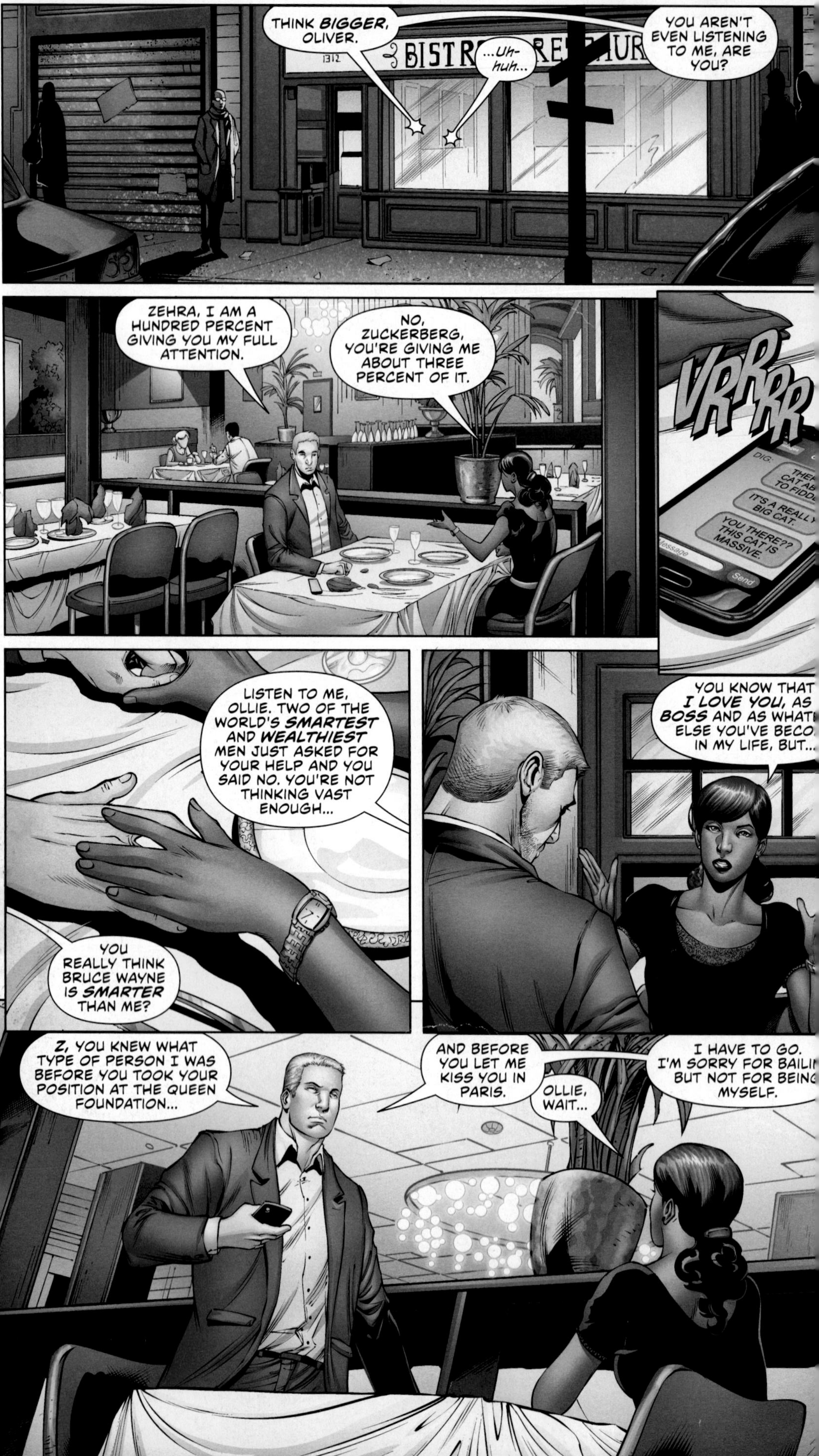
THINK BIGGER, OLIVER.
...Uh-huh...
YOU AREN'T EVEN LISTENING TO ME, ARE YOU?
ZEHRA, I AM A HUNDRED PERCENT GIVING YOU MY FULL ATTENTION.
NO, ZUCKERBERG, YOU'RE GIVING ME ABOUT THREE PERCENT OF IT.
VRRRR
DIG:
IT'S A REALLY BIG CAT.
YOU THERE?? THIS CAT IS MASSIVE.
Send
LISTEN TO ME, OLLIE. TWO OF THE WORLD'S SMARTEST AND WEALTHIEST MEN JUST ASKED FOR YOUR HELP AND YOU SAID NO. YOU'RE NOT THINKING VAST ENOUGH...
YOU REALLY THINK BRUCE WAYNE IS SMARTER THAN ME?
YOU KNOW THAT I LOVE YOU, AS BOSS AND AS WHAT ELSE YOU'VE BECO IN MY LIFE, BUT...
Z, YOU KNEW WHAT TYPE OF PERSON I WAS BEFORE YOU TOOK YOUR POSITION AT THE QUEEN FOUNDATION...
AND BEFORE YOU LET ME KISS YOU IN PARIS.
OLLIE, WAIT...
I HAVE TO GO. I'M SORRY FOR BAILI BUT NOT FOR BEING MYSELF.

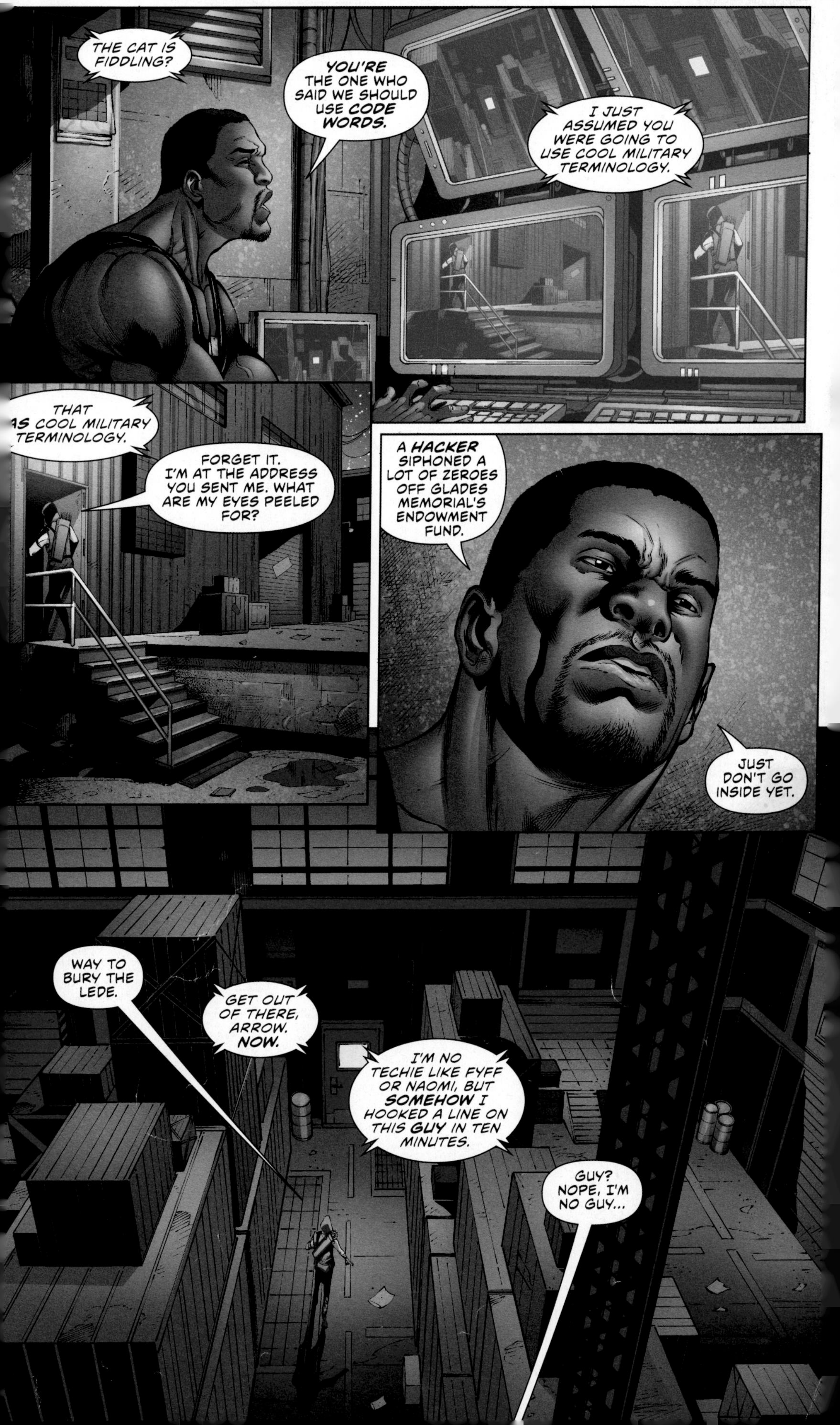
THE CAT IS FIDDLING?
YOU'RE THE ONE WHO SAID WE SHOULD USE CODE WORDS.
I JUST ASSUMED YOU WERE GOING TO USE COOL MILITARY TERMINOLOGY.
THAT AS COOL MILITARY TERMINOLOGY.
FORGET IT. I'M AT THE ADDRESS YOU SENT ME. WHAT ARE MY EYES PEELED FOR?
A HACKER SIPHONED A LOT OF ZEROES OFF GLADES MEMORIAL'S ENDOWMENT FUND.
JUST DON'T GO INSIDE YET.
WAY TO BURY THE LEDE.
GET OUT OF THERE, ARROW. NOW.
I'M NO TECHIE LIKE FYFF OR NAOMI, BUT SOMEHOW I HOOKED A LINE ON THIS GUY IN TEN MINUTES.
GUY? NOPE, I'M NO GUY...

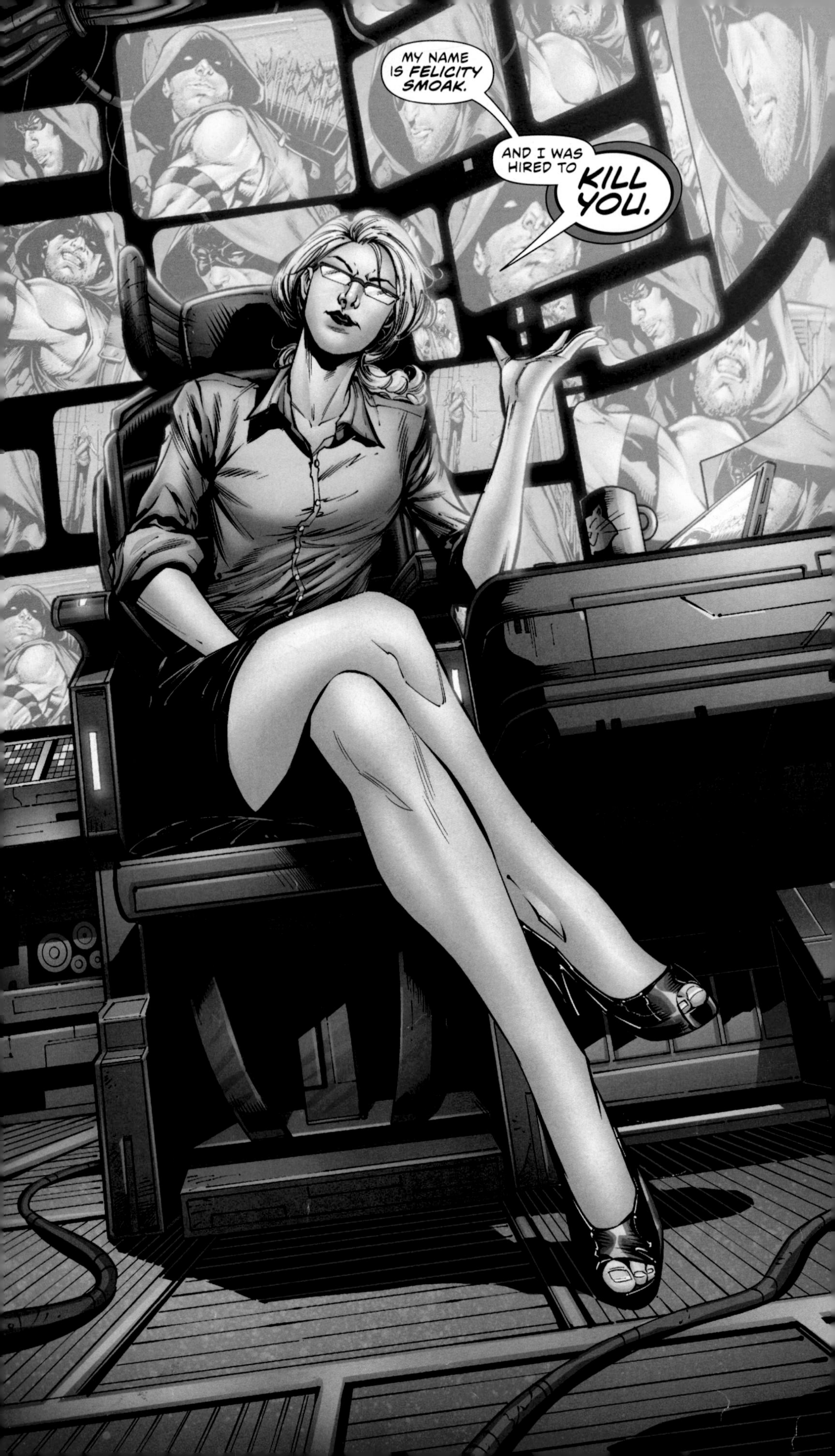
MY NAME IS FELICITY SMOAK.
AND I WAS HIRED TO KILL YOU.

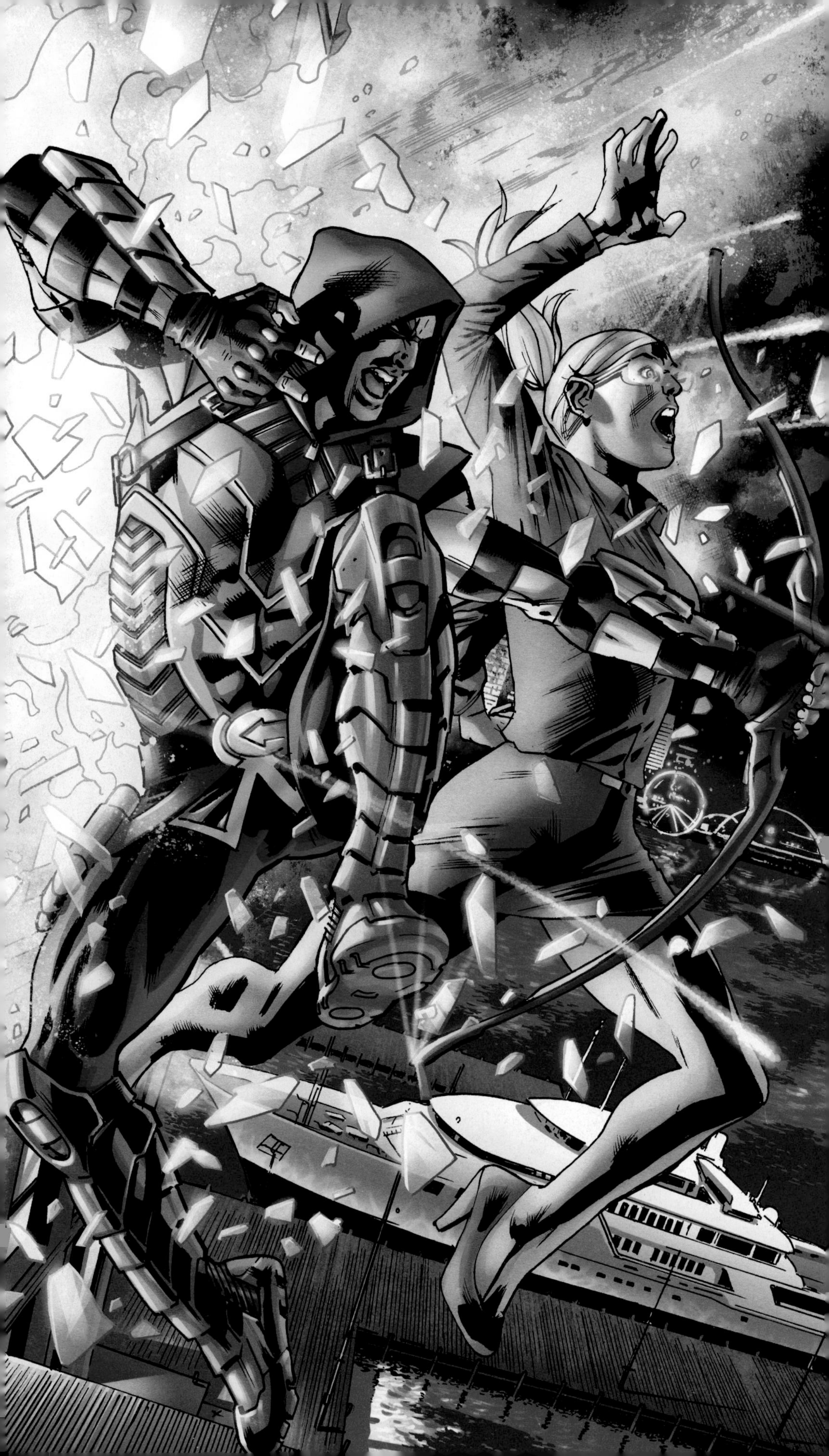

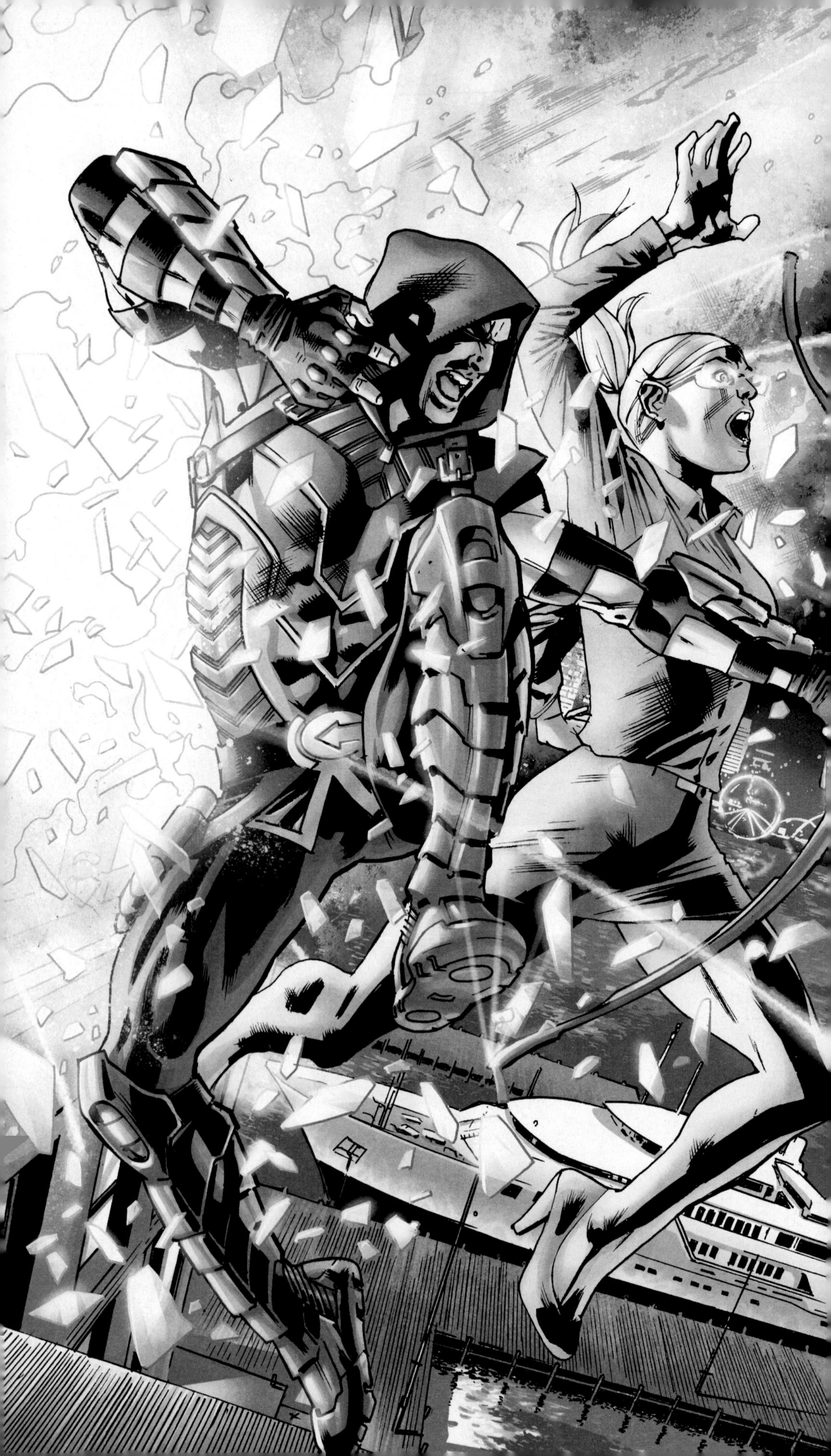

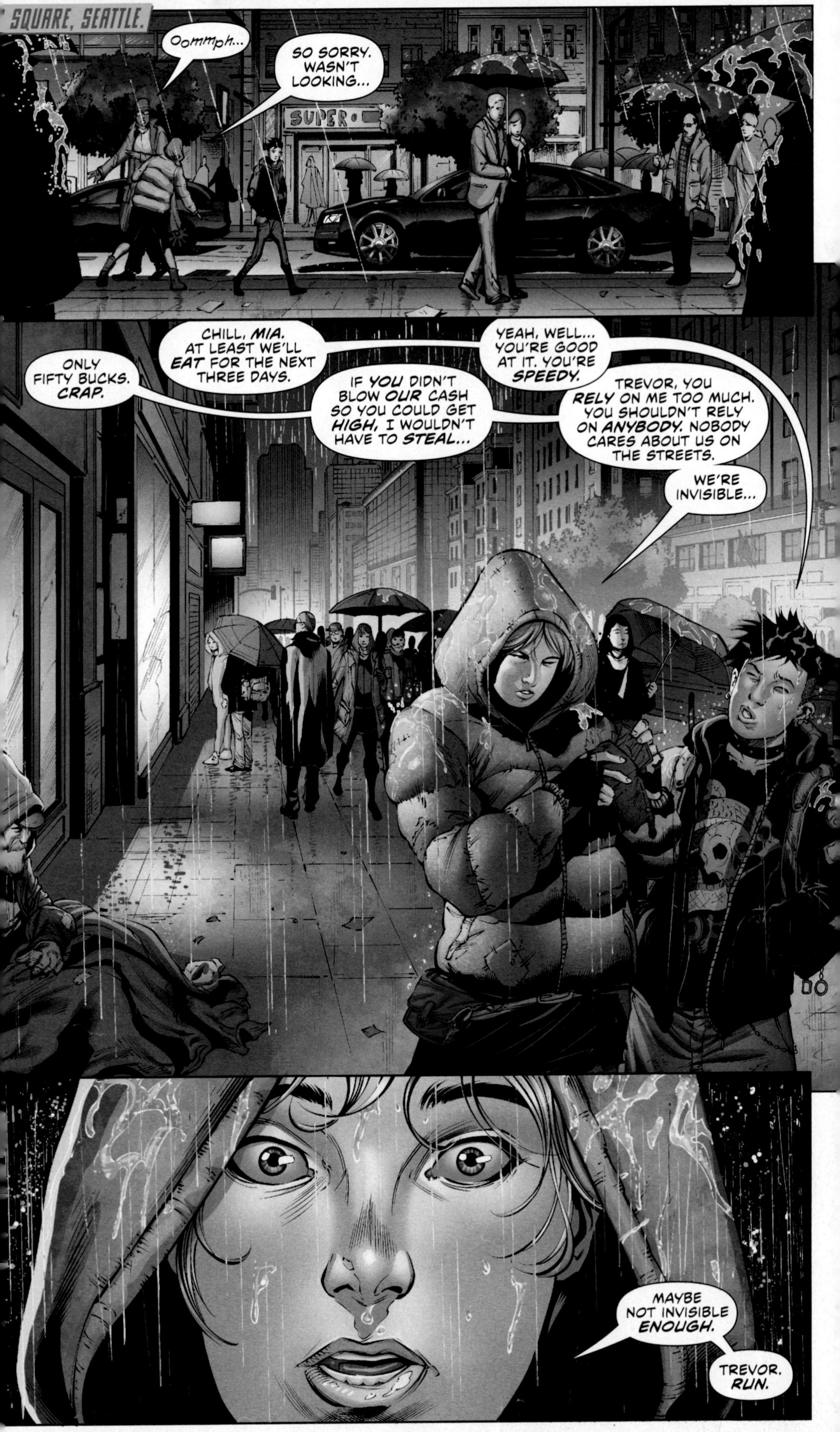
SQUARE, SEATTLE.
Oommph...
SO SORRY. WASN'T LOOKING...
SUPER
ONLY FIFTY BUCKS. CRAP.
CHILL, MIA. AT LEAST WE'LL EAT FOR THE NEXT THREE DAYS.
IF YOU DIDN'T BLOW OUR CASH SO YOU COULD GET HIGH, I WOULDN'T HAVE TO STEAL...
YEAH, WELL... YOU'RE GOOD AT IT. YOU'RE SPEEDY.
TREVOR, YOU RELY ON ME TOO MUCH. YOU SHOULDN'T RELY ON ANYBODY. NOBODY CARES ABOUT US ON THE STREETS.
WE'RE INVISIBLE...
MAYBE NOT INVISIBLE ENOUGH.
TREVOR. RUN.

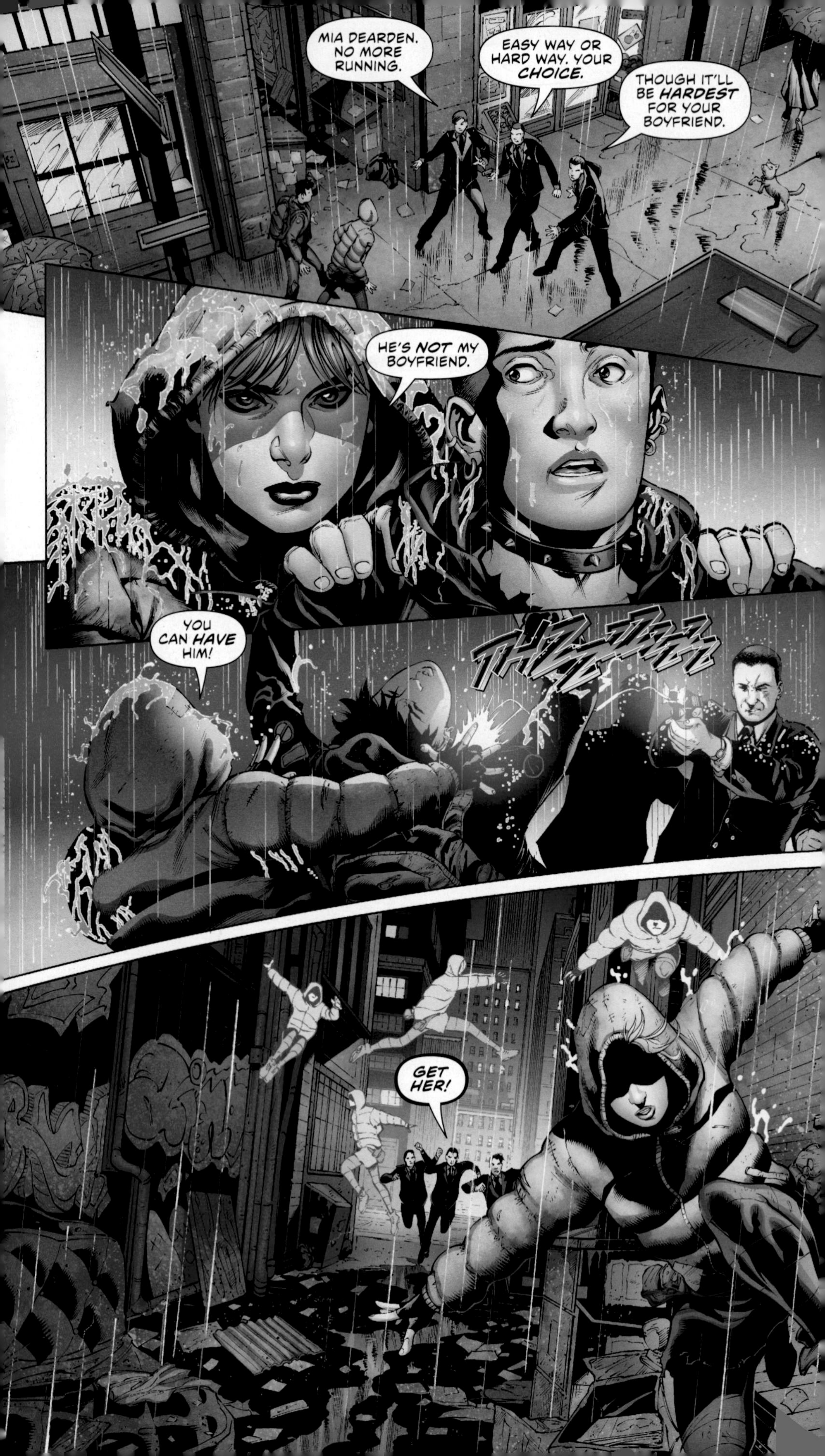
MIA DEARDEN. NO MORE RUNNING.
EASY WAY OR HARD WAY. YOUR CHOICE.
THOUGH IT'LL BE HARDEST FOR YOUR BOYFRIEND.
HE'S NOT MY BOYFRIEND.
YOU CAN HAVE HIM!
THZZZZZT
GET HER!

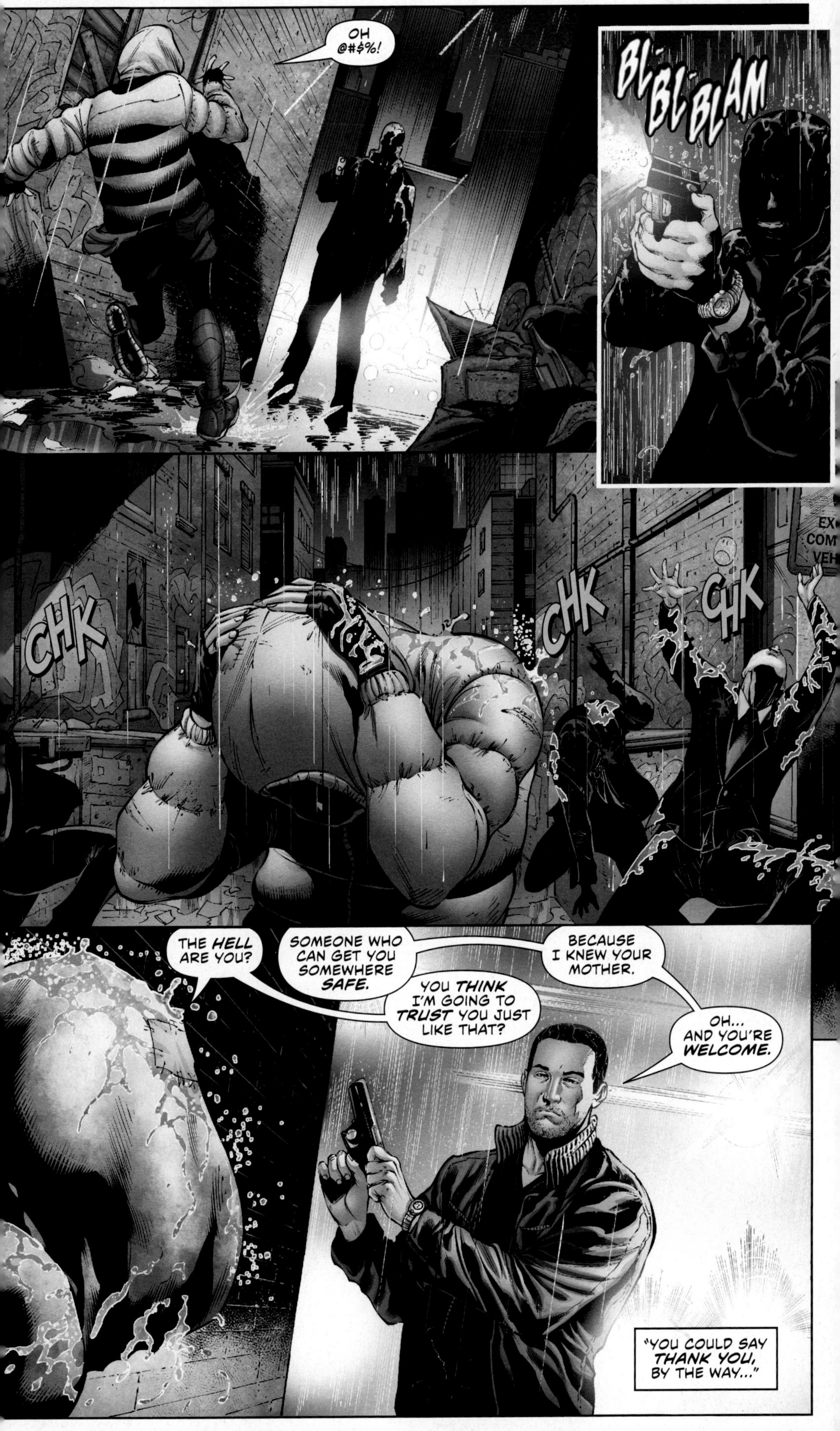

OH @#$%!
BL-BL-BLAM
CHK
CHK
CHK
EX
COM
VEH
THE HELL ARE YOU?
SOMEONE WHO CAN GET YOU SOMEWHERE SAFE.
YOU THINK I'M GOING TO TRUST YOU JUST LIKE THAT?
BECAUSE I KNEW YOUR MOTHER.
OH... AND YOU'RE WELCOME.
"YOU COULD SAY THANK YOU, BY THE WAY..."

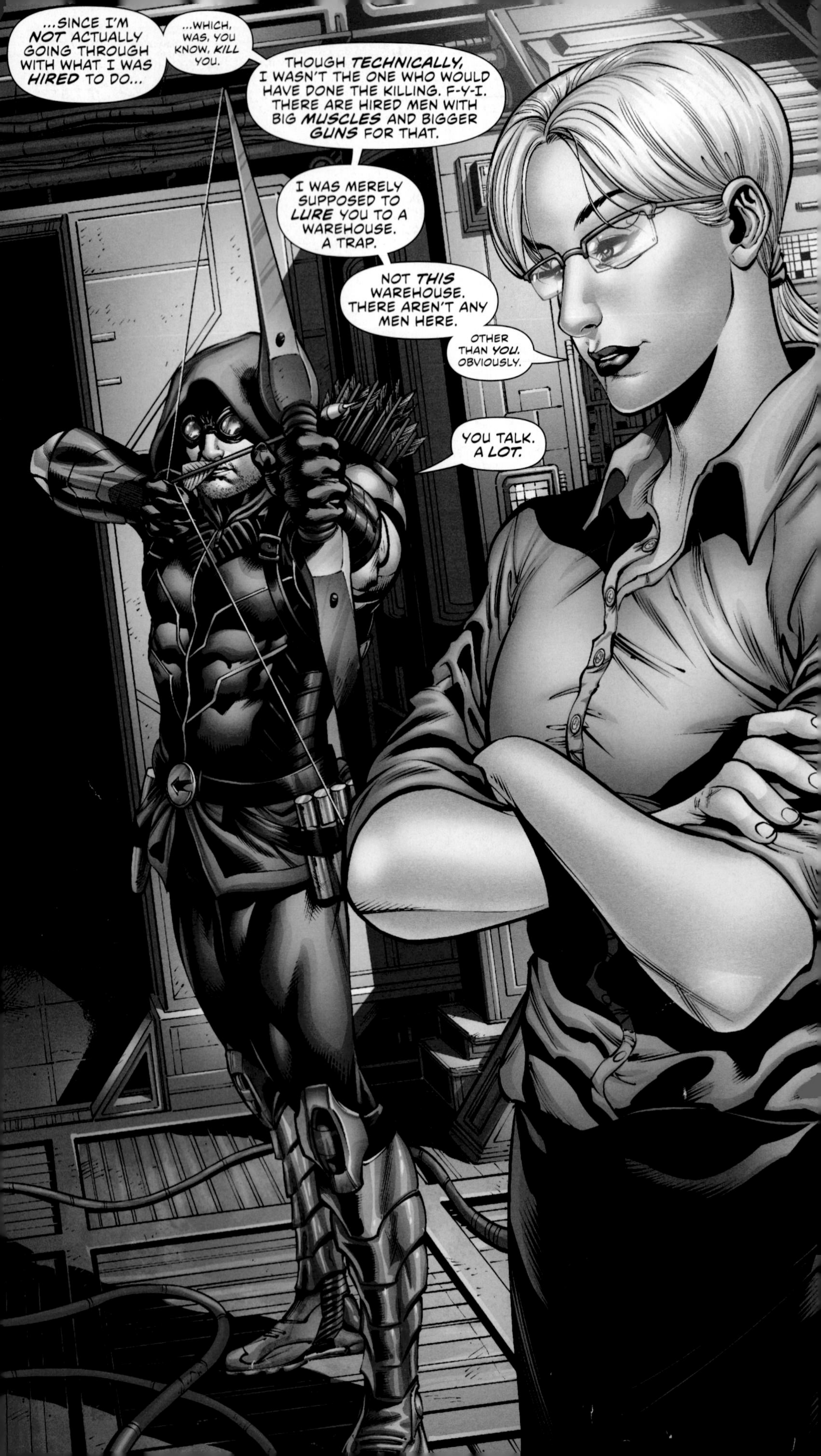
...SINCE I'M NOT ACTUALLY GOING THROUGH WITH WHAT I WAS HIRED TO DO...
...WHICH, WAS, YOU KNOW, KILL YOU.
THOUGH TECHNICALLY, I WASN'T THE ONE WHO WOULD HAVE DONE THE KILLING. F-Y-I. THERE ARE HIRED MEN WITH BIG MUSCLES AND BIGGER GUNS FOR THAT.
I WAS MERELY SUPPOSED TO LURE YOU TO A WAREHOUSE. A TRAP.
NOT THIS WAREHOUSE. THERE AREN'T ANY MEN HERE.
OTHER THAN YOU. OBVIOUSLY.
YOU TALK. A LOT.

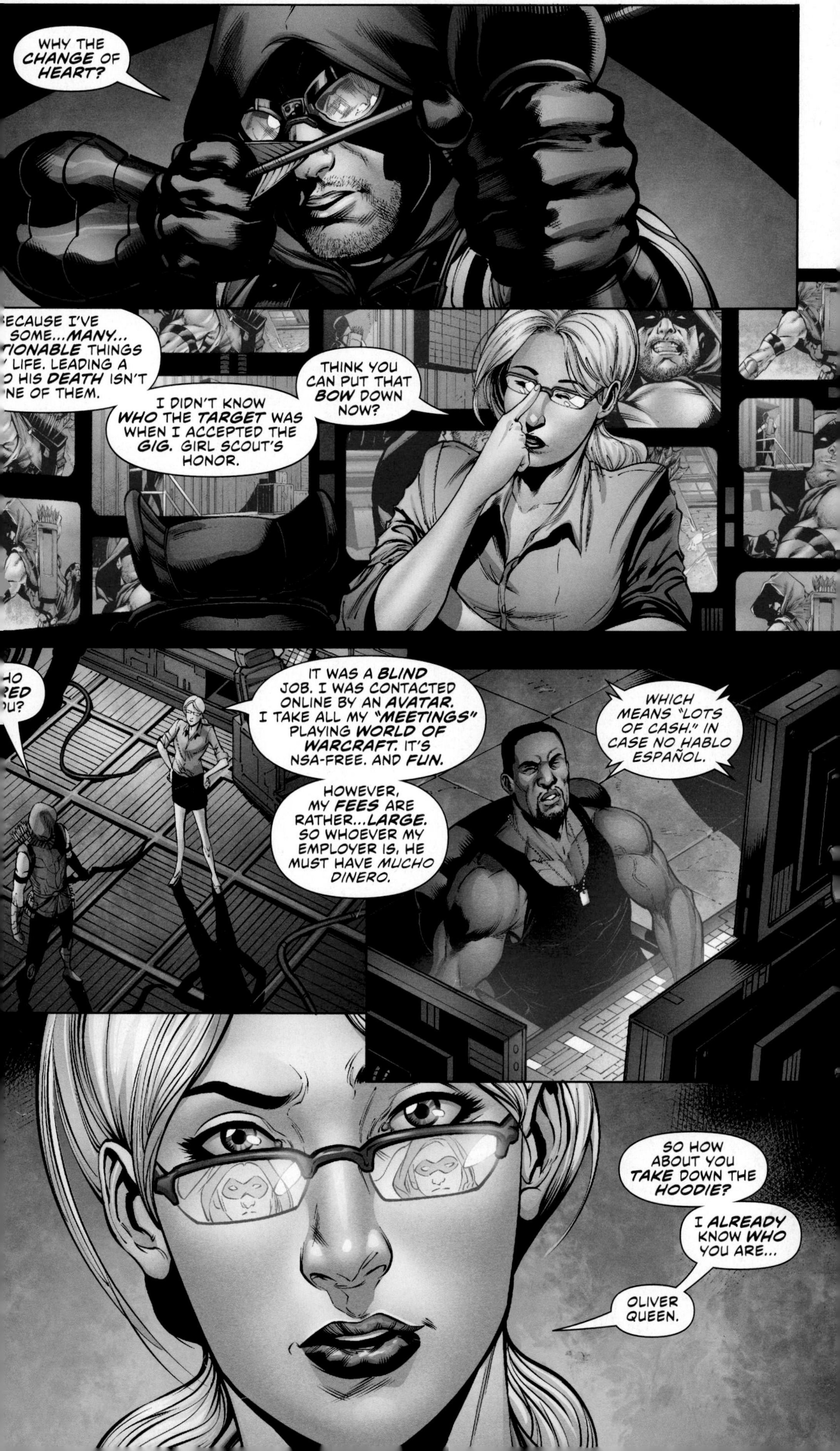

WHY THE CHANGE OF HEART?
ECAUSE I'VE SOME...MANY... TIONABLE THINGS LIFE. LEADING A O HIS DEATH ISN'T NE OF THEM.
I DIDN'T KNOW WHO THE TARGET WAS WHEN I ACCEPTED THE GIG. GIRL SCOUT'S HONOR.
THINK YOU CAN PUT THAT BOW DOWN NOW?
HO RED OU?
IT WAS A BLIND JOB. I WAS CONTACTED ONLINE BY AN AVATAR. I TAKE ALL MY "MEETINGS" PLAYING WORLD OF WARCRAFT. IT'S NSA-FREE. AND FUN.
HOWEVER, MY FEES ARE RATHER...LARGE. SO WHOEVER MY EMPLOYER IS, HE MUST HAVE MUCHO DINERO.
WHICH MEANS "LOTS OF CASH." IN CASE NO HABLO ESPAÑOL.
SO HOW ABOUT YOU TAKE DOWN THE HOODIE?
I ALREADY KNOW WHO YOU ARE...
OLIVER QUEEN.

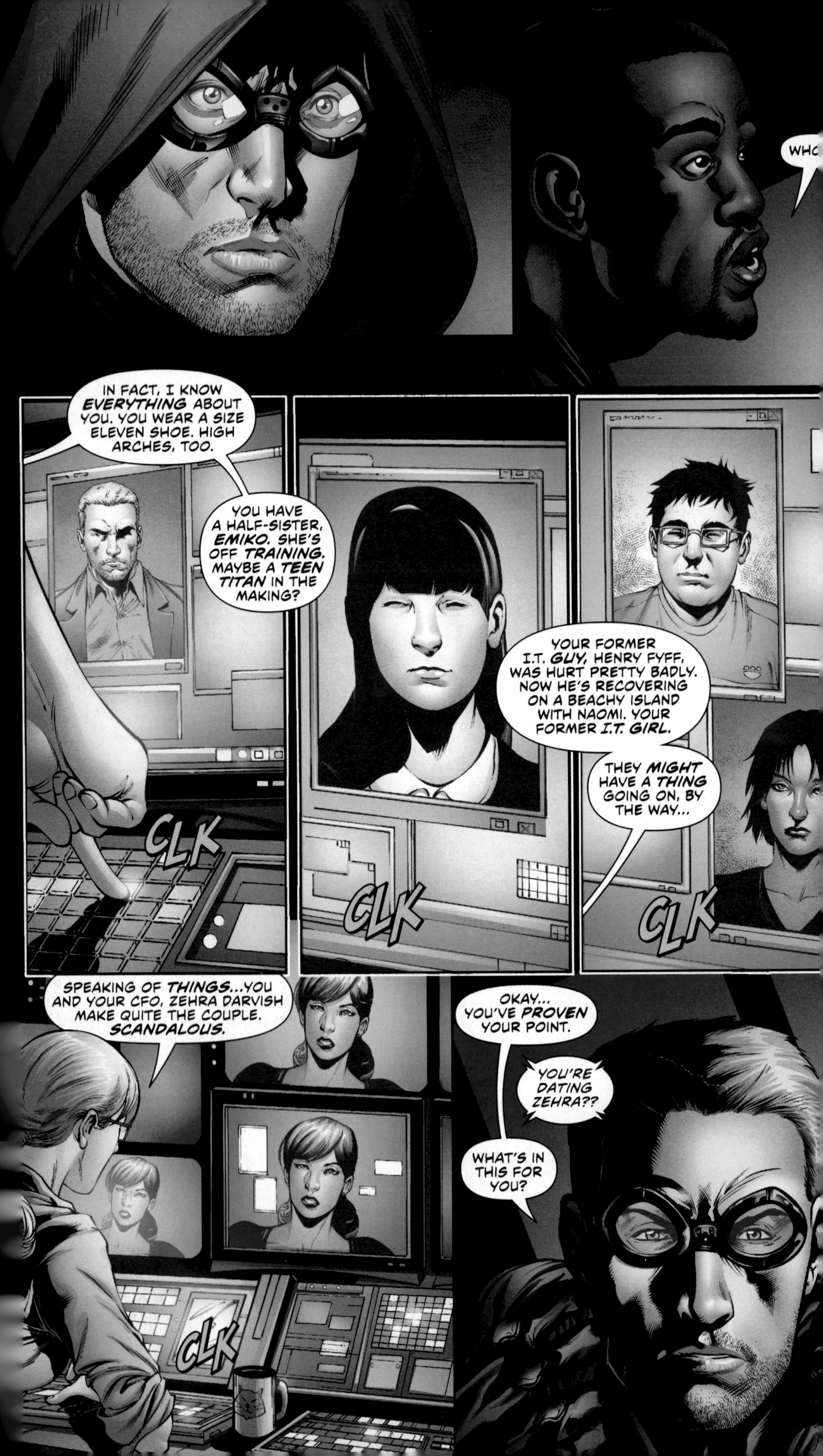
WHO
IN FACT, I KNOW EVERYTHING ABOUT YOU. YOU WEAR A SIZE ELEVEN SHOE. HIGH ARCHES, TOO.
YOU HAVE A HALF-SISTER, EMIKO. SHE'S OFF TRAINING. MAYBE A TEEN TITAN IN THE MAKING?
CLK
CLK
YOUR FORMER I.T. GUY, HENRY FYFF, WAS HURT PRETTY BADLY. NOW HE'S RECOVERING ON A BEACHY ISLAND WITH NAOMI. YOUR FORMER I.T. GIRL.
THEY MIGHT HAVE A THING GOING ON, BY THE WAY...
CLK
SPEAKING OF THINGS...YOU AND YOUR CFO, ZEHRA DARVISH MAKE QUITE THE COUPLE. SCANDALOUS.
CLK
OKAY... YOU'VE PROVEN YOUR POINT.
YOU'RE DATING ZEHRA??
WHAT'S IN THIS FOR YOU?

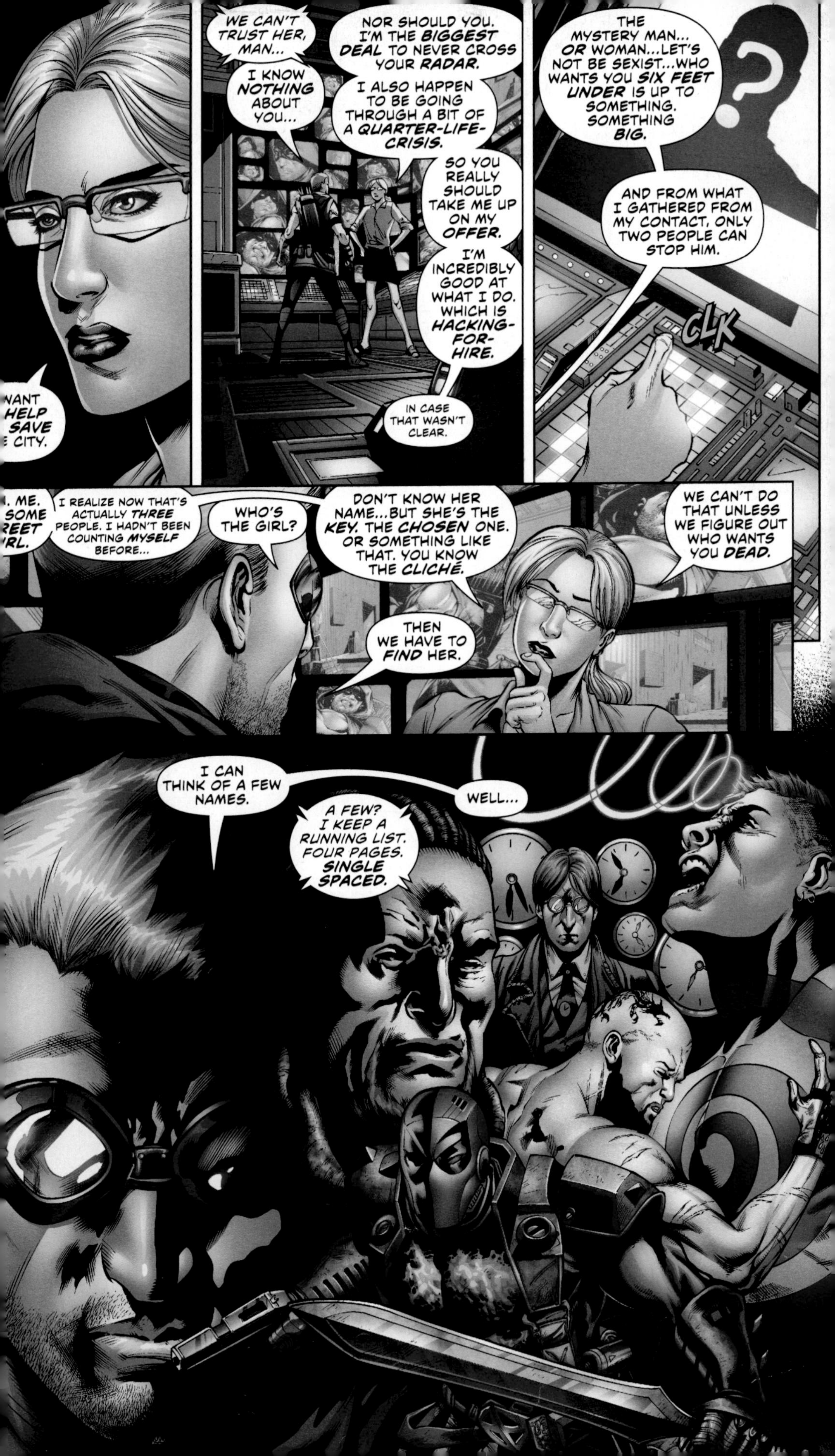

WANT
HELP
SAVE
CITY.
WE CAN'T TRUST HER, MAN...
I KNOW NOTHING ABOUT YOU...
NOR SHOULD YOU. I'M THE BIGGEST DEAL TO NEVER CROSS YOUR RADAR.
I ALSO HAPPEN TO BE GOING THROUGH A BIT OF A QUARTER-LIFE-CRISIS.
SO YOU REALLY SHOULD TAKE ME UP ON MY OFFER.
I'M INCREDIBLY GOOD AT WHAT I DO. WHICH IS HACKING-FOR-HIRE.
IN CASE THAT WASN'T CLEAR.
THE MYSTERY MAN... OR WOMAN...LET'S NOT BE SEXIST...WHO WANTS YOU SIX FEET UNDER IS UP TO SOMETHING. SOMETHING BIG.
AND FROM WHAT I GATHERED FROM MY CONTACT, ONLY TWO PEOPLE CAN STOP HIM.
CLK
ME.
SOME
REET
IRL.
I REALIZE NOW THAT'S ACTUALLY THREE PEOPLE. I HADN'T BEEN COUNTING MYSELF BEFORE...
WHO'S THE GIRL?
DON'T KNOW HER NAME...BUT SHE'S THE KEY. THE CHOSEN ONE. OR SOMETHING LIKE THAT. YOU KNOW THE CLICHÉ.
THEN WE HAVE TO FIND HER.
WE CAN'T DO THAT UNLESS WE FIGURE OUT WHO WANTS YOU DEAD.
I CAN THINK OF A FEW NAMES.
WELL...
A FEW? I KEEP A RUNNING LIST. FOUR PAGES. SINGLE SPACED.

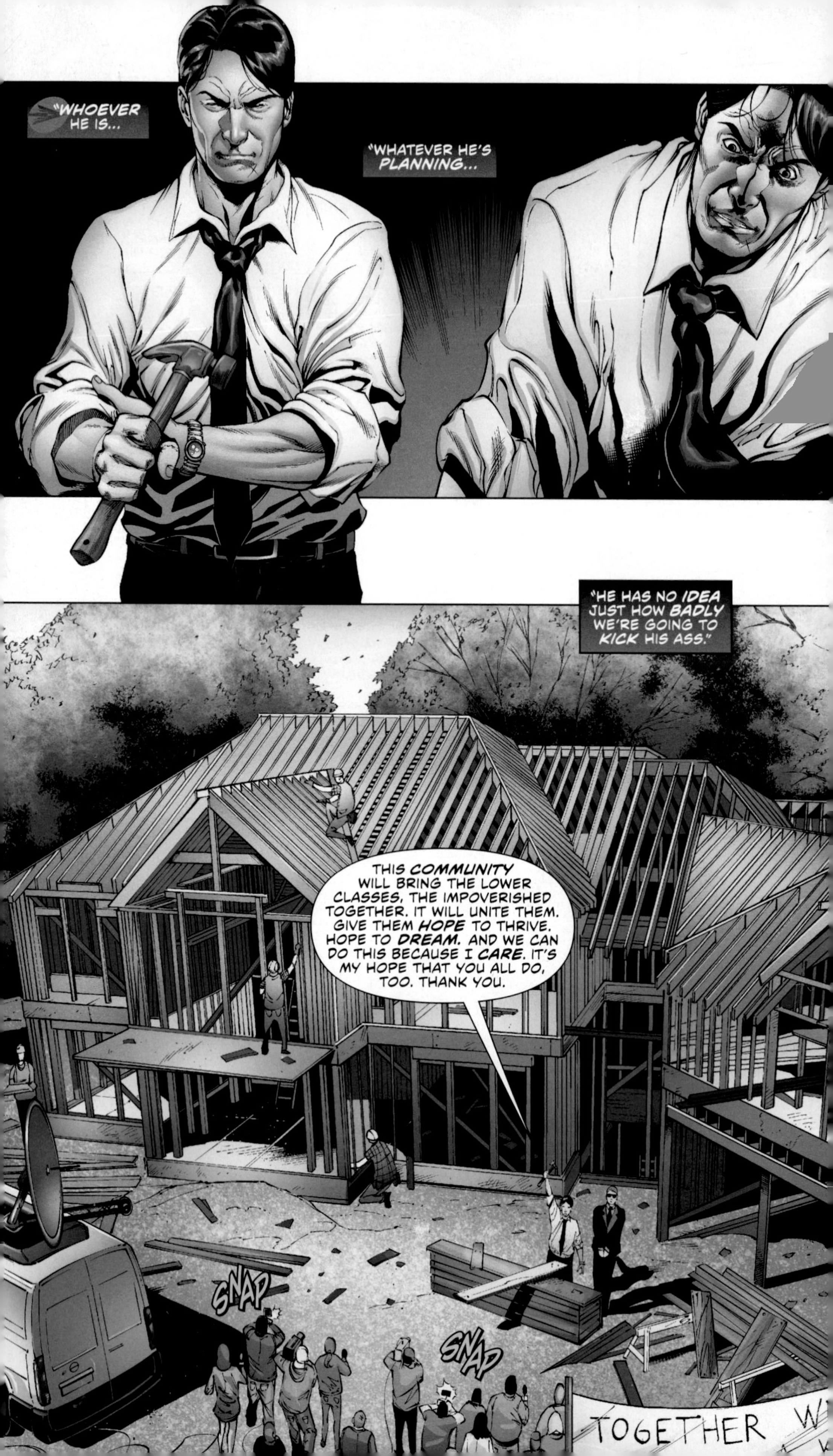
"WHOEVER HE IS...
"WHATEVER HE'S PLANNING...
"HE HAS NO IDEA JUST HOW BADLY WE'RE GOING TO KICK HIS ASS."
THIS COMMUNITY WILL BRING THE LOWER CLASSES, THE IMPOVERISHED TOGETHER. IT WILL UNITE THEM. GIVE THEM HOPE TO THRIVE. HOPE TO DREAM. AND WE CAN DO THIS BECAUSE I CARE. IT'S MY HOPE THAT YOU ALL DO, TOO. THANK YOU.
SNAP
SNAP
TOGETHER W

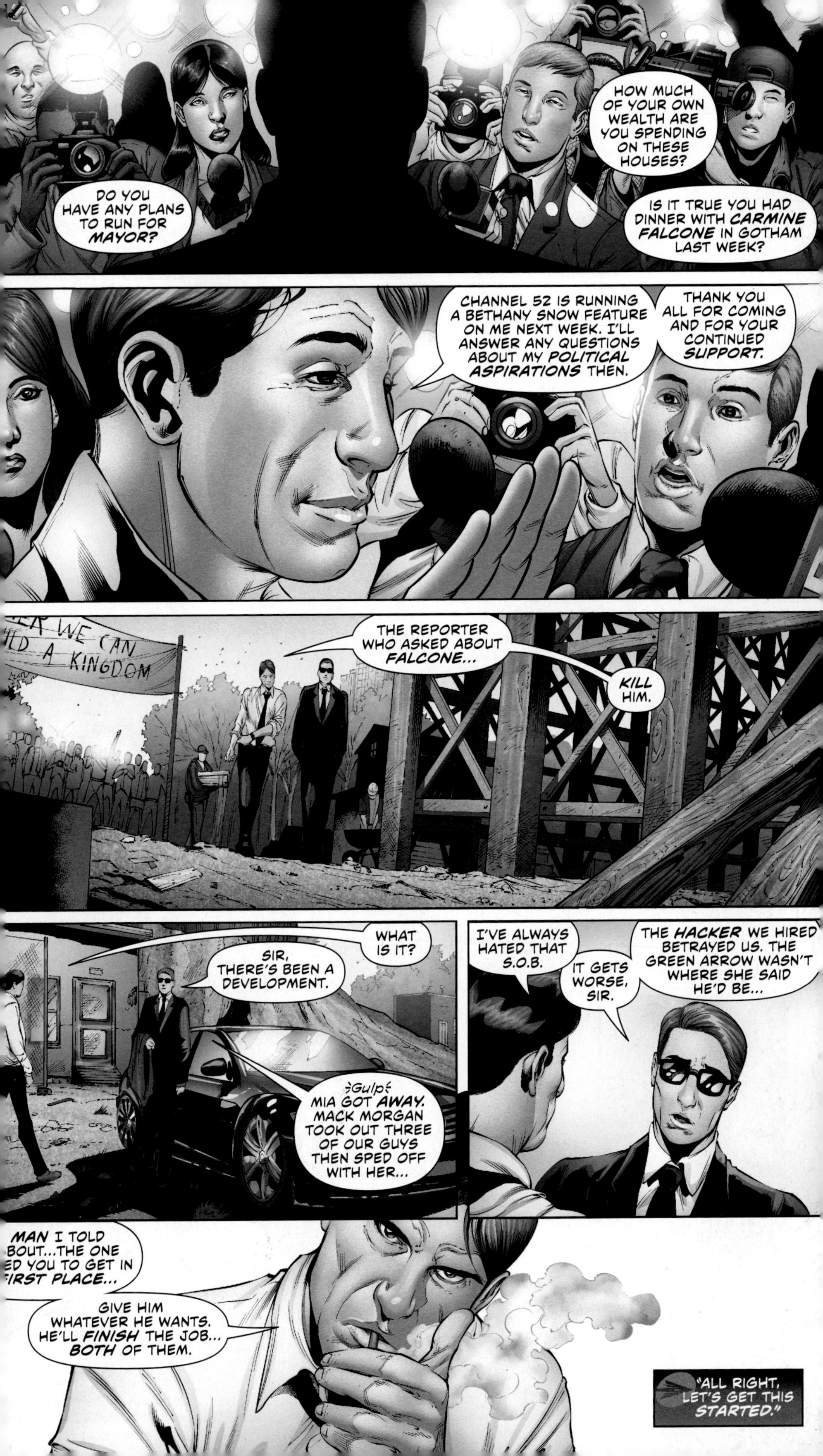

DO YOU HAVE ANY PLANS TO RUN FOR MAYOR?
HOW MUCH OF YOUR OWN WEALTH ARE YOU SPENDING ON THESE HOUSES?
IS IT TRUE YOU HAD DINNER WITH CARMINE FALCONE IN GOTHAM LAST WEEK?
CHANNEL 52 IS RUNNING A BETHANY SNOW FEATURE ON ME NEXT WEEK. I'LL ANSWER ANY QUESTIONS ABOUT MY POLITICAL ASPIRATIONS THEN.
THANK YOU ALL FOR COMING AND FOR YOUR CONTINUED SUPPORT.
WE CAN
A KINGDOM
THE REPORTER WHO ASKED ABOUT FALCONE...
KILL HIM.
WHAT IS IT?
SIR, THERE'S BEEN A DEVELOPMENT.
Gulp
MIA GOT AWAY. MACK MORGAN TOOK OUT THREE OF OUR GUYS THEN SPED OFF WITH HER...
I'VE ALWAYS HATED THAT S.O.B.
IT GETS WORSE, SIR.
THE HACKER WE HIRED BETRAYED US. THE GREEN ARROW WASN'T WHERE SHE SAID HE'D BE...
MAN I TOLD
BOUT...THE ONE
ED YOU TO GET IN
IRST PLACE...
GIVE HIM WHATEVER HE WANTS. HE'LL FINISH THE JOB... BOTH OF THEM.
"ALL RIGHT, LET'S GET THIS STARTED."

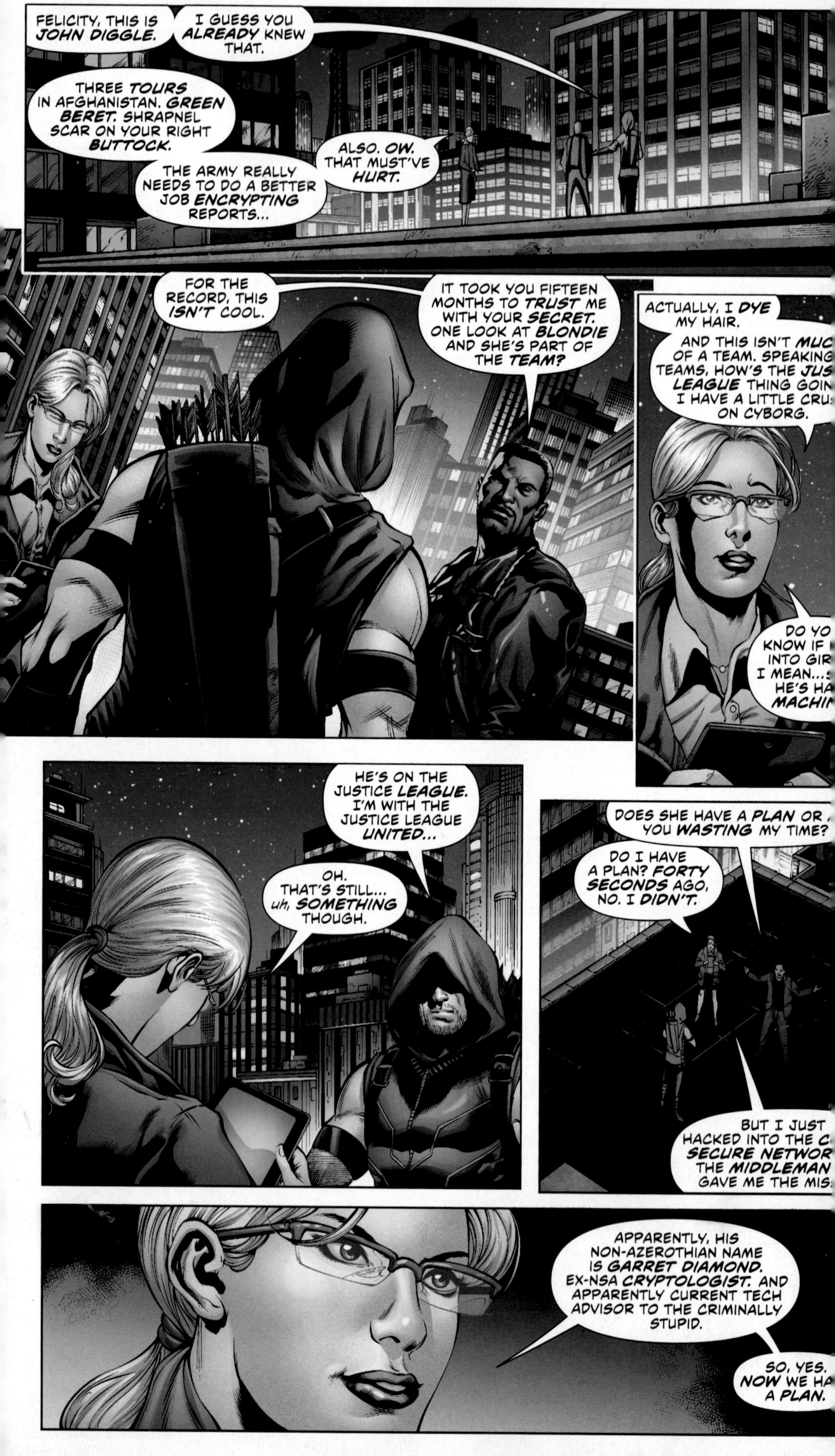

FELICITY, THIS IS JOHN DIGGLE.
I GUESS YOU ALREADY KNEW THAT.
THREE TOURS IN AFGHANISTAN. GREEN BERET. SHRAPNEL SCAR ON YOUR RIGHT BUTTOCK.
THE ARMY REALLY NEEDS TO DO A BETTER JOB ENCRYPTING REPORTS...
ALSO. OW. THAT MUST'VE HURT.
FOR THE RECORD, THIS ISN'T COOL.
IT TOOK YOU FIFTEEN MONTHS TO TRUST ME WITH YOUR SECRET. ONE LOOK AT BLONDIE AND SHE'S PART OF THE TEAM?
ACTUALLY, I DYE MY HAIR.
AND THIS ISN'T MUC OF A TEAM. SPEAKING TEAMS, HOW'S THE JUS LEAGUE THING GOIN I HAVE A LITTLE CRU ON CYBORG.
DO YO KNOW IF INTO GIR I MEAN... HE'S HA MACHI
HE'S ON THE JUSTICE LEAGUE. I'M WITH THE JUSTICE LEAGUE UNITED...
OH. THAT'S STILL... uh, SOMETHING THOUGH.
DOES SHE HAVE A PLAN OR YOU WASTING MY TIME?
DO I HAVE A PLAN? FORTY SECONDS AGO, NO. I DIDN'T.
BUT I JUST HACKED INTO THE C SECURE NETWOR THE MIDDLEMAN GAVE ME THE MIS
APPARENTLY, HIS NON-AZEROTHIAN NAME IS GARRET DIAMOND. EX-NSA CRYPTOLOGIST. AND APPARENTLY CURRENT TECH ADVISOR TO THE CRIMINALLY STUPID.
SO, YES. NOW WE HA A PLAN.

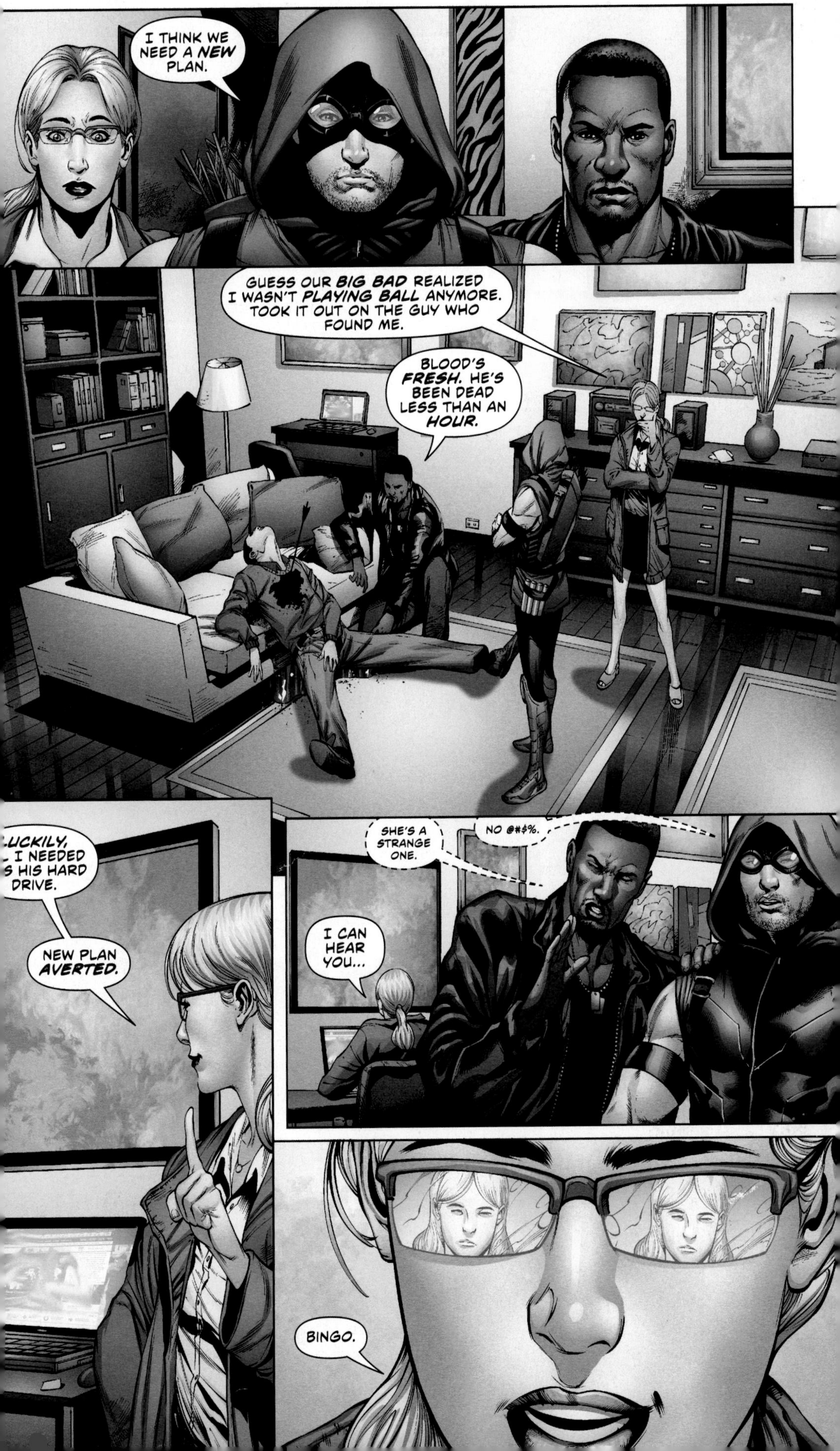
I THINK WE NEED A *NEW* PLAN.
GUESS OUR *BIG BAD* REALIZED I WASN'T *PLAYING BALL* ANYMORE. TOOK IT OUT ON THE GUY WHO FOUND ME.
BLOOD'S *FRESH.* HE'S BEEN DEAD LESS THAN AN *HOUR.*
UCKILY, I NEEDED S HIS HARD DRIVE.
NEW PLAN *AVERTED.*
SHE'S A STRANGE ONE.
NO @#$%.
I CAN HEAR YOU...
BINGO.

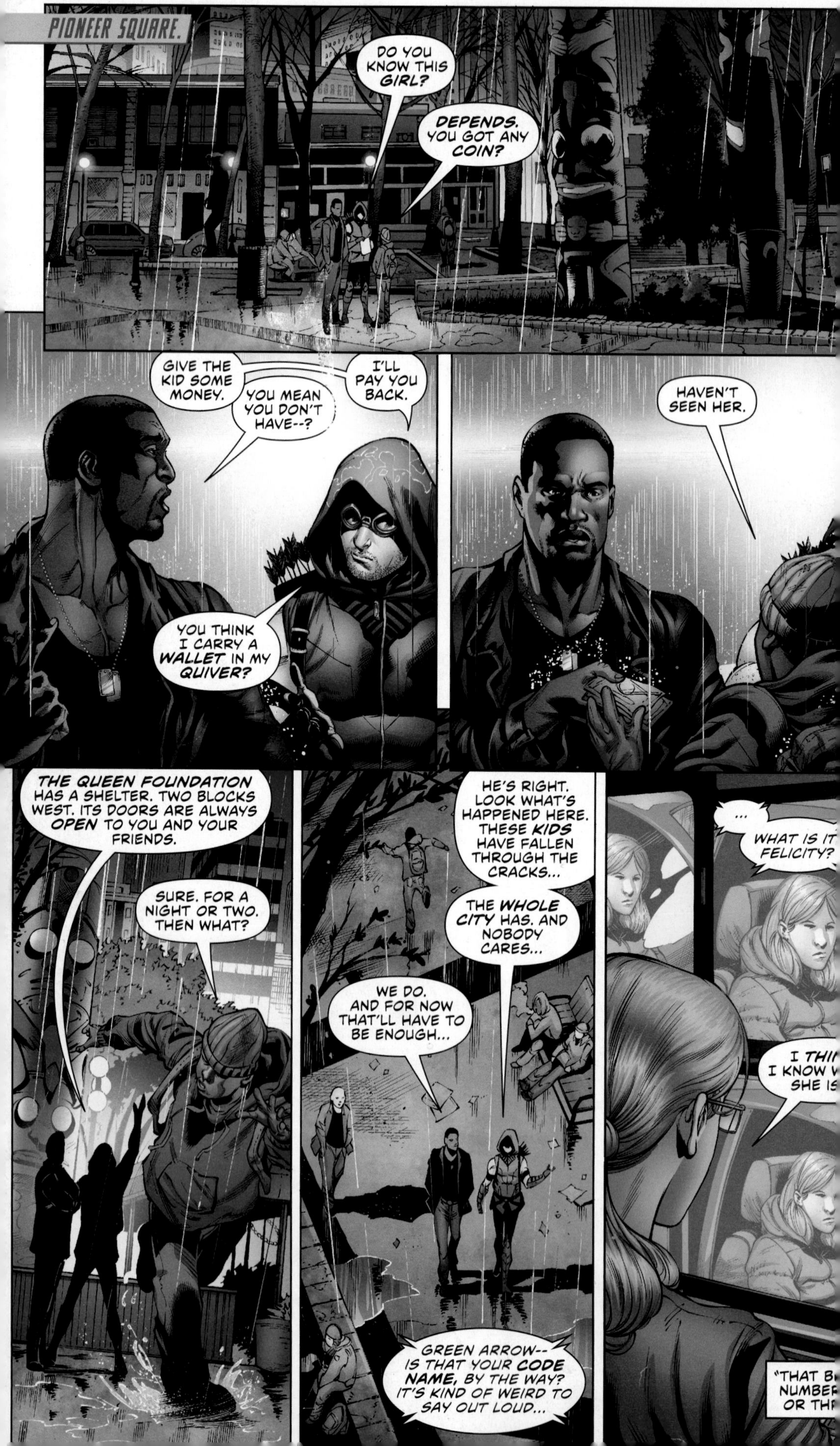

PIONEER SQUARE.
DO YOU KNOW THIS GIRL?
DEPENDS. YOU GOT ANY COIN?
GIVE THE KID SOME MONEY.
YOU MEAN YOU DON'T HAVE--?
I'LL PAY YOU BACK.
YOU THINK I CARRY A WALLET IN MY QUIVER?
HAVEN'T SEEN HER.
THE QUEEN FOUNDATION HAS A SHELTER. TWO BLOCKS WEST. ITS DOORS ARE ALWAYS OPEN TO YOU AND YOUR FRIENDS.
SURE. FOR A NIGHT OR TWO. THEN WHAT?
HE'S RIGHT. LOOK WHAT'S HAPPENED HERE. THESE KIDS HAVE FALLEN THROUGH THE CRACKS...
THE WHOLE CITY HAS. AND NOBODY CARES...
WE DO. AND FOR NOW THAT'LL HAVE TO BE ENOUGH...
GREEN ARROW-- IS THAT YOUR CODE NAME, BY THE WAY? IT'S KIND OF WEIRD TO SAY OUT LOUD...
...
WHAT IS IT FELICITY?

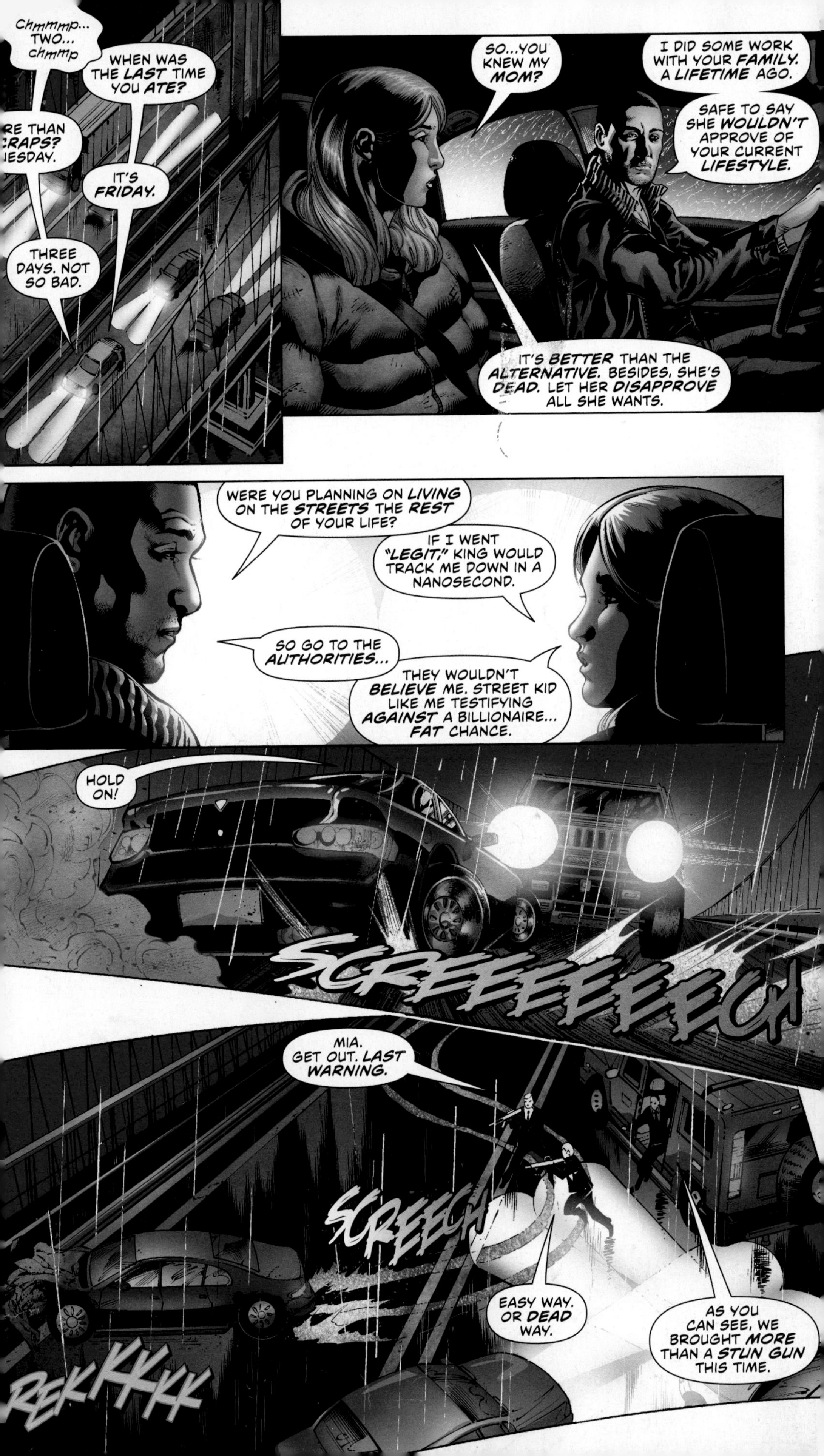
Chmmmp... TWO... chmmp
WHEN WAS THE LAST TIME YOU ATE?
IT'S FRIDAY.
THREE DAYS. NOT SO BAD.
SO...YOU KNEW MY MOM?
I DID SOME WORK WITH YOUR FAMILY. A LIFETIME AGO.
SAFE TO SAY SHE WOULDN'T APPROVE OF YOUR CURRENT LIFESTYLE.
IT'S BETTER THAN THE ALTERNATIVE. BESIDES, SHE'S DEAD. LET HER DISAPPROVE ALL SHE WANTS.
WERE YOU PLANNING ON LIVING ON THE STREETS THE REST OF YOUR LIFE?
IF I WENT "LEGIT," KING WOULD TRACK ME DOWN IN A NANOSECOND.
SO GO TO THE AUTHORITIES...
THEY WOULDN'T BELIEVE ME. STREET KID LIKE ME TESTIFYING AGAINST A BILLIONAIRE... FAT CHANCE.
HOLD ON!
SCREEEEEEECH
MIA. GET OUT. LAST WARNING.
SCREECH
EASY WAY. OR DEAD WAY.
AS YOU CAN SEE, WE BROUGHT MORE THAN A STUN GUN THIS TIME.
REKKKKK

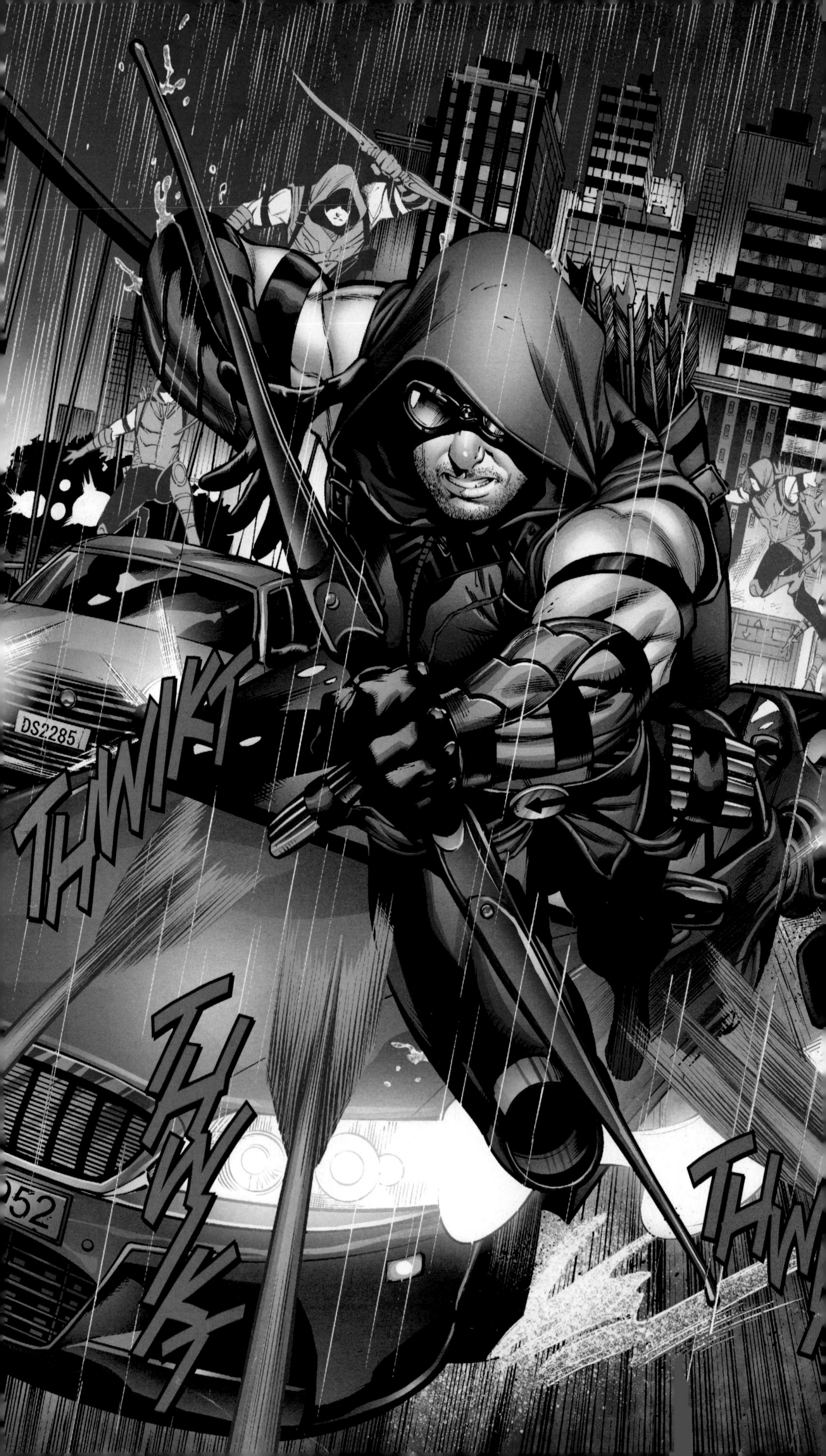
THWIK!
THWIK
THW

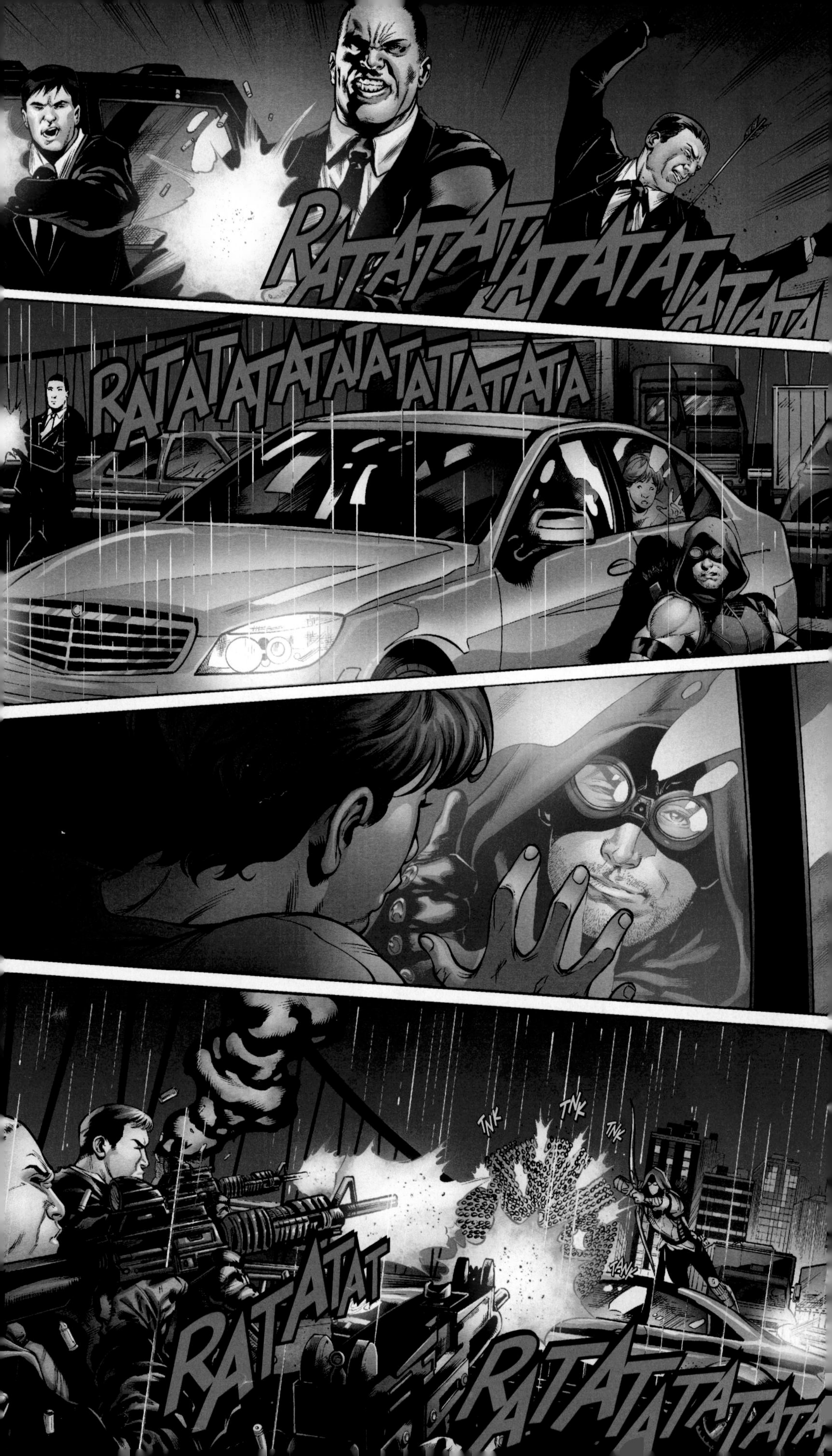
RATATATATATATATATATA
RATATATATATATATATATA
TNK
TNK
TNK
TANK
RATATAT
RATATATATATA

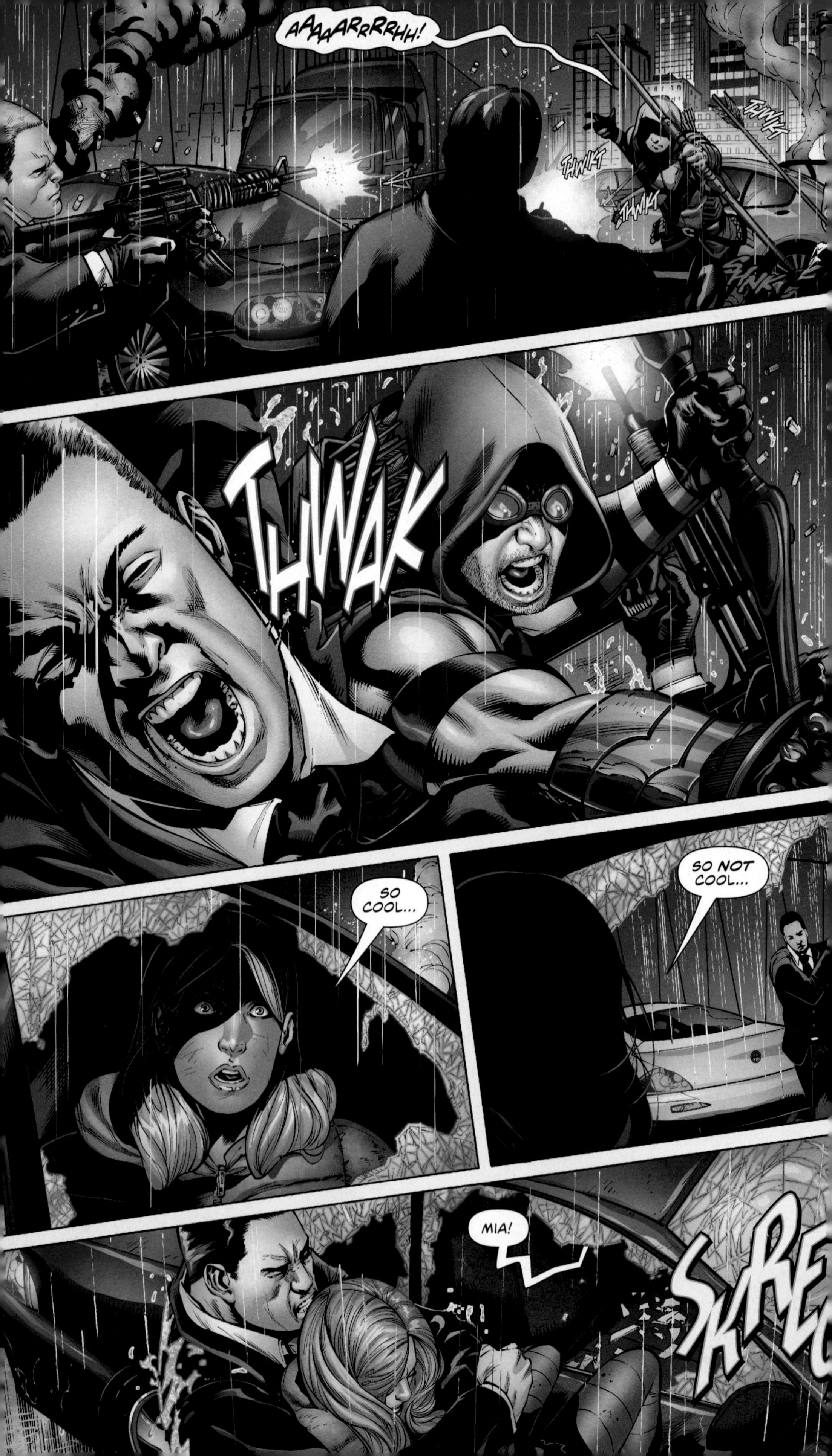
AAAAARRRRHH!
THWIKT
THWIKT
THWIKT
THWAK
SO COOL...
SO NOT COOL...
MIA!
SKREE

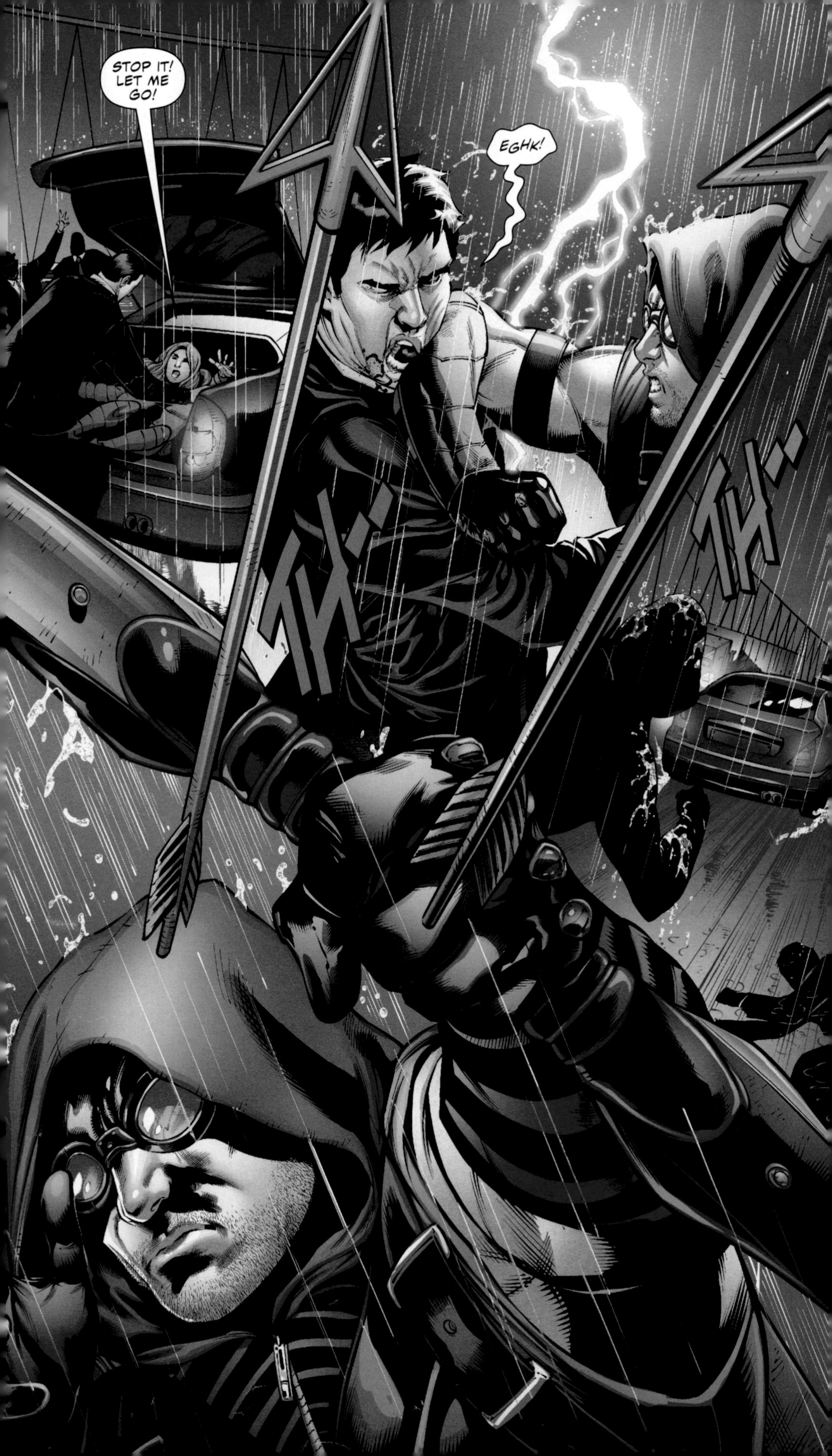
STOP IT! LET ME GO!
EGHK!
TVK!
TVK--

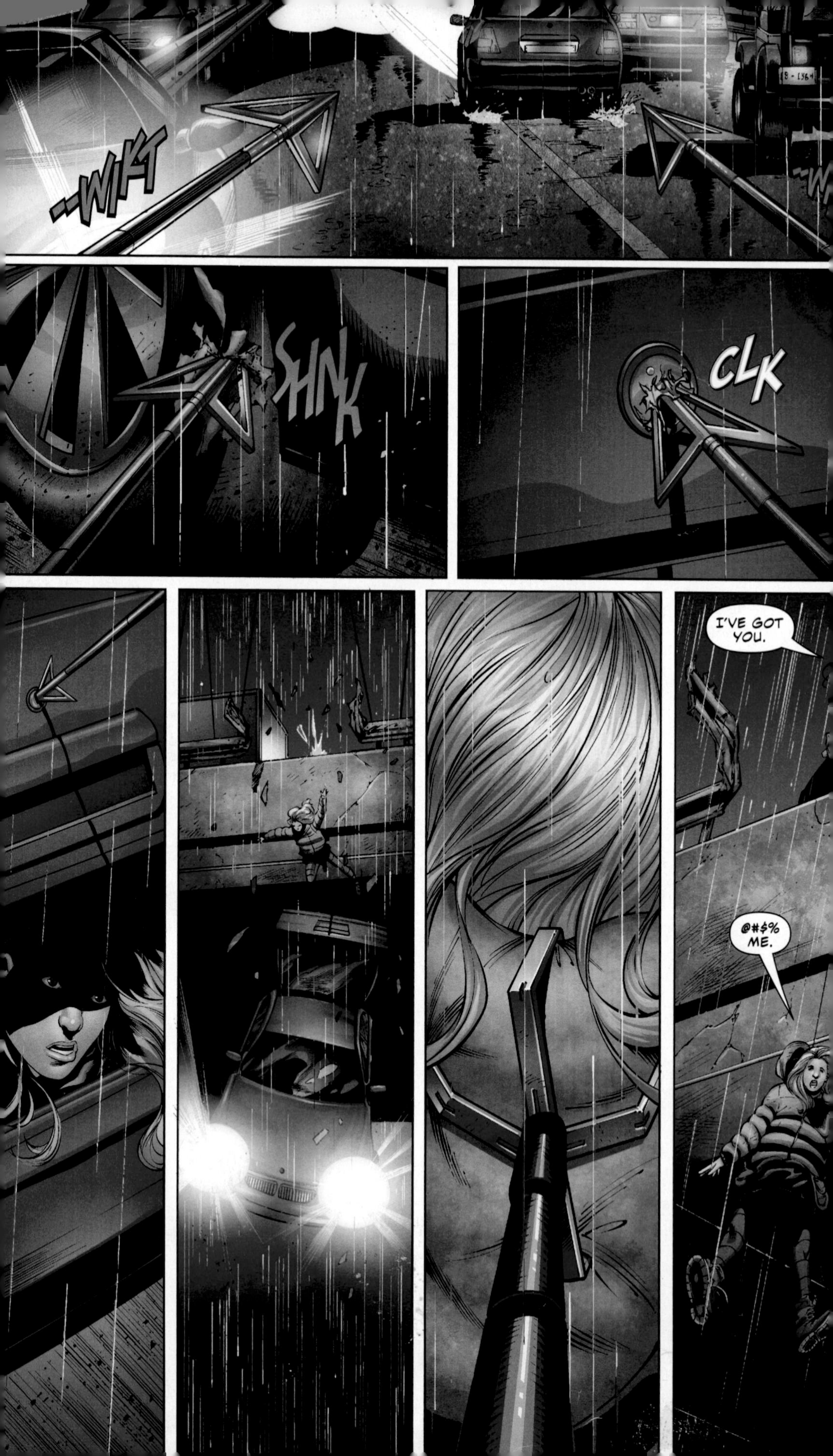
--WIKT
SHNK
CLK
I'VE GOT YOU.
@#$% ME.

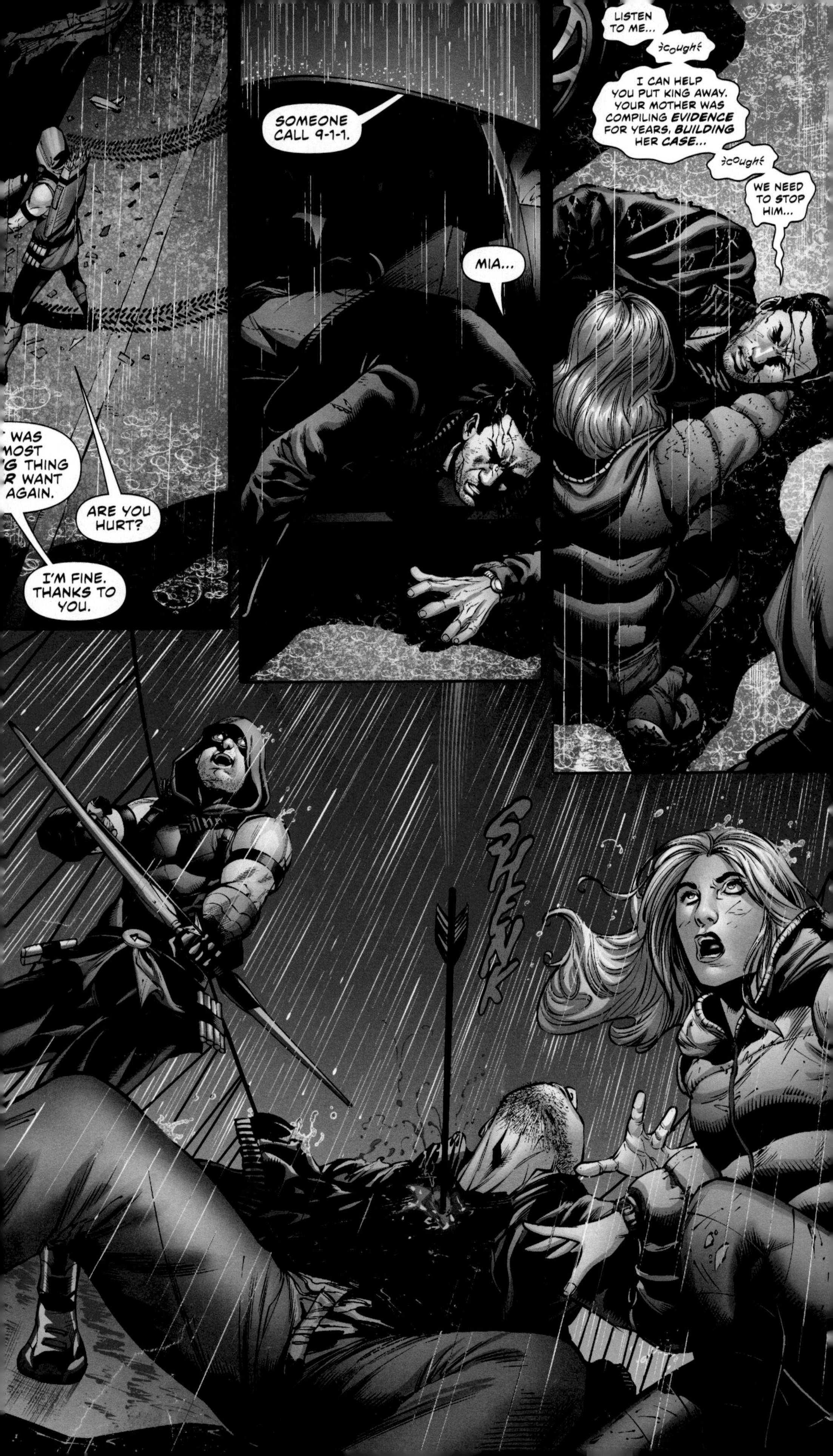
WAS MOST G THING R WANT AGAIN.
ARE YOU HURT?
I'M FINE. THANKS TO YOU.
SOMEONE CALL 9-1-1.
MIA...
LISTEN TO ME...
cough
I CAN HELP YOU PUT KING AWAY. YOUR MOTHER WAS COMPILING EVIDENCE FOR YEARS, BUILDING HER CASE...
cough
WE NEED TO STOP HIM...
SHENK

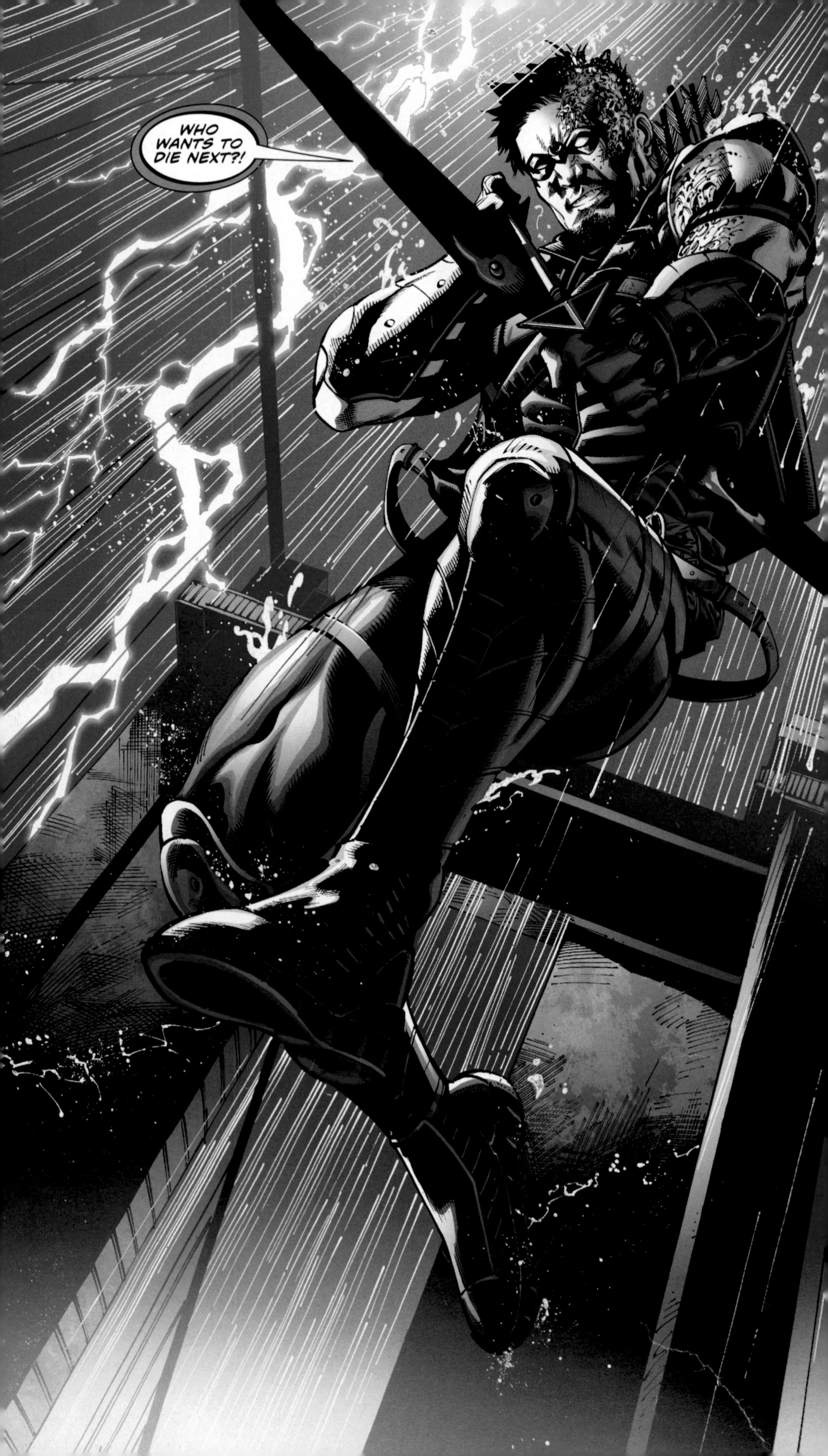
WHO WANTS TO DIE NEXT?!

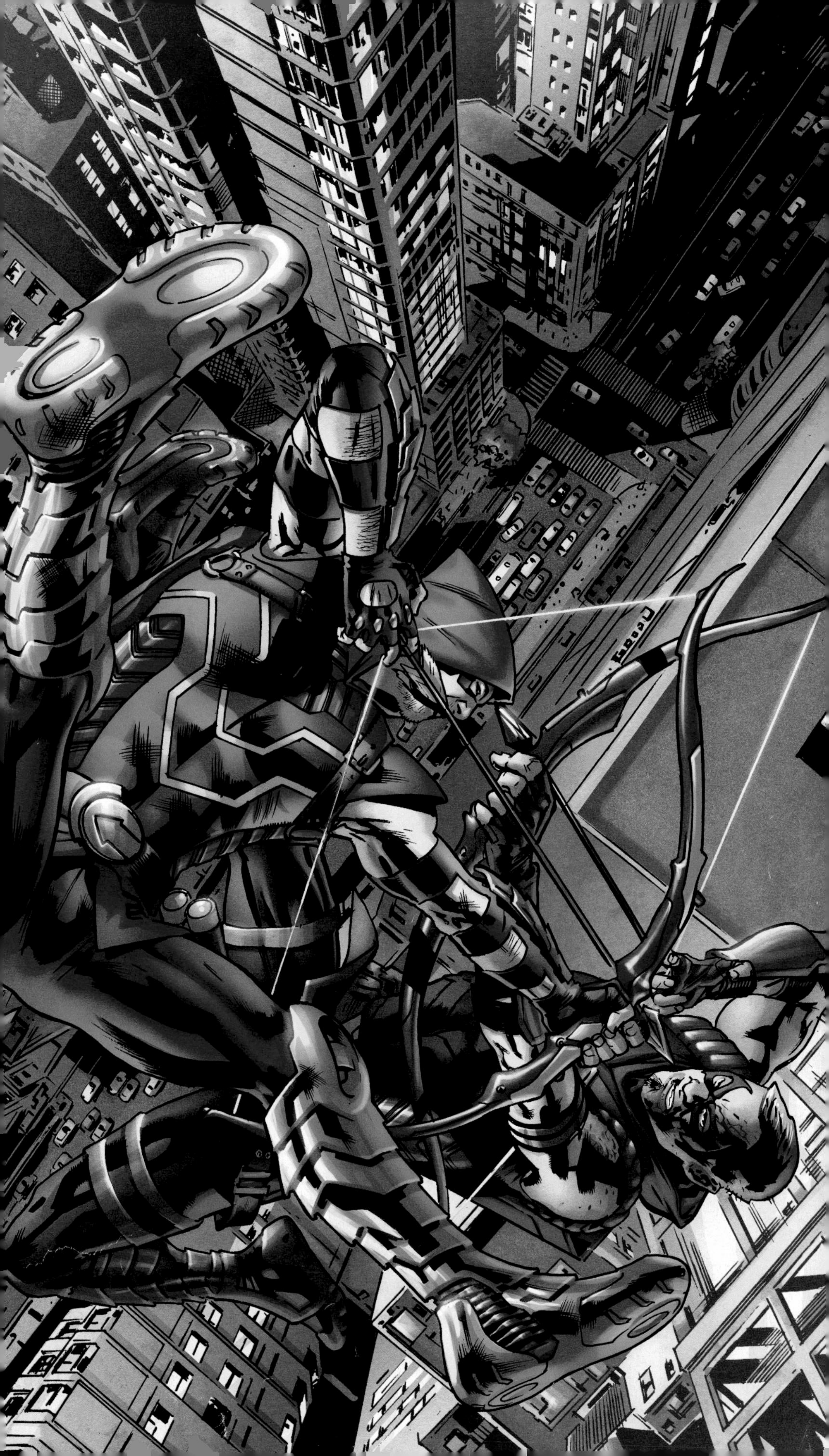

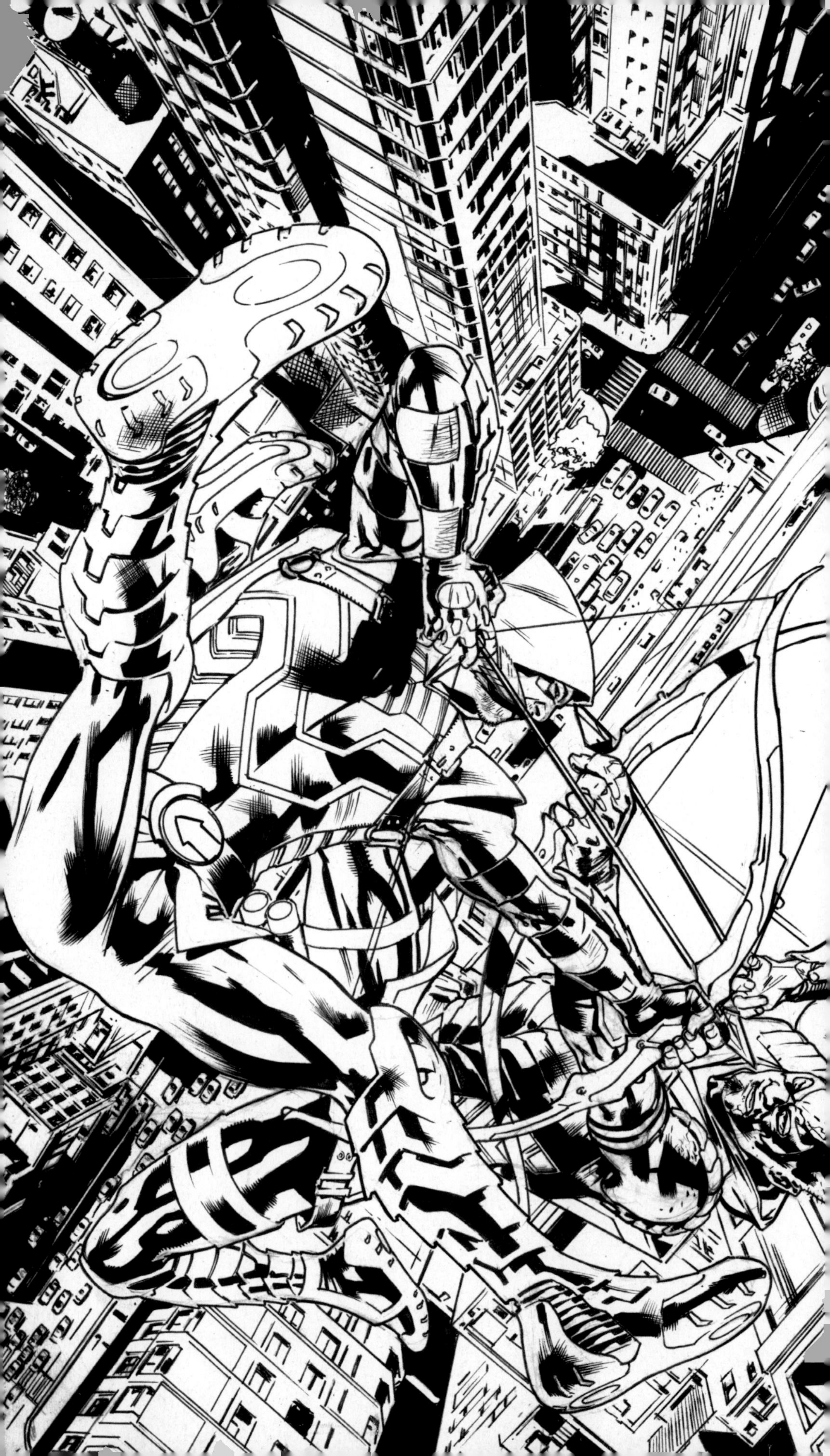

THE KING HAS BEEN NOTHING BUT *GENEROUS* AND *LOVING* TO YOU. IS THAT NOT *TRUE?*

YES. YES. HE HAS BEEN. HE PAID FOR MY *DAUGHTER'S* CHEMOTHERAPY...

YOU LOYAL CT, ARE NOT?

YES. YES...

THEN DO NOT COME TO THE GREEN ARROW'S AID RIGHT NOW. DO YOU *UNDERSTAND?*

BUT...

...I UNDERSTAND.

VERY WELL.

CLK

ARE ING

THEY'RE *TEARING* THE STREET APART.

WE'RE NOT TO ENGAGE OR INTERFERE...

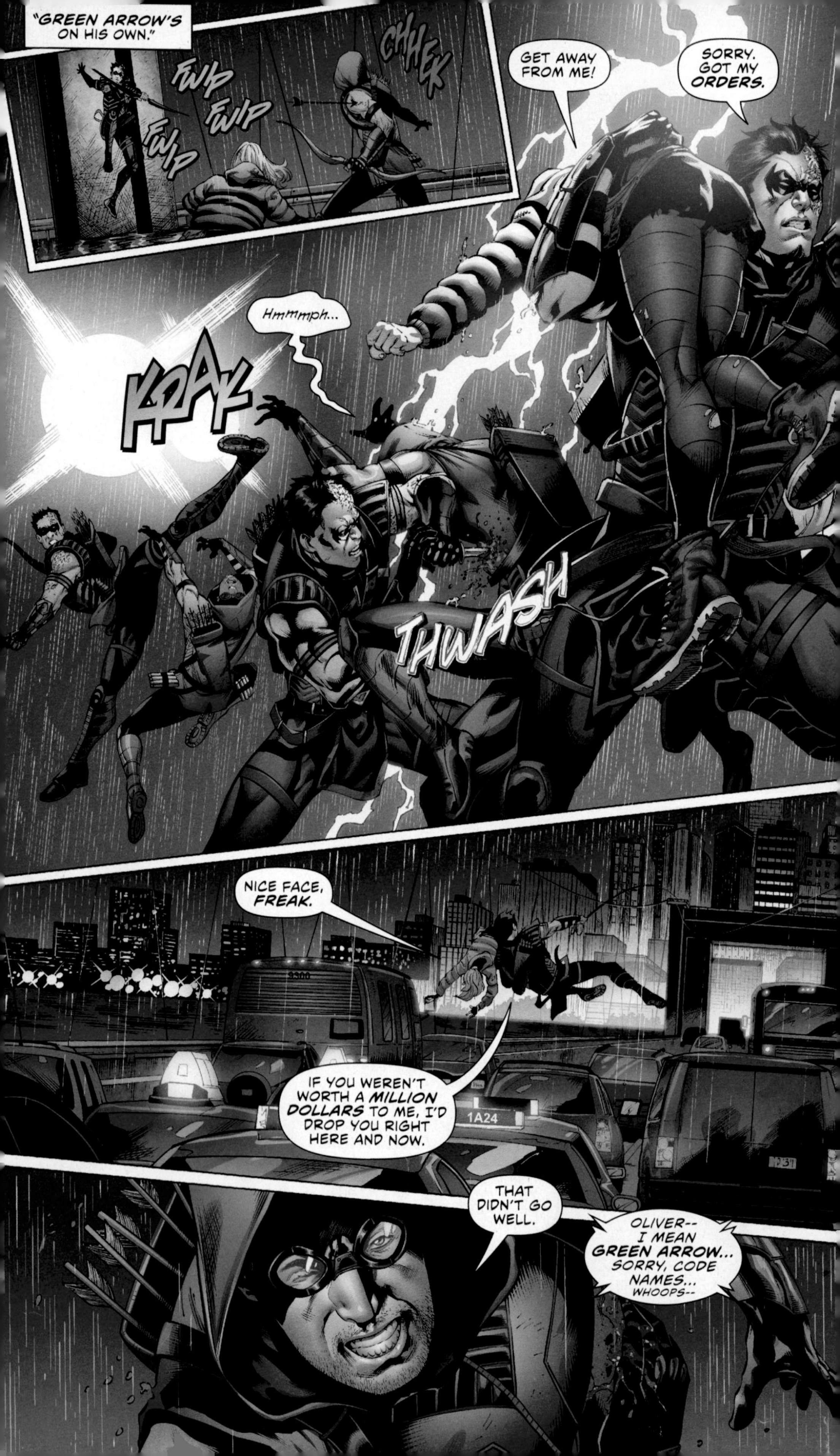
"GREEN ARROW'S ON HIS OWN."
FWIP FWIP FWIP
CHHEK
GET AWAY FROM ME!
SORRY. GOT MY ORDERS.
Hmmmph...
KRAK
THWASH
NICE FACE, FREAK.
IF YOU WEREN'T WORTH A MILLION DOLLARS TO ME, I'D DROP YOU RIGHT HERE AND NOW.
THAT DIDN'T GO WELL.
OLIVER-- I MEAN GREEN ARROW... SORRY, CODE NAMES... WHOOPS--

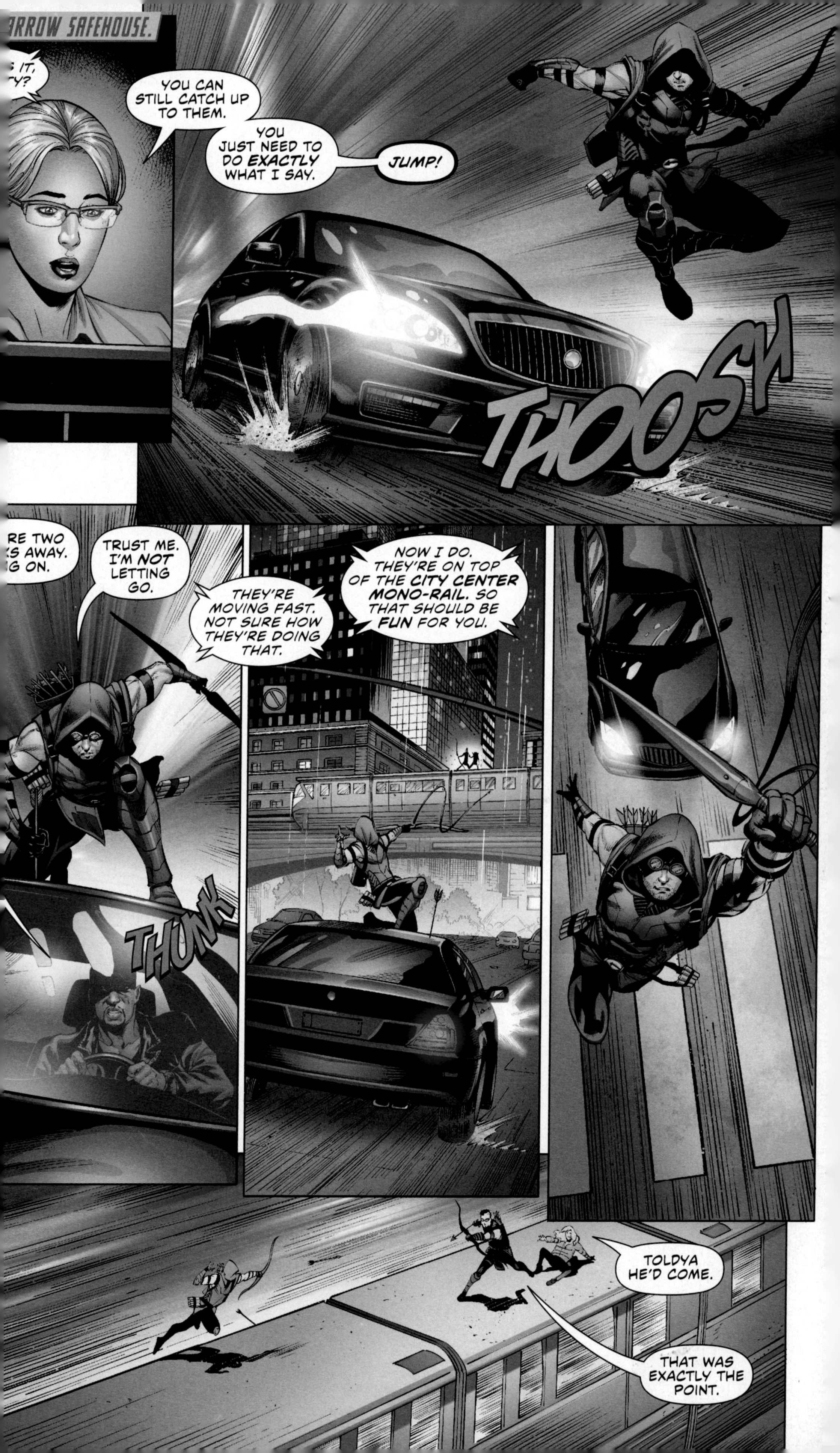

ARROW SAFEHOUSE.
YOU CAN STILL CATCH UP TO THEM.
YOU JUST NEED TO DO EXACTLY WHAT I SAY.
JUMP!
THOOSH
TRUST ME. I'M NOT LETTING GO.
THUNK
THEY'RE MOVING FAST. NOT SURE HOW THEY'RE DOING THAT.
NOW I DO. THEY'RE ON TOP OF THE CITY CENTER MONO-RAIL. SO THAT SHOULD BE FUN FOR YOU.
TOLDYA HE'D COME.
THAT WAS EXACTLY THE POINT.

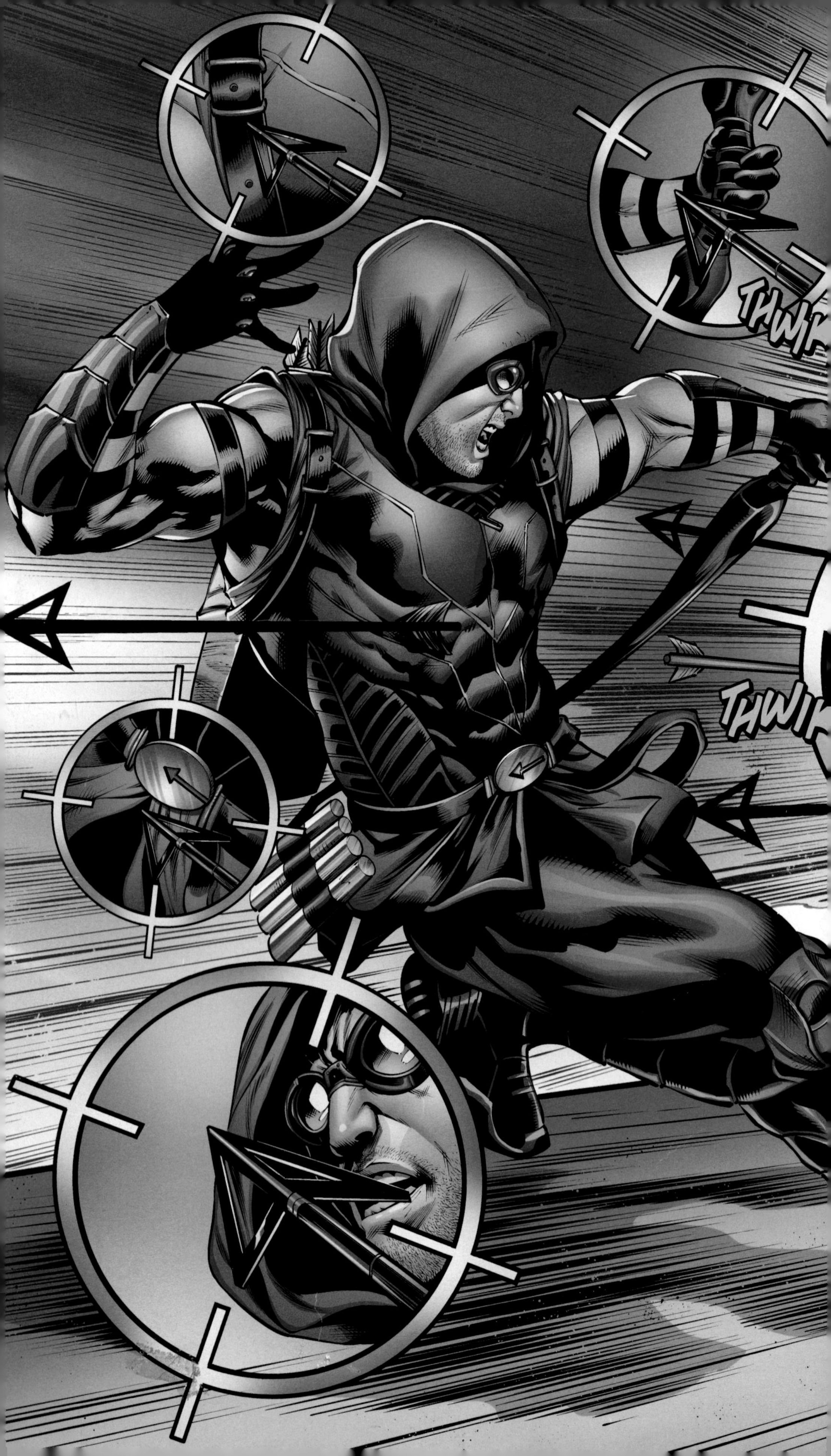
THWI
THWI

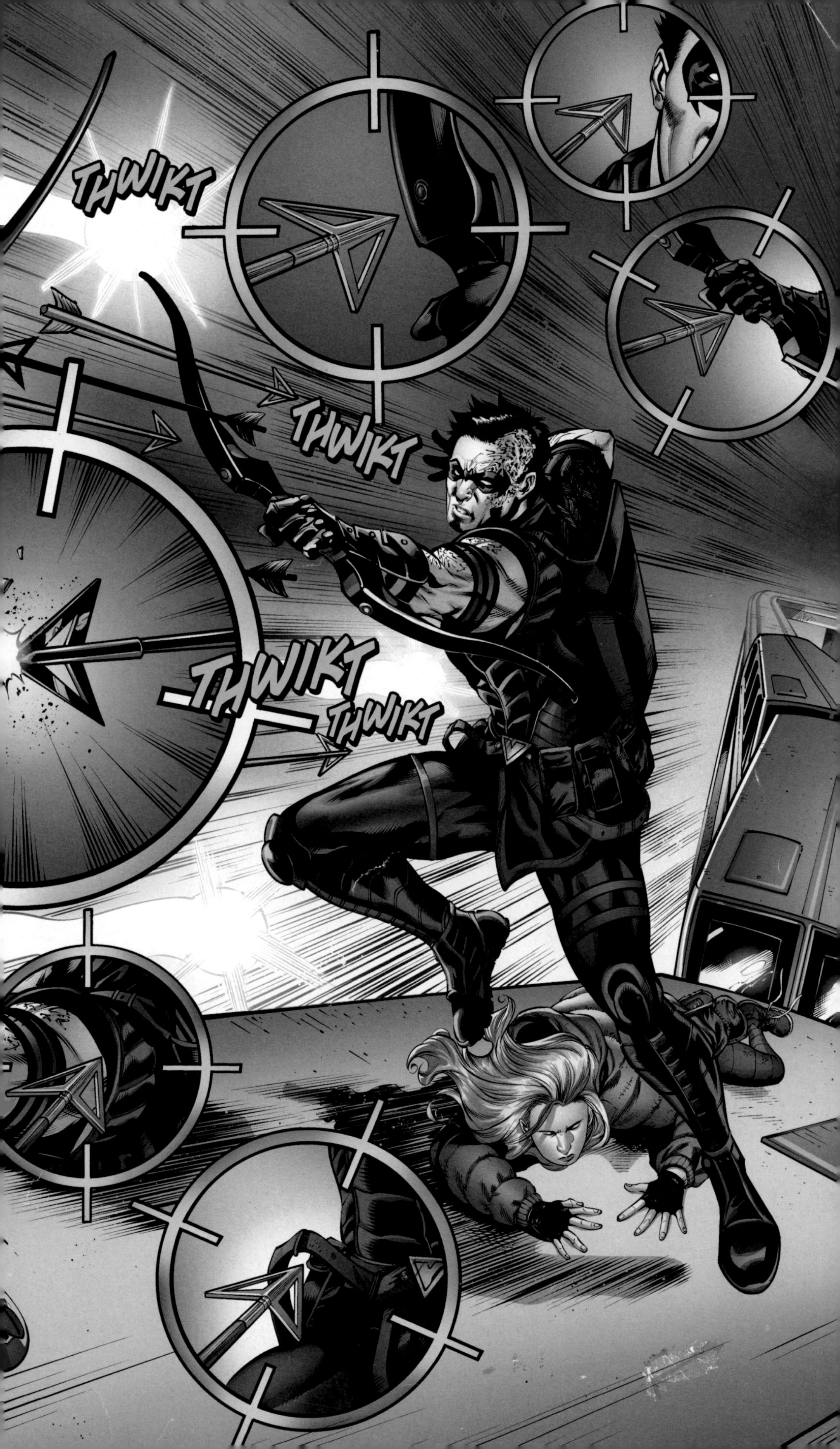
THWIKT
THWIKT
THWIKT
THWIKT

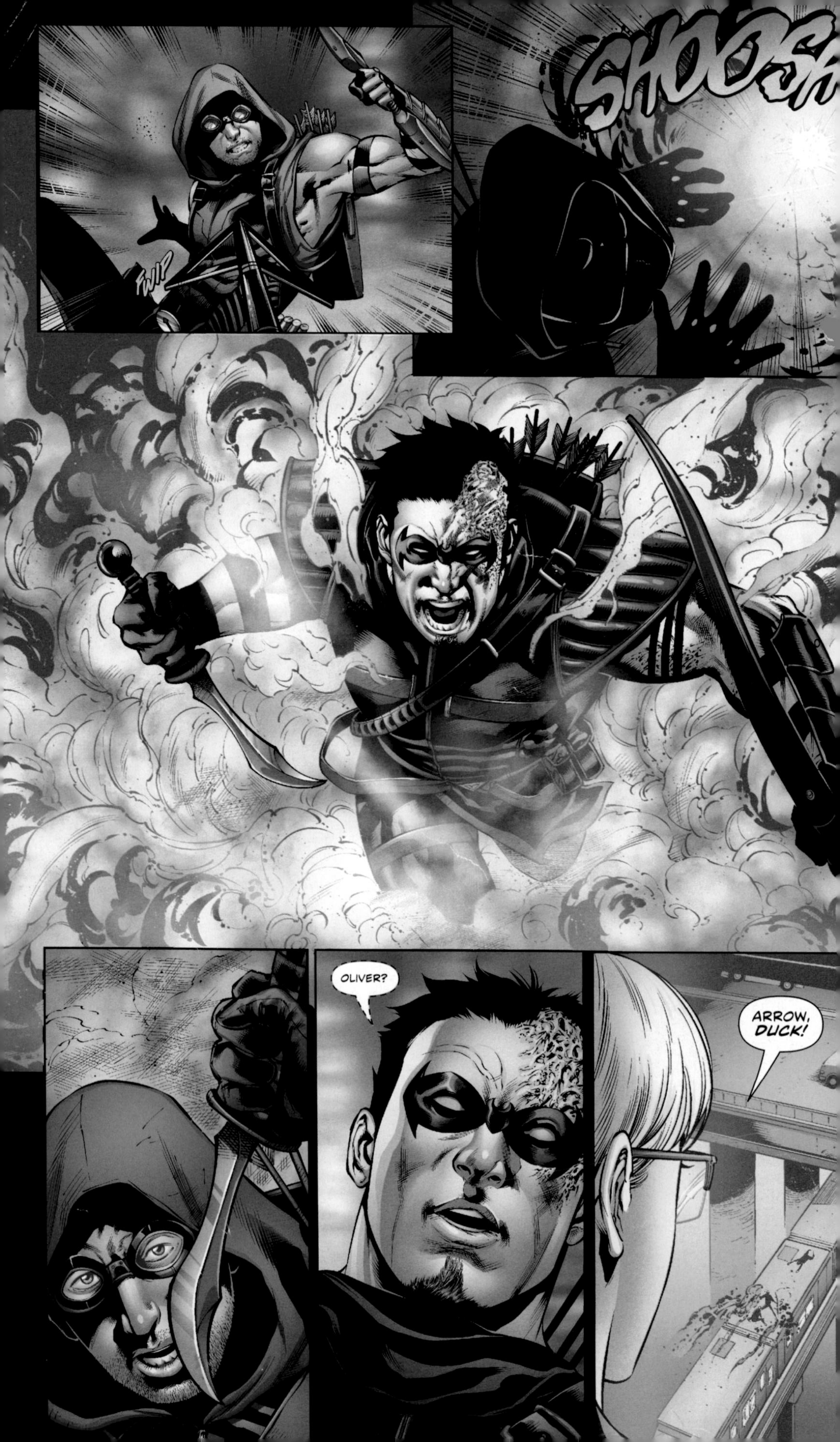
SHOOSH
FWIP
OLIVER?
ARROW, DUCK!

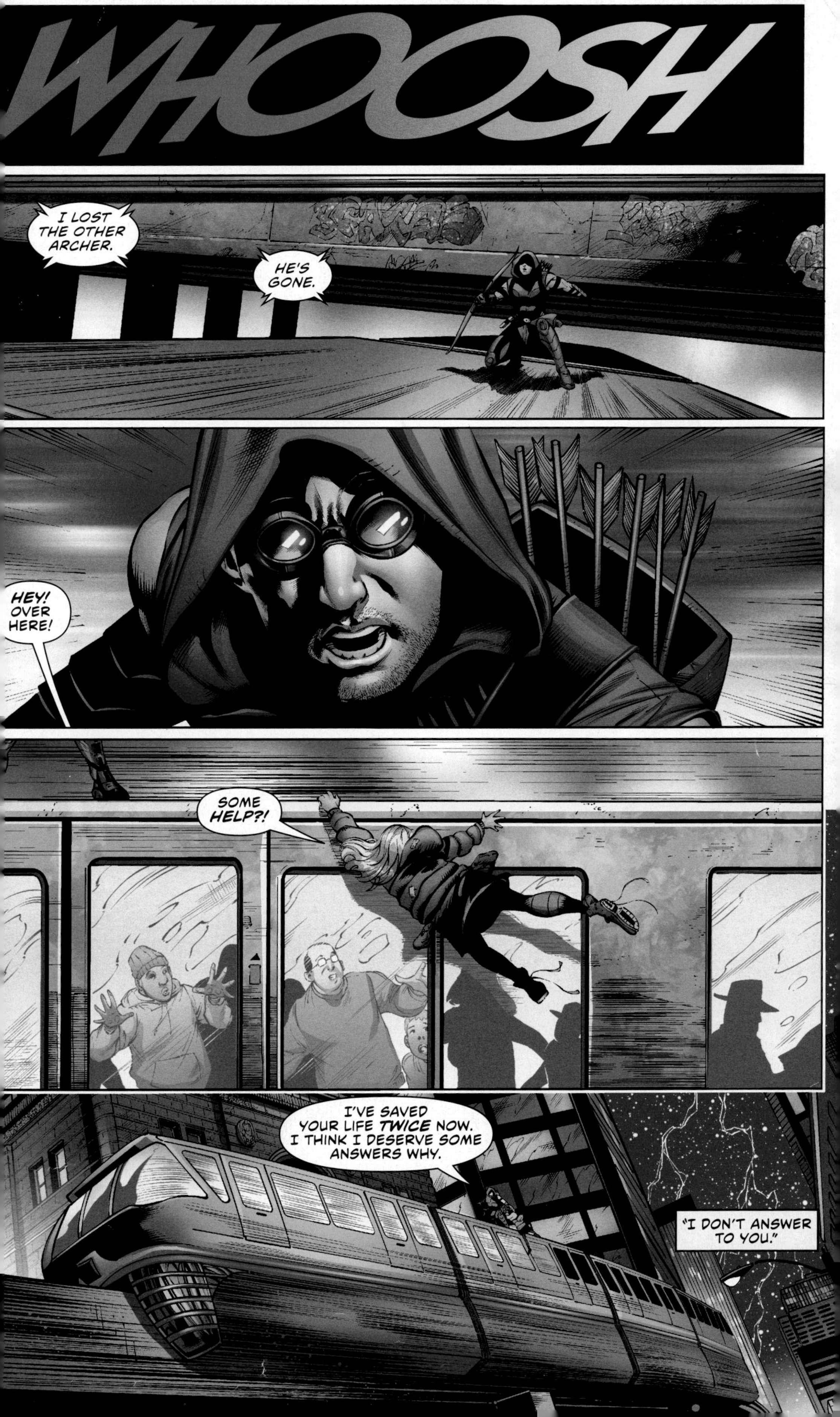
WHOOSH
I LOST THE OTHER ARCHER.
HE'S GONE.
HEY! OVER HERE!
SOME HELP?!
I'VE SAVED YOUR LIFE TWICE NOW. I THINK I DESERVE SOME ANSWERS WHY.
"I DON'T ANSWER TO YOU."

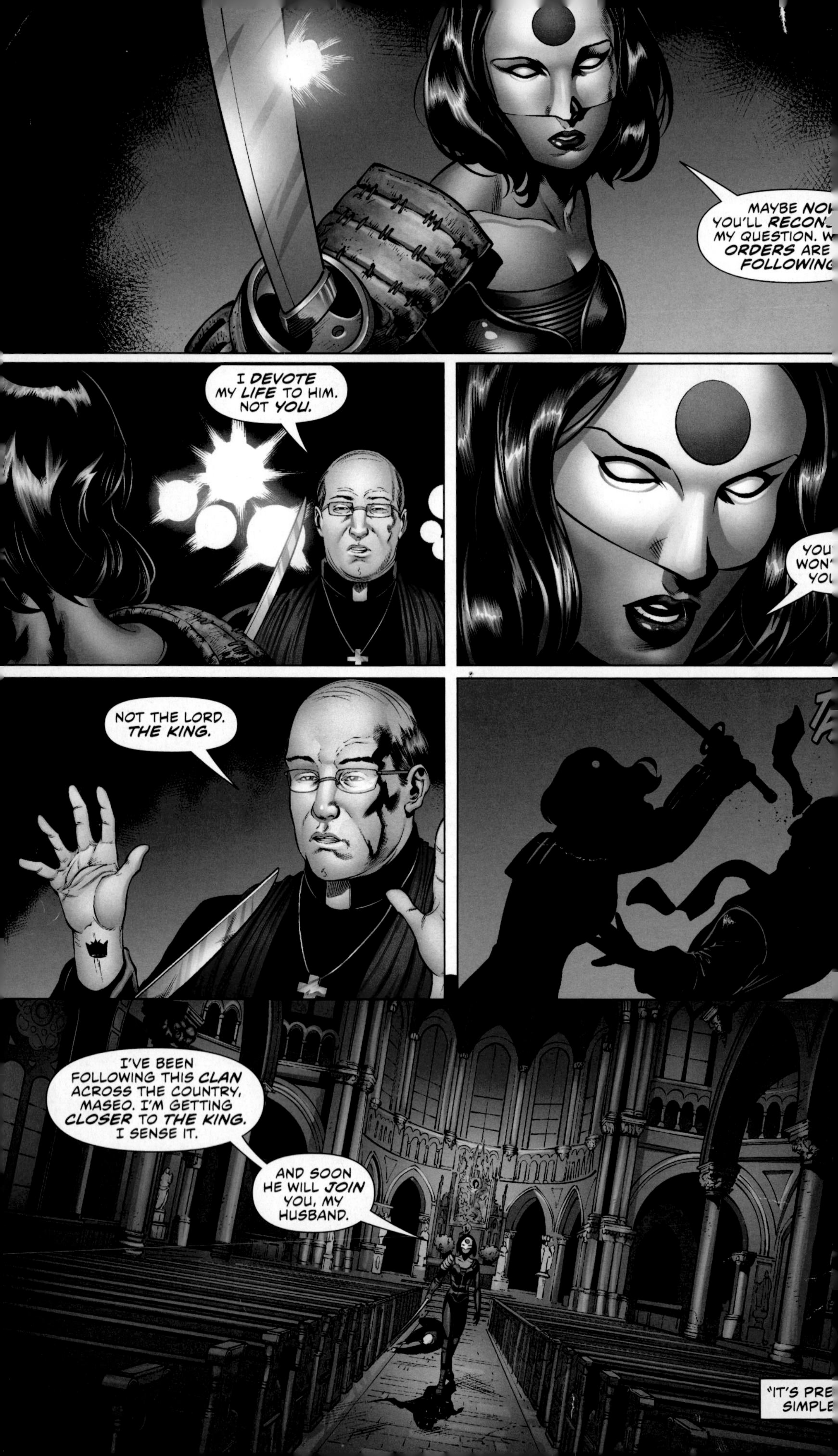
MAYBE NO YOU'LL RECON MY QUESTION. ORDERS ARE FOLLOWING
I DEVOTE MY LIFE TO HIM. NOT YOU.
YOU WON'
NOT THE LORD. THE KING.
I'VE BEEN FOLLOWING THIS CLAN ACROSS THE COUNTRY, MASEO. I'M GETTING CLOSER TO THE KING. I SENSE IT.
AND SOON HE WILL JOIN YOU, MY HUSBAND.
"IT'S PRE SIMPLE

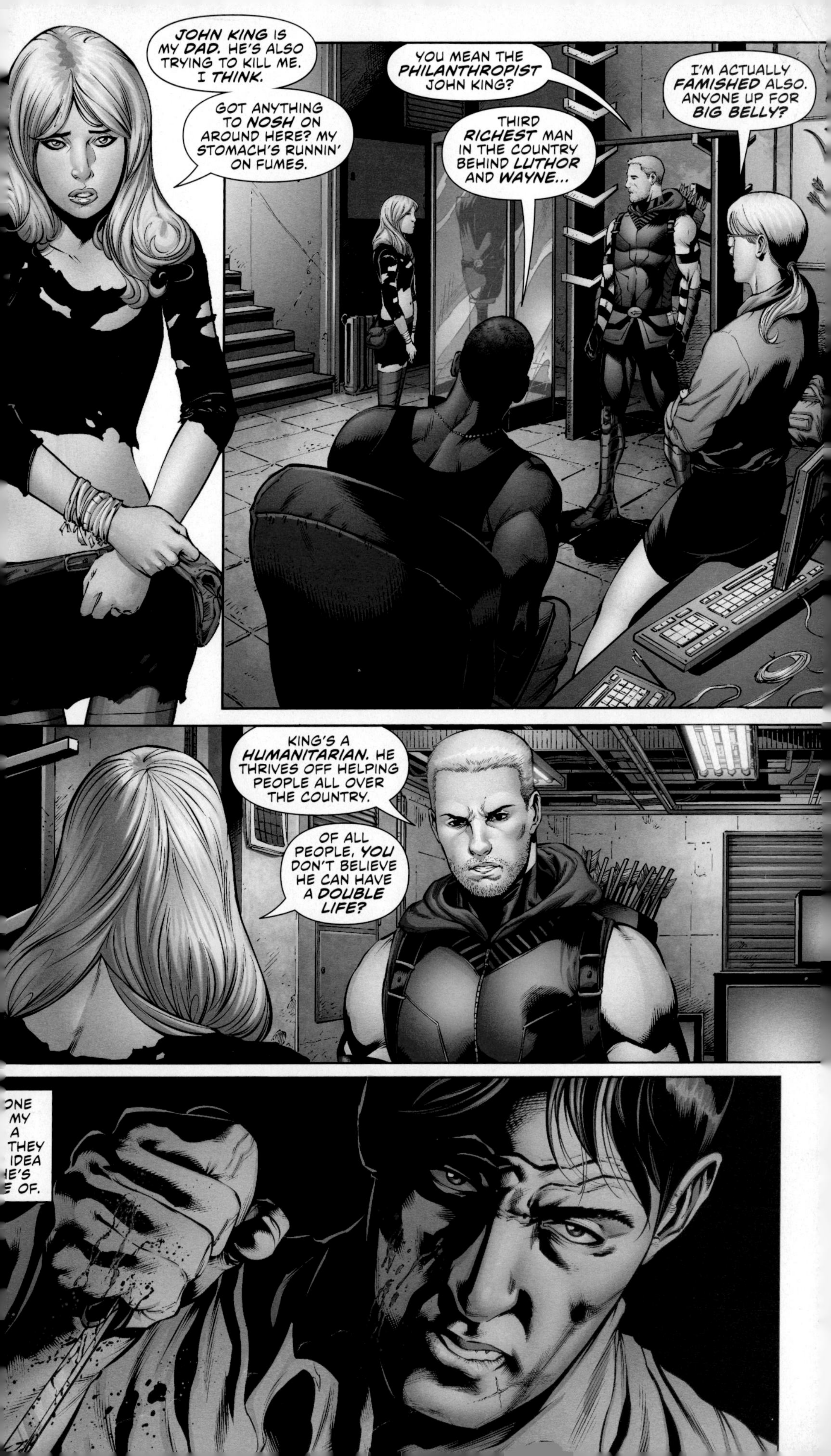

JOHN KING IS MY DAD. HE'S ALSO TRYING TO KILL ME. I THINK.
GOT ANYTHING TO NOSH ON AROUND HERE? MY STOMACH'S RUNNIN' ON FUMES.
YOU MEAN THE PHILANTHROPIST JOHN KING?
THIRD RICHEST MAN IN THE COUNTRY BEHIND LUTHOR AND WAYNE...
I'M ACTUALLY FAMISHED ALSO. ANYONE UP FOR BIG BELLY?
KING'S A HUMANITARIAN. HE THRIVES OFF HELPING PEOPLE ALL OVER THE COUNTRY.
OF ALL PEOPLE, YOU DON'T BELIEVE HE CAN HAVE A DOUBLE LIFE?
ONE
MY
A
THEY
IDEA
HE'S
E OF.

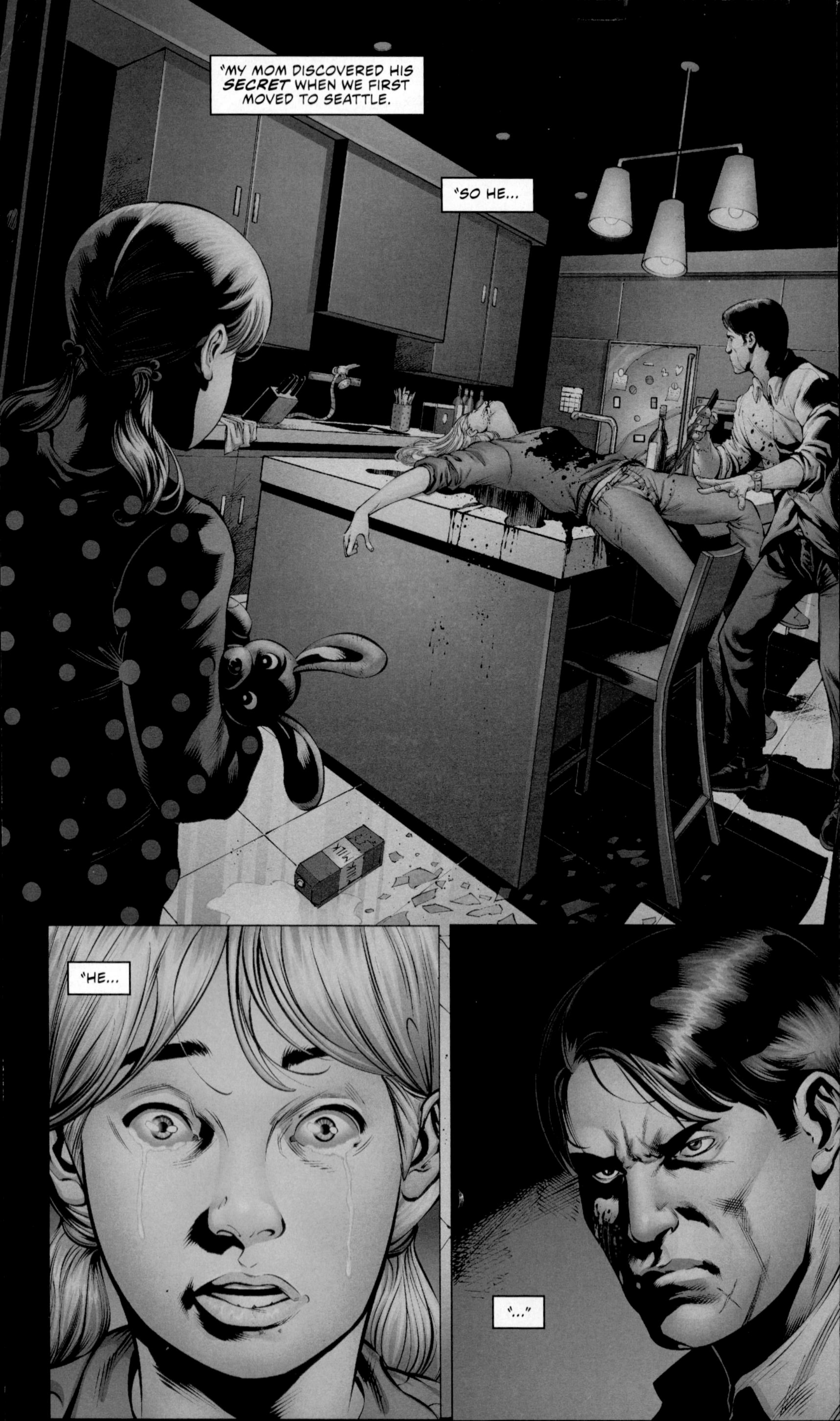
"MY MOM DISCOVERED HIS SECRET WHEN WE FIRST MOVED TO SEATTLE.
"SO HE...
"HE...
"..."

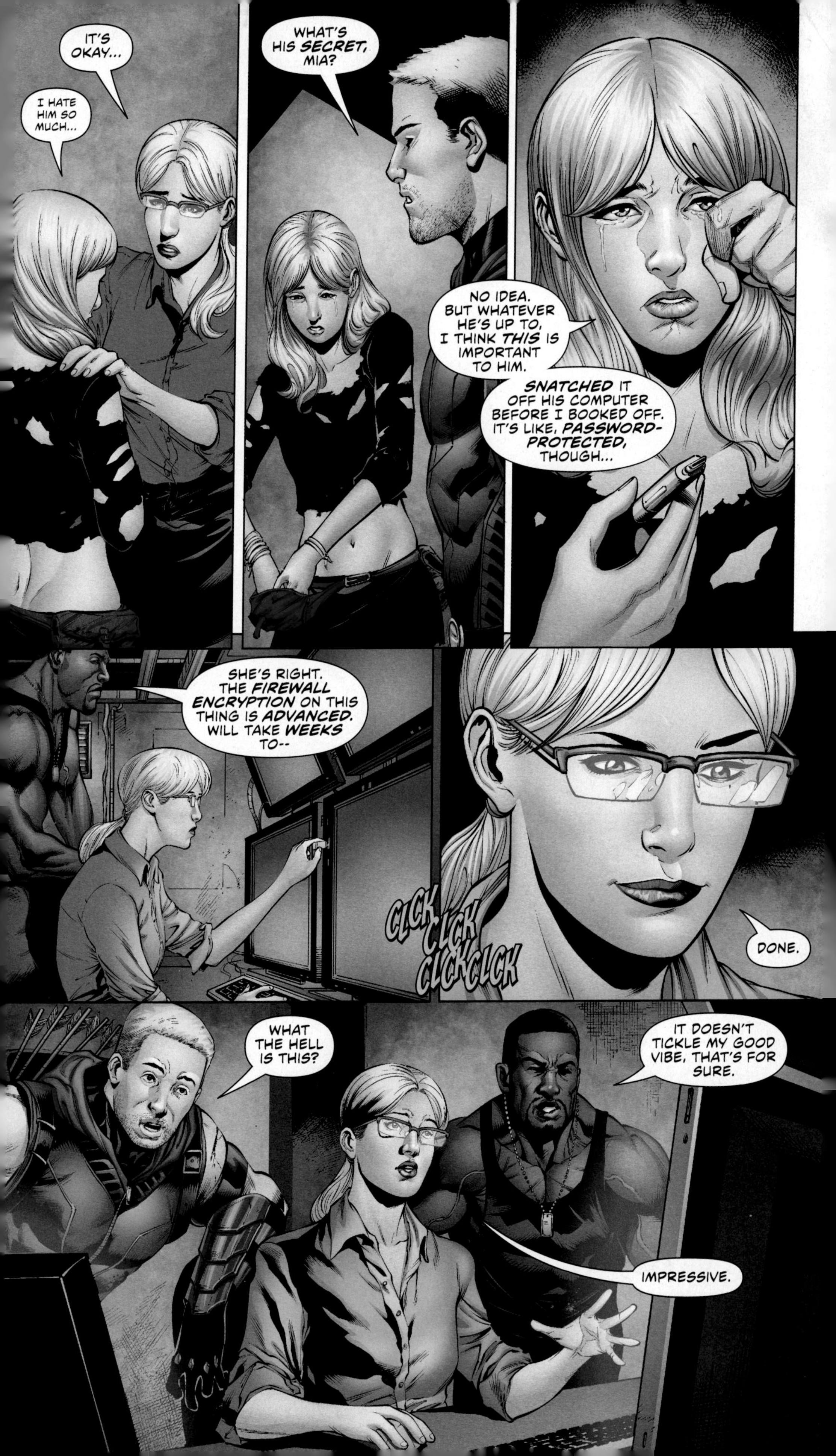
IT'S OKAY...
I HATE HIM SO MUCH...
WHAT'S HIS SECRET, MIA?
NO IDEA. BUT WHATEVER HE'S UP TO, I THINK THIS IS IMPORTANT TO HIM.
SNATCHED IT OFF HIS COMPUTER BEFORE I BOOKED OFF. IT'S LIKE, PASSWORD-PROTECTED, THOUGH...
SHE'S RIGHT. THE FIREWALL ENCRYPTION ON THIS THING IS ADVANCED. WILL TAKE WEEKS TO--
CLCK CLCK CLCKCLCK
DONE.
WHAT THE HELL IS THIS?
IT DOESN'T TICKLE MY GOOD VIBE, THAT'S FOR SURE.
IMPRESSIVE.

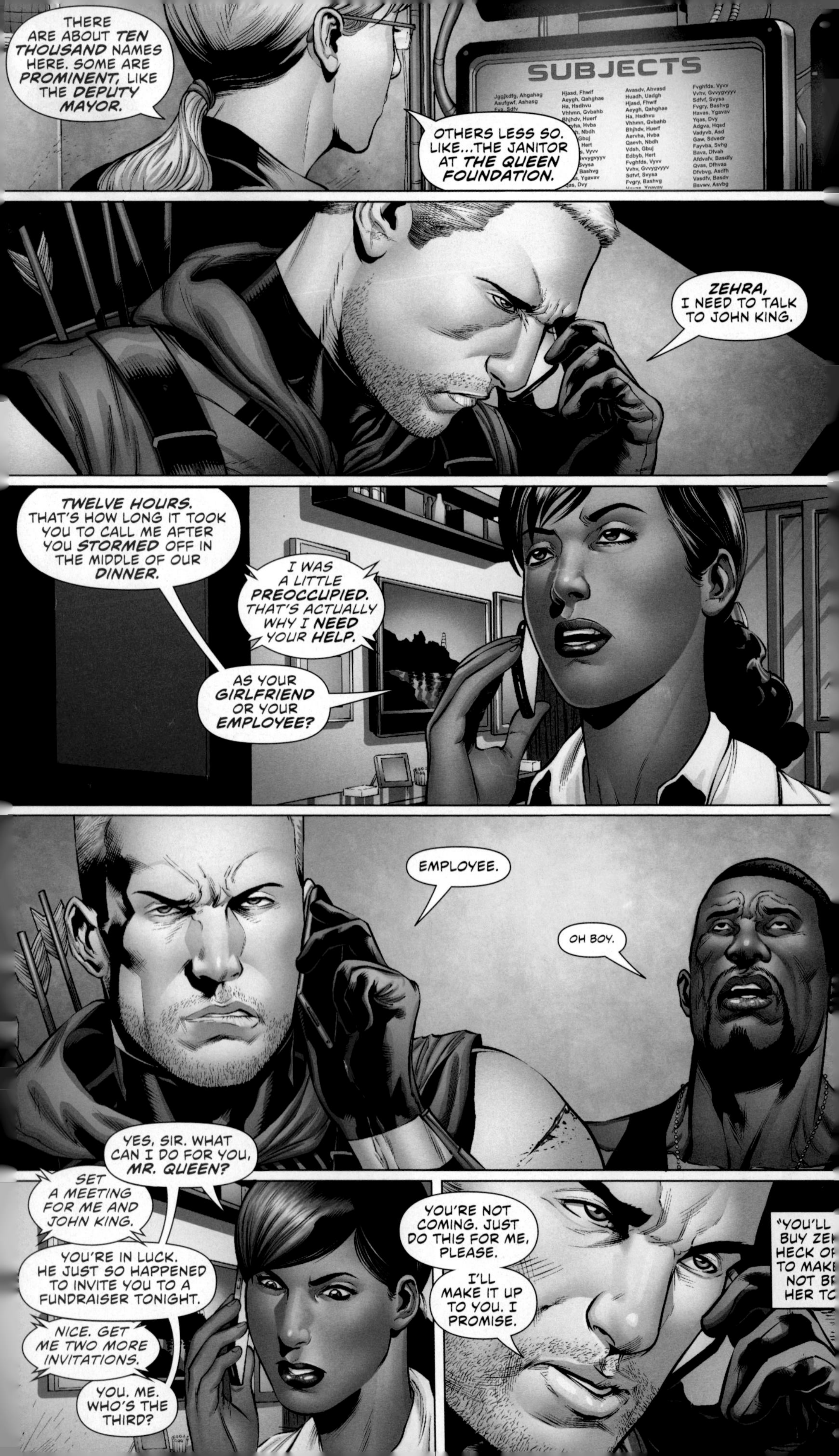
THERE ARE ABOUT TEN THOUSAND NAMES HERE. SOME ARE PROMINENT, LIKE THE DEPUTY MAYOR.
SUBJECTS
OTHERS LESS SO. LIKE...THE JANITOR AT THE QUEEN FOUNDATION.
ZEHRA, I NEED TO TALK TO JOHN KING.
TWELVE HOURS. THAT'S HOW LONG IT TOOK YOU TO CALL ME AFTER YOU STORMED OFF IN THE MIDDLE OF OUR DINNER.
I WAS A LITTLE PREOCCUPIED. THAT'S ACTUALLY WHY I NEED YOUR HELP.
AS YOUR GIRLFRIEND OR YOUR EMPLOYEE?
EMPLOYEE.
OH BOY.
YES, SIR. WHAT CAN I DO FOR YOU, MR. QUEEN?
SET A MEETING FOR ME AND JOHN KING.
YOU'RE IN LUCK. HE JUST SO HAPPENED TO INVITE YOU TO A FUNDRAISER TONIGHT.
NICE. GET ME TWO MORE INVITATIONS.
YOU. ME. WHO'S THE THIRD?
YOU'RE NOT COMING. JUST DO THIS FOR ME, PLEASE.
I'LL MAKE IT UP TO YOU. I PROMISE.

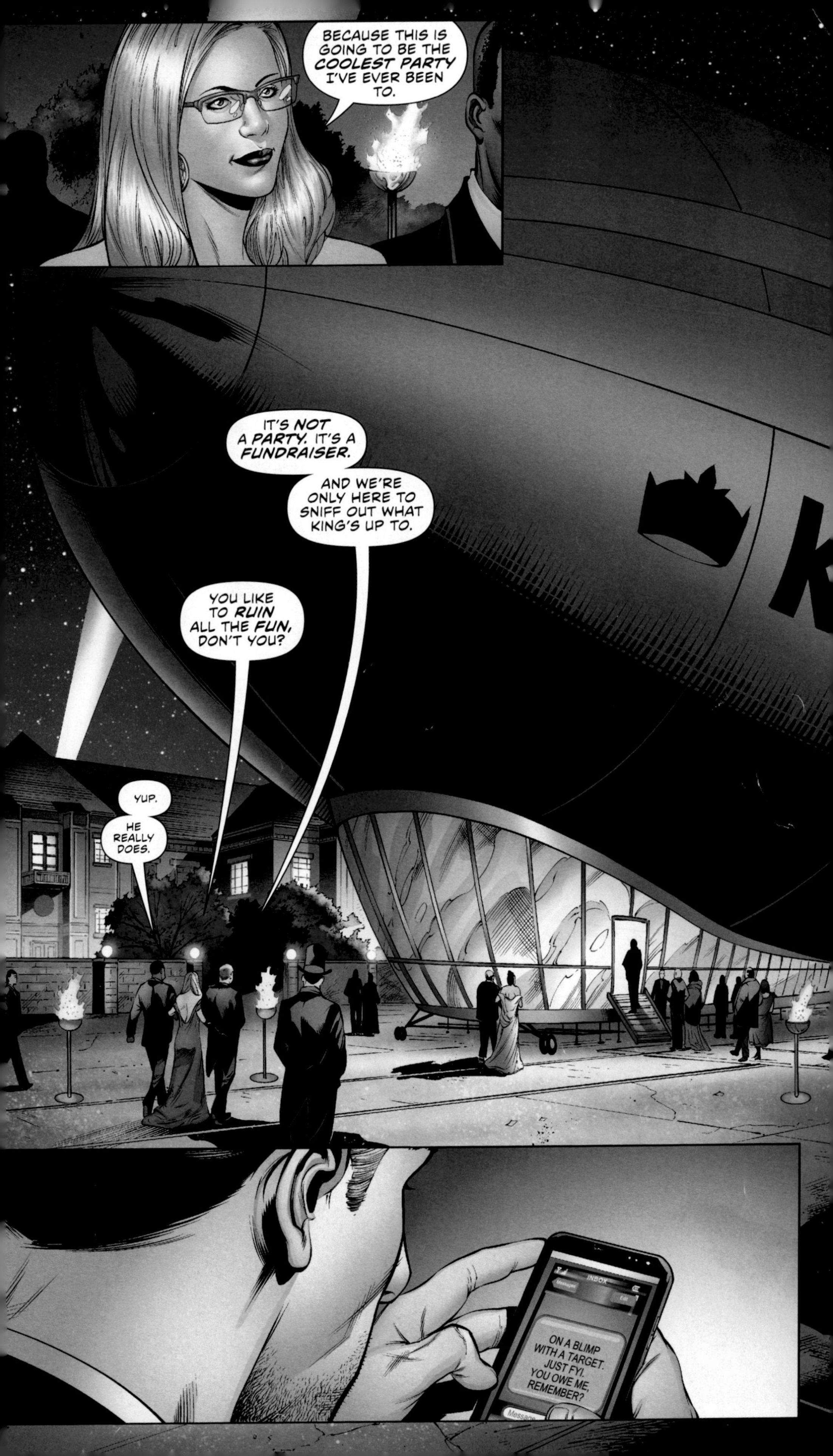
BECAUSE THIS IS GOING TO BE THE COOLEST PARTY I'VE EVER BEEN TO.
IT'S NOT A PARTY. IT'S A FUNDRAISER.
AND WE'RE ONLY HERE TO SNIFF OUT WHAT KING'S UP TO.
YOU LIKE TO RUIN ALL THE FUN, DON'T YOU?
YUP.
HE REALLY DOES.
INBOX
ON A BLIMP WITH A TARGET. JUST FYI. YOU OWE ME, REMEMBER?

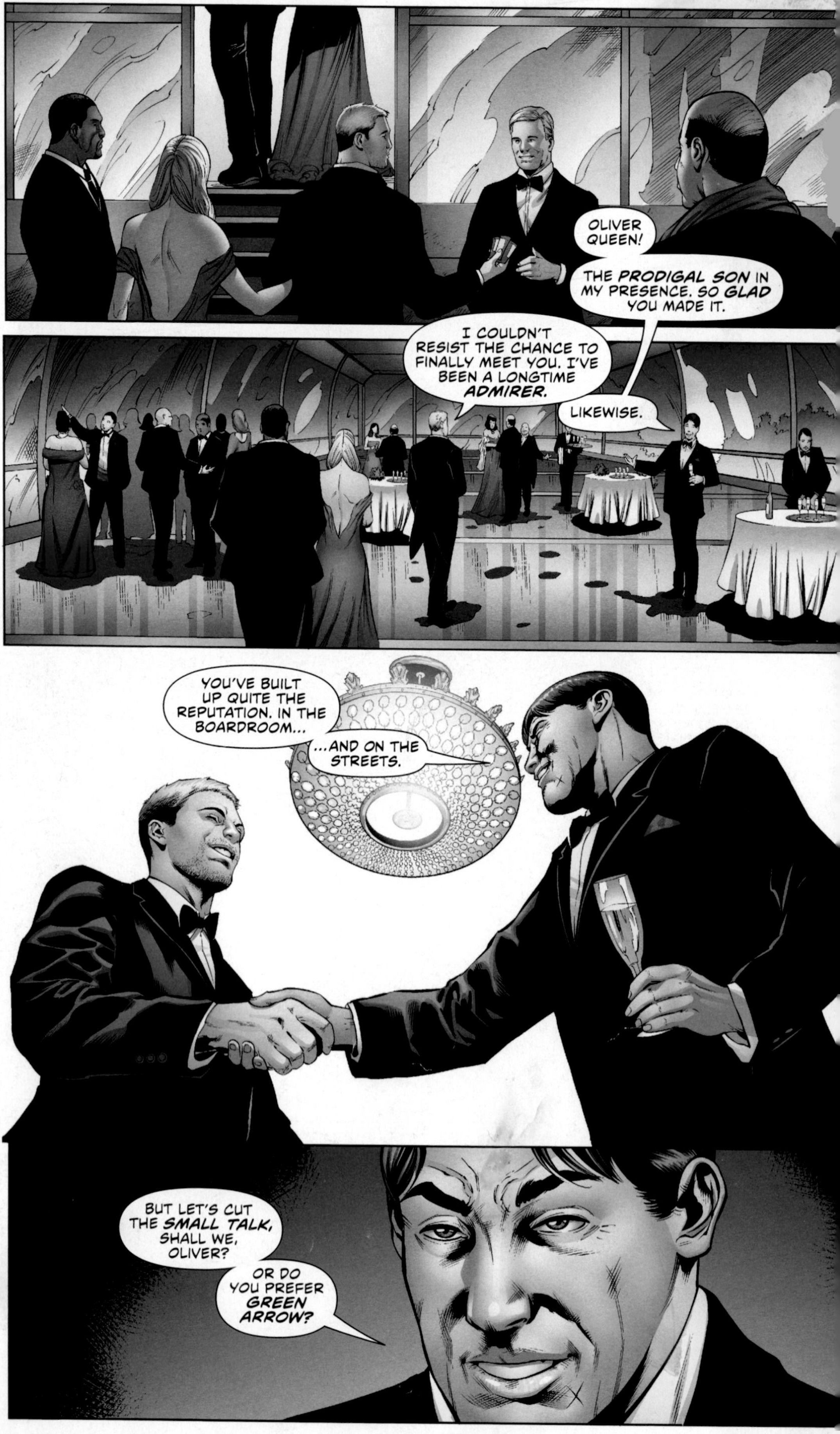
OLIVER QUEEN!
THE PRODIGAL SON IN MY PRESENCE. SO GLAD YOU MADE IT.
I COULDN'T RESIST THE CHANCE TO FINALLY MEET YOU. I'VE BEEN A LONGTIME ADMIRER.
LIKEWISE.
YOU'VE BUILT UP QUITE THE REPUTATION. IN THE BOARDROOM...
...AND ON THE STREETS.
BUT LET'S CUT THE SMALL TALK, SHALL WE, OLIVER?
OR DO YOU PREFER GREEN ARROW?

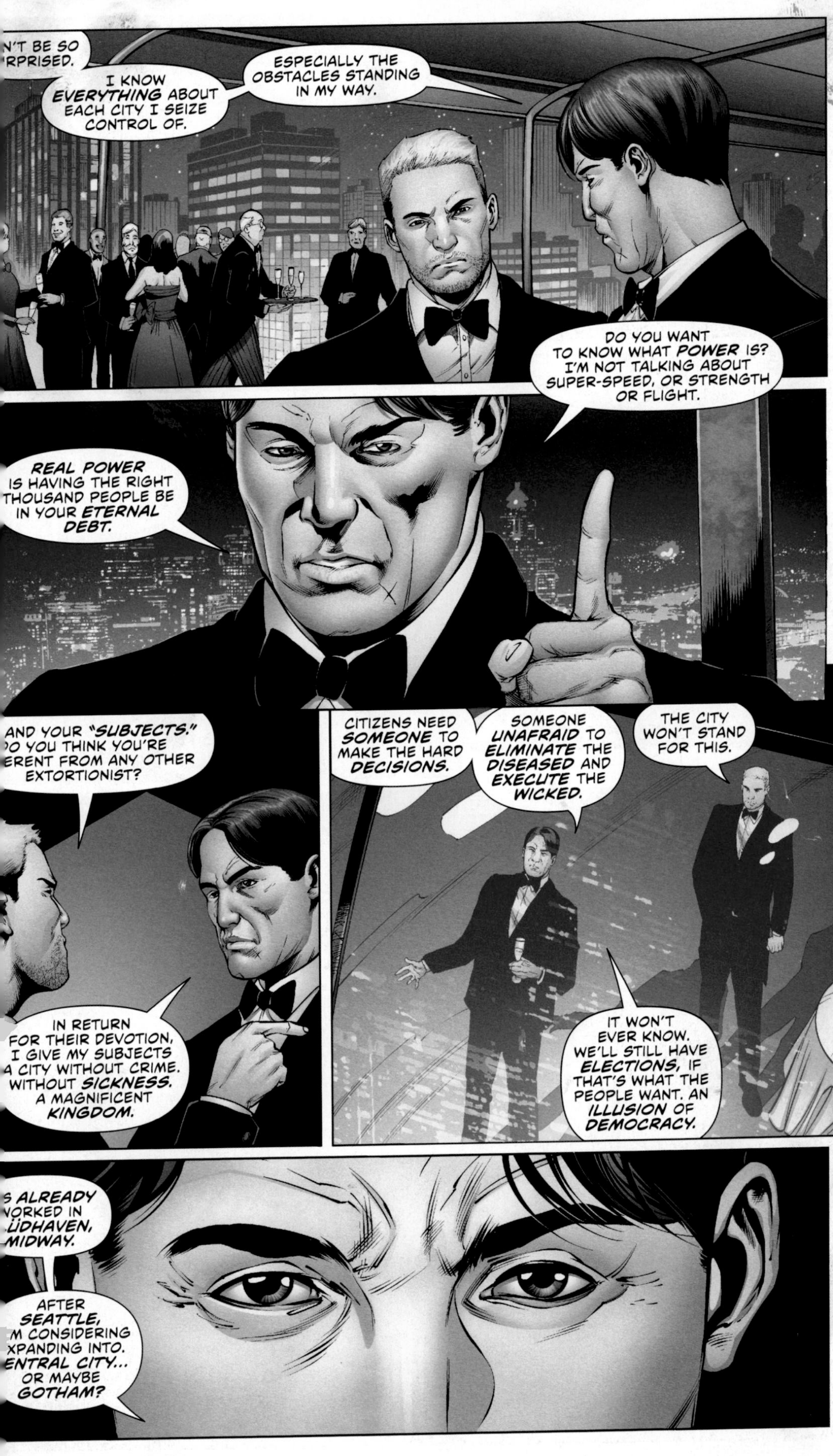
N'T BE SO
RPRISED.
I KNOW EVERYTHING ABOUT EACH CITY I SEIZE CONTROL OF.
ESPECIALLY THE OBSTACLES STANDING IN MY WAY.
DO YOU WANT TO KNOW WHAT POWER IS? I'M NOT TALKING ABOUT SUPER-SPEED, OR STRENGTH OR FLIGHT.
REAL POWER IS HAVING THE RIGHT THOUSAND PEOPLE BE IN YOUR ETERNAL DEBT.
AND YOUR "SUBJECTS." O YOU THINK YOU'RE ERENT FROM ANY OTHER EXTORTIONIST?
IN RETURN FOR THEIR DEVOTION, I GIVE MY SUBJECTS A CITY WITHOUT CRIME. WITHOUT SICKNESS. A MAGNIFICENT KINGDOM.
CITIZENS NEED SOMEONE TO MAKE THE HARD DECISIONS.
SOMEONE UNAFRAID TO ELIMINATE THE DISEASED AND EXECUTE THE WICKED.
THE CITY WON'T STAND FOR THIS.
IT WON'T EVER KNOW. WE'LL STILL HAVE ELECTIONS, IF THAT'S WHAT THE PEOPLE WANT. AN ILLUSION OF DEMOCRACY.
S ALREADY WORKED IN LÜDHAVEN, MIDWAY.
AFTER SEATTLE, M CONSIDERING XPANDING INTO. ENTRAL CITY... OR MAYBE GOTHAM?

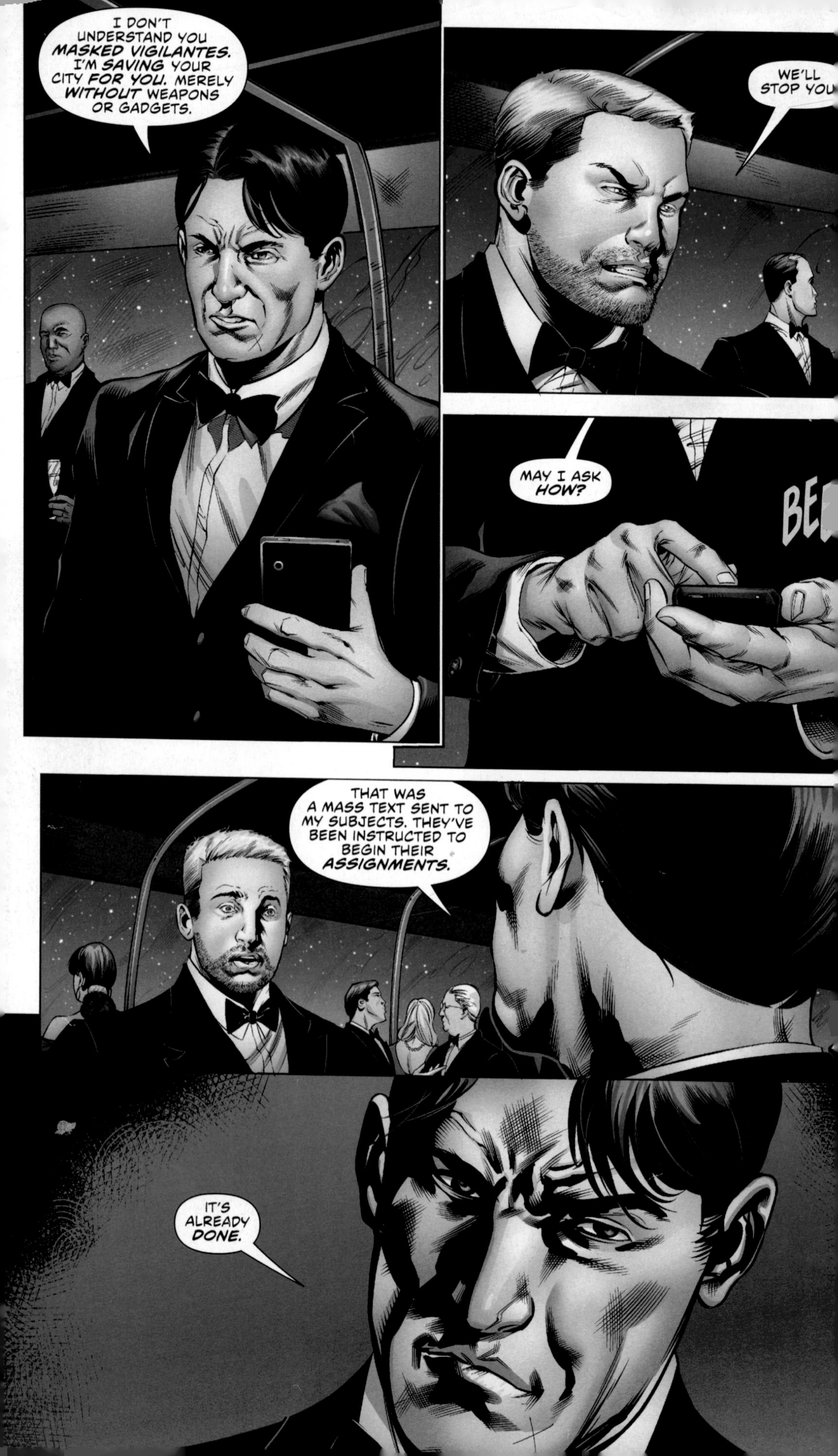
I DON'T UNDERSTAND YOU MASKED VIGILANTES. I'M SAVING YOUR CITY FOR YOU. MERELY WITHOUT WEAPONS OR GADGETS.
WE'LL STOP YOU
MAY I ASK HOW?
THAT WAS A MASS TEXT SENT TO MY SUBJECTS. THEY'VE BEEN INSTRUCTED TO BEGIN THEIR ASSIGNMENTS.
IT'S ALREADY DONE.

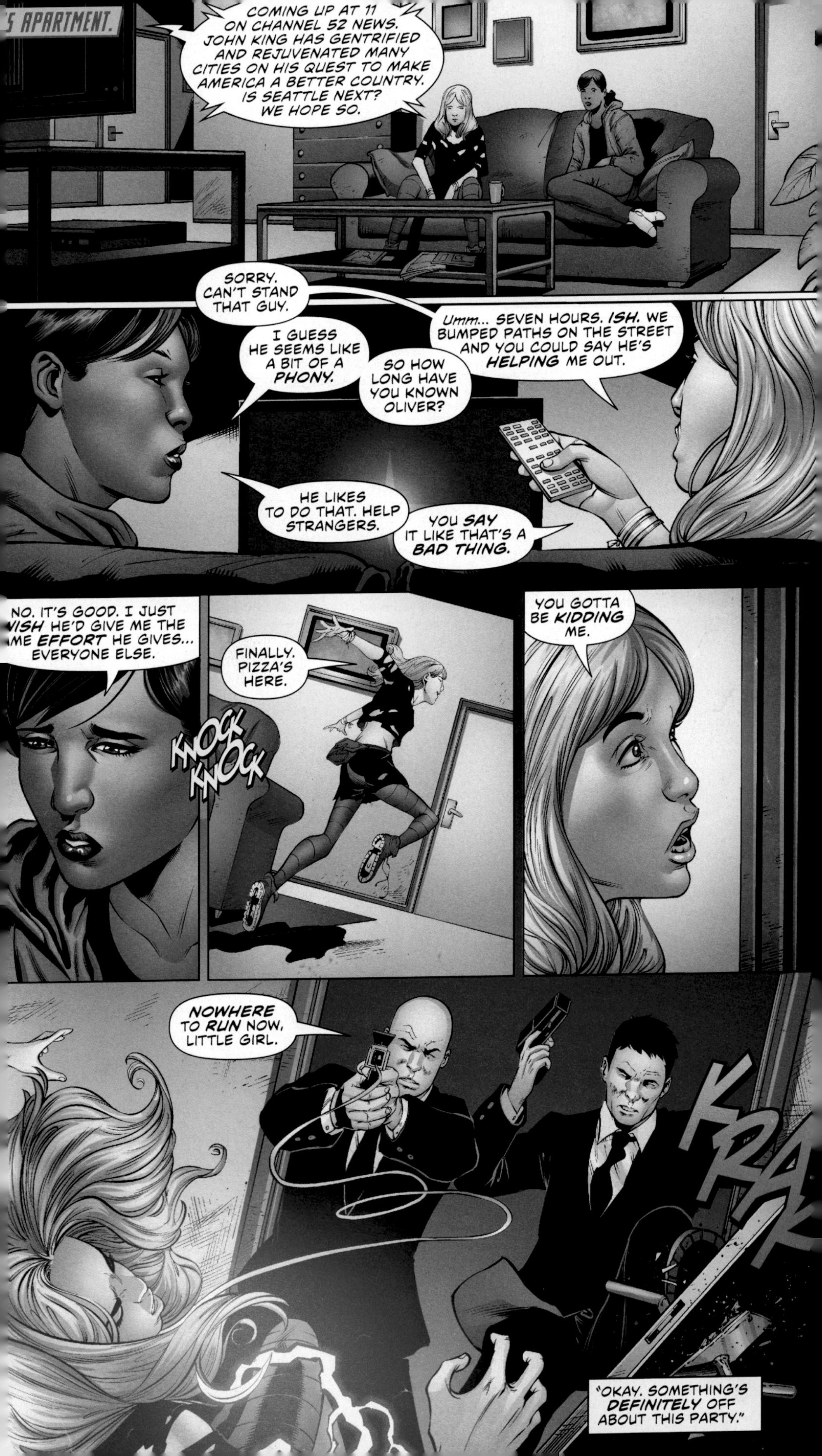

'S APARTMENT.
COMING UP AT 11 ON CHANNEL 52 NEWS. JOHN KING HAS GENTRIFIED AND REJUVENATED MANY CITIES ON HIS QUEST TO MAKE AMERICA A BETTER COUNTRY. IS SEATTLE NEXT? WE HOPE SO.
SORRY. CAN'T STAND THAT GUY.
I GUESS HE SEEMS LIKE A BIT OF A PHONY.
SO HOW LONG HAVE YOU KNOWN OLIVER?
Umm... SEVEN HOURS. ISH. WE BUMPED PATHS ON THE STREET AND YOU COULD SAY HE'S HELPING ME OUT.
HE LIKES TO DO THAT. HELP STRANGERS.
YOU SAY IT LIKE THAT'S A BAD THING.
NO. IT'S GOOD. I JUST WISH HE'D GIVE ME THE ME EFFORT HE GIVES... EVERYONE ELSE.
KNOCK KNOCK
FINALLY. PIZZA'S HERE.
YOU GOTTA BE KIDDING ME.
NOWHERE TO RUN NOW, LITTLE GIRL.
KRA
"OKAY. SOMETHING'S DEFINITELY OFF ABOUT THIS PARTY."

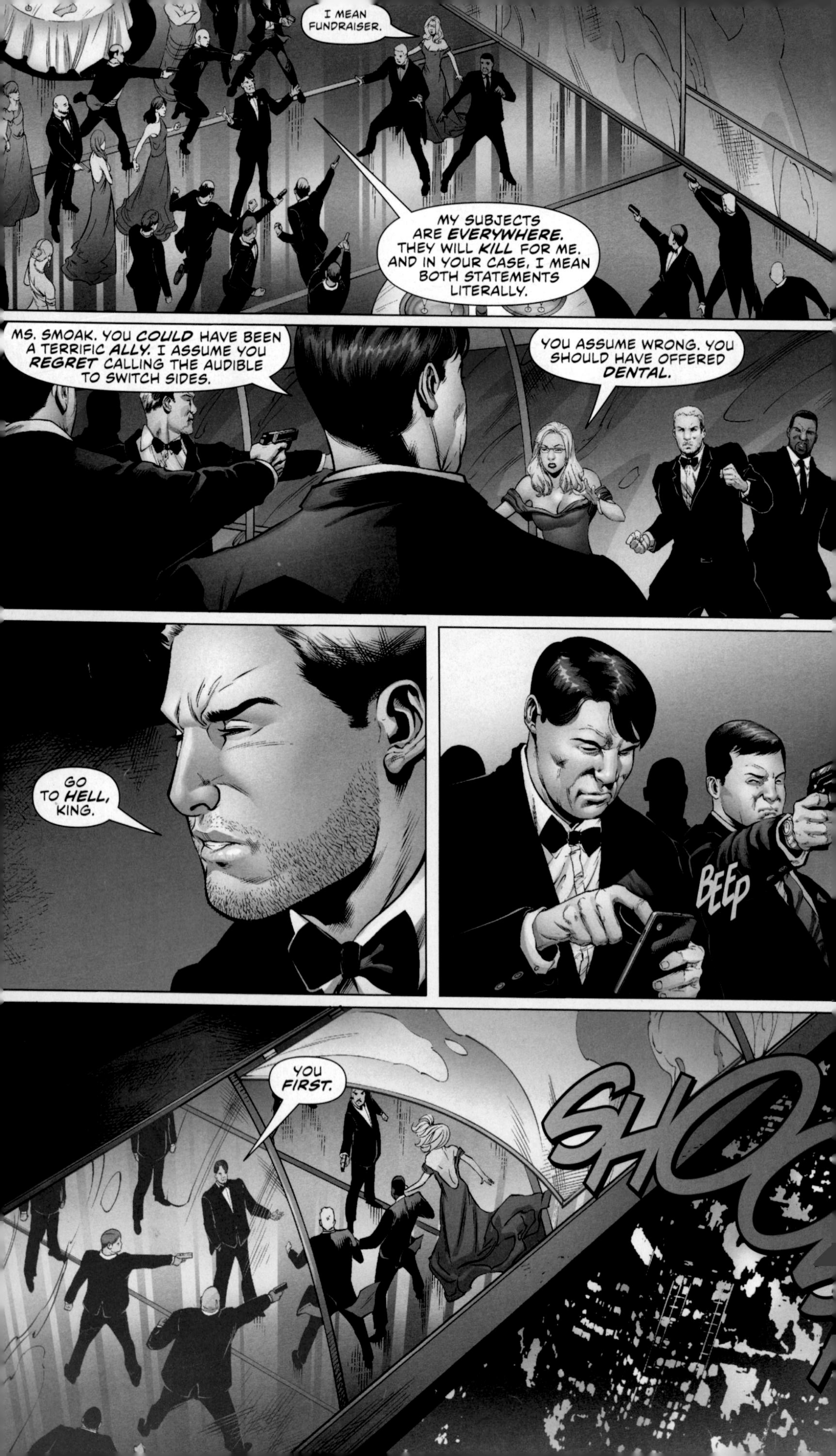
I MEAN FUNDRAISER.
MY SUBJECTS ARE EVERYWHERE. THEY WILL KILL FOR ME. AND IN YOUR CASE, I MEAN BOTH STATEMENTS LITERALLY.
MS. SMOAK. YOU COULD HAVE BEEN A TERRIFIC ALLY. I ASSUME YOU REGRET CALLING THE AUDIBLE TO SWITCH SIDES.
YOU ASSUME WRONG. YOU SHOULD HAVE OFFERED DENTAL.
GO TO HELL, KING.
BEEP
YOU FIRST.
SHO

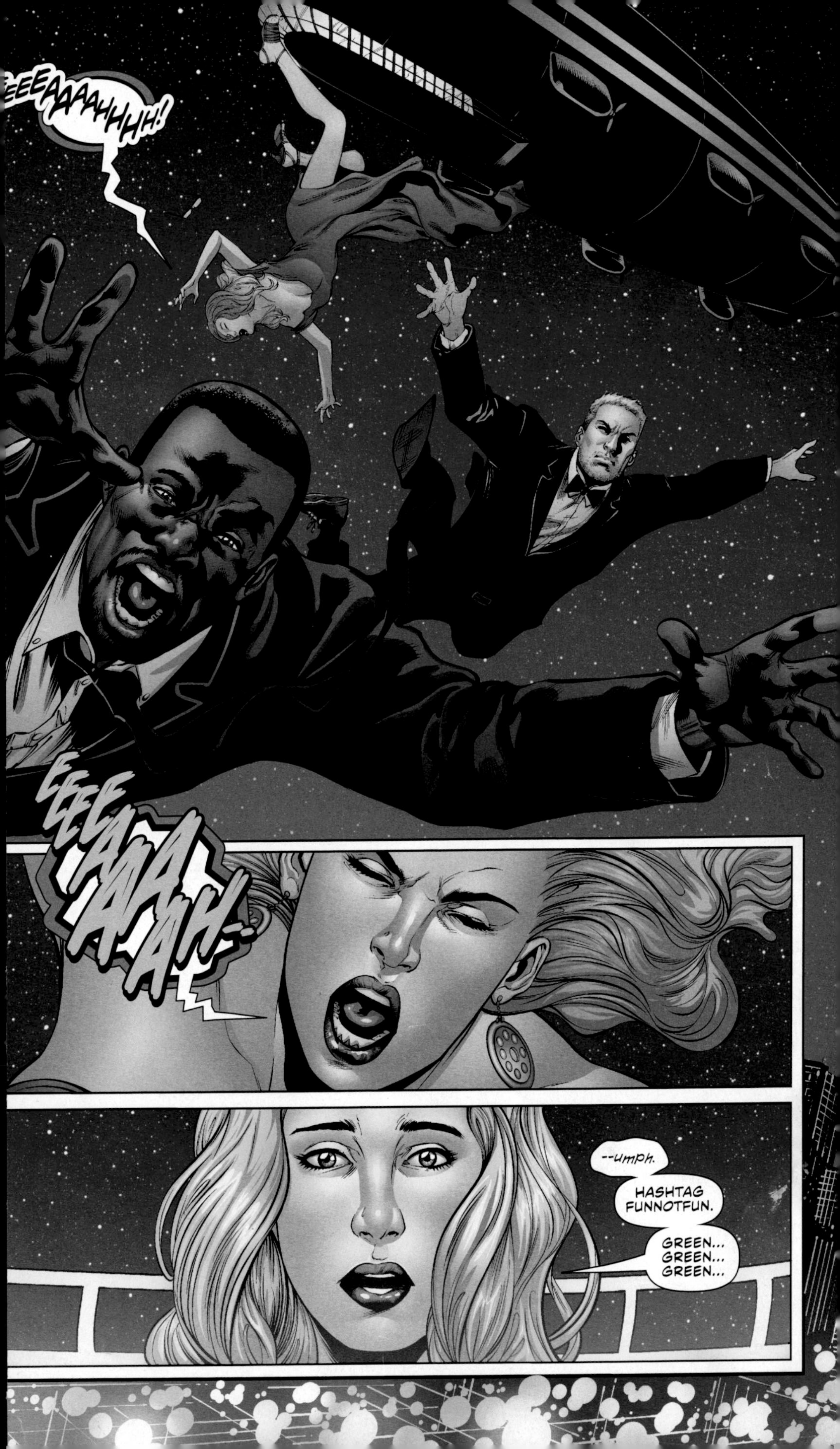
EEEEAAAAHHHH!
EEEEAAAAAAAAAH--
--umph.
HASHTAG FUNNOTFUN.
GREEN... GREEN... GREEN...

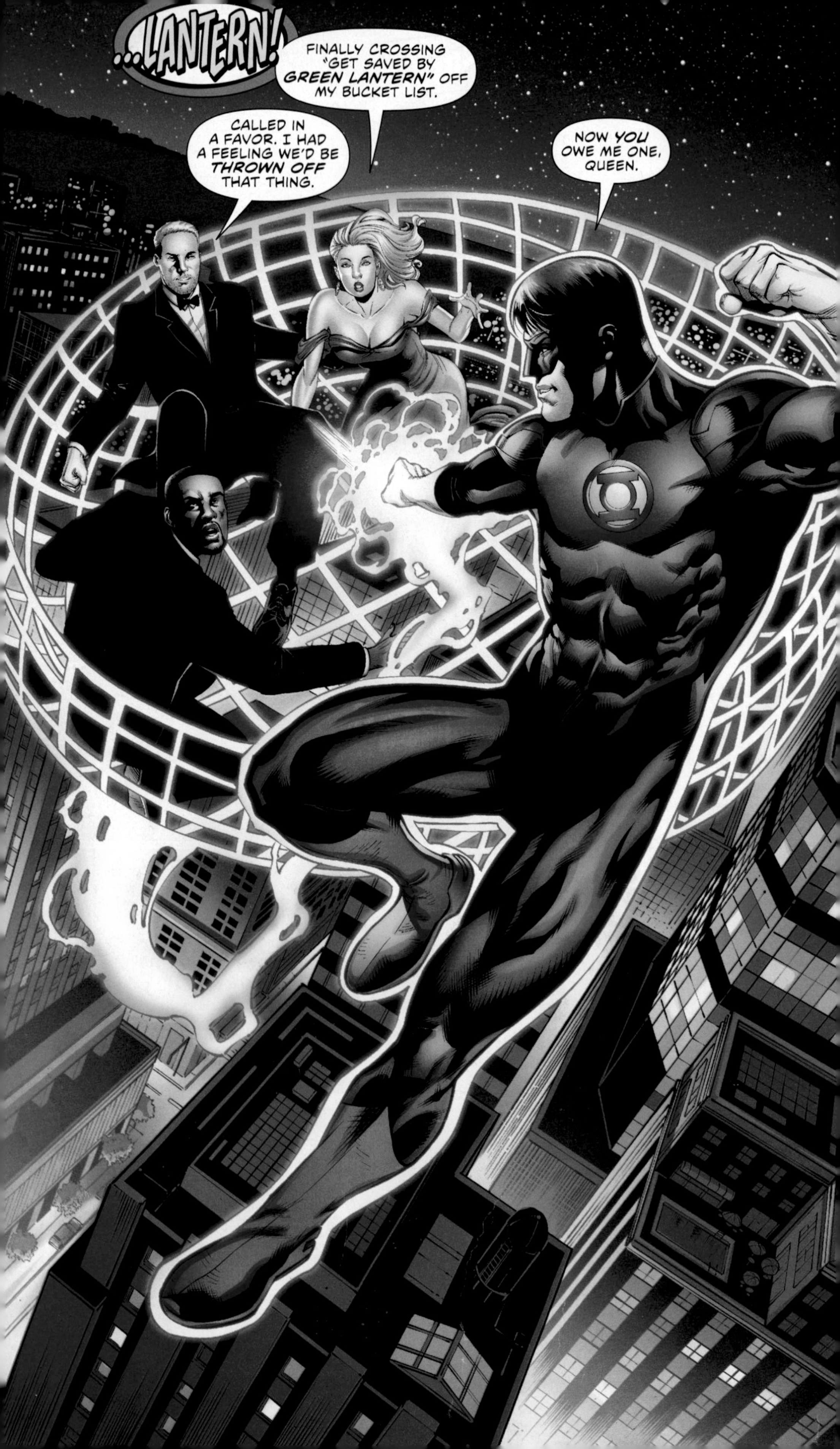
...LANTERN!
FINALLY CROSSING "GET SAVED BY GREEN LANTERN" OFF MY BUCKET LIST.
CALLED IN A FAVOR. I HAD A FEELING WE'D BE THROWN OFF THAT THING.
NOW YOU OWE ME ONE, QUEEN.

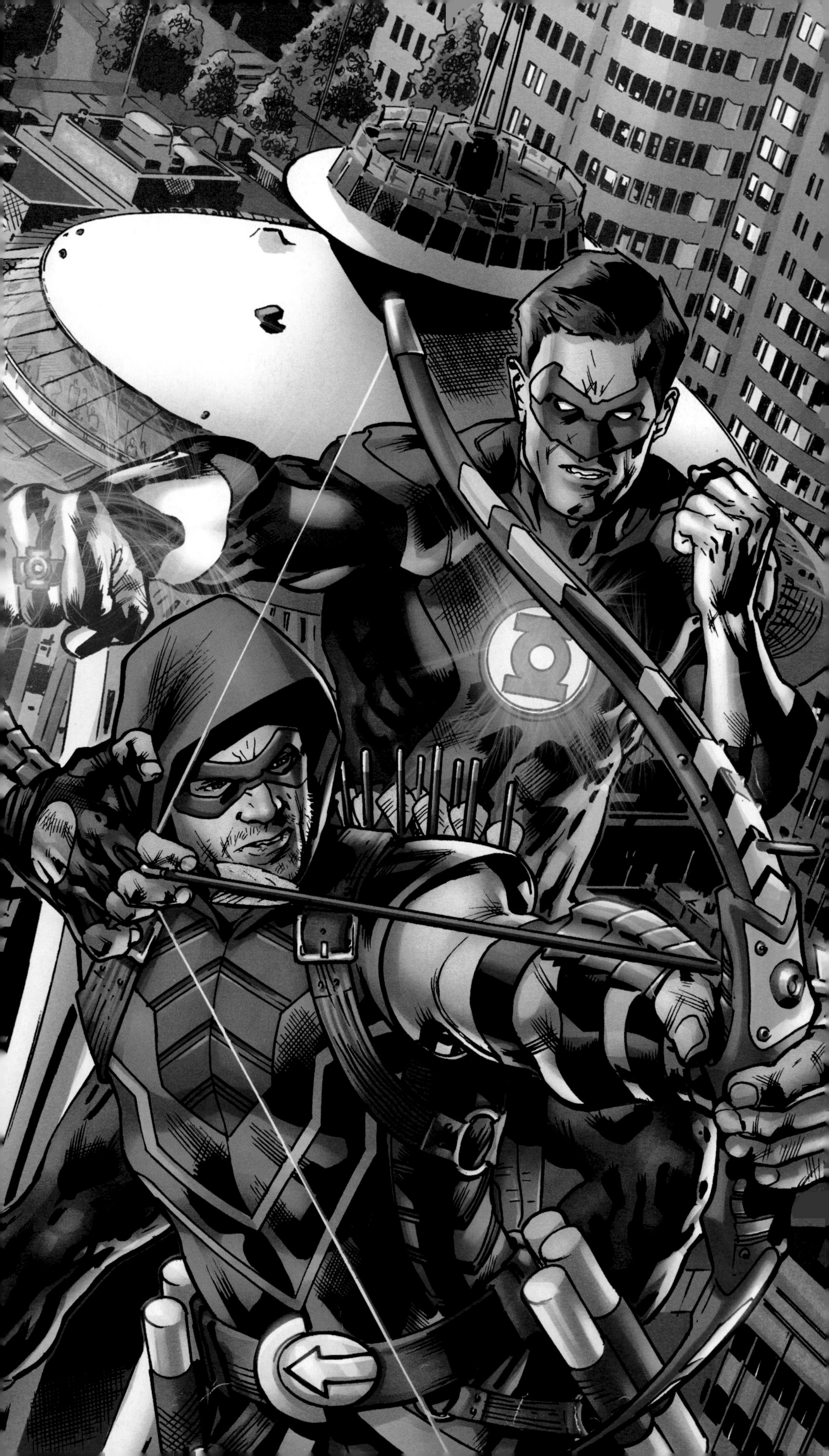

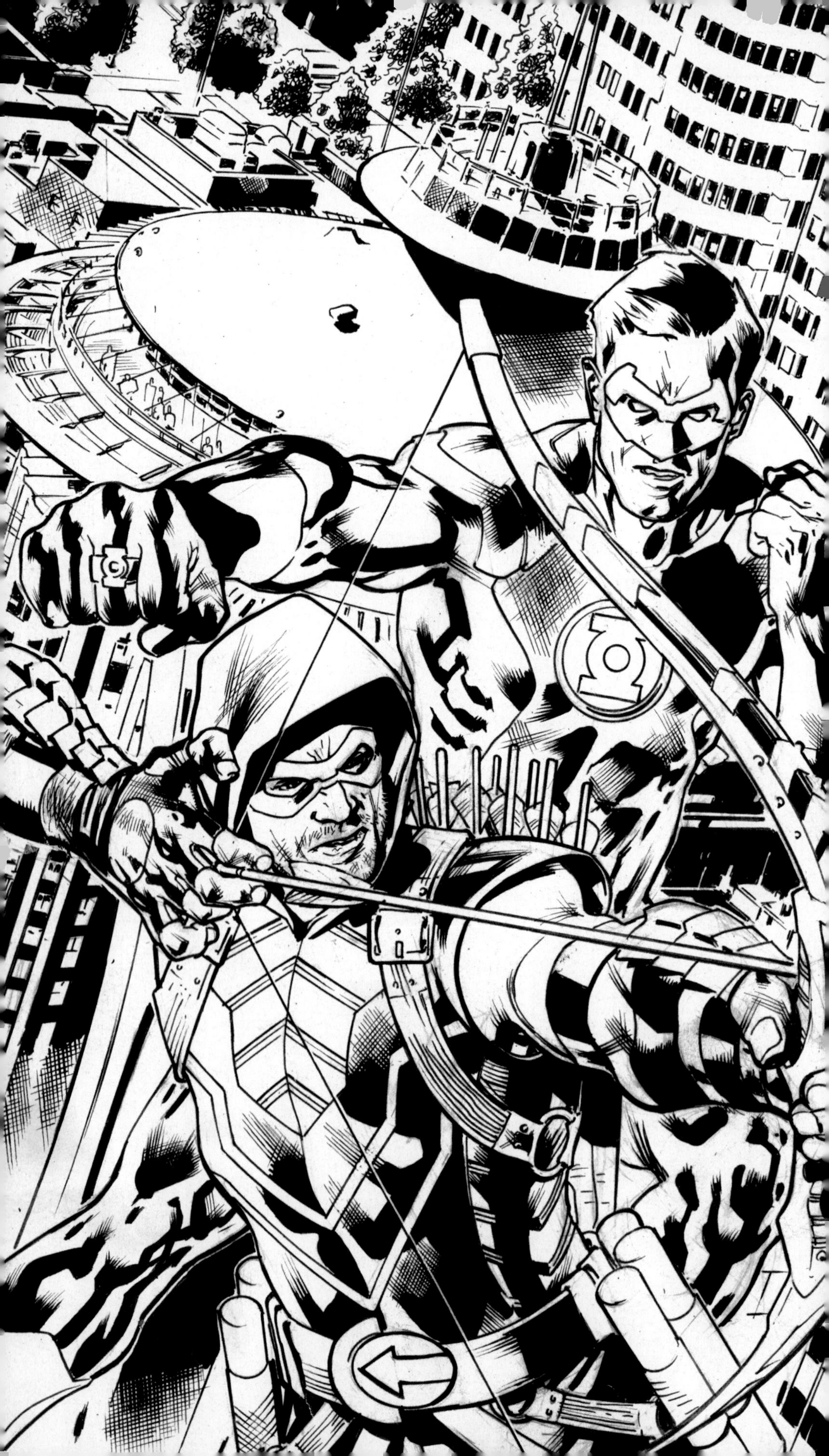

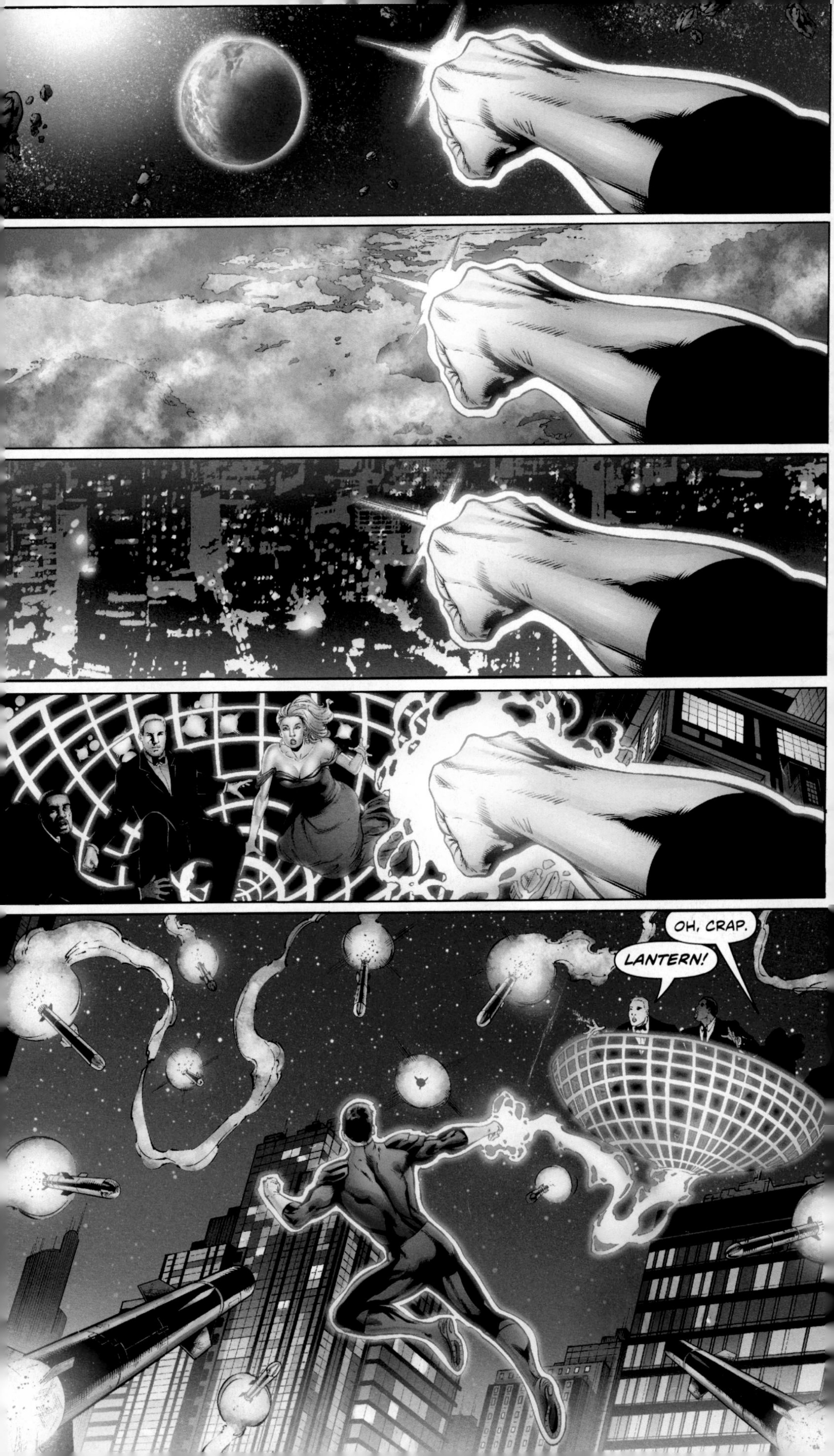
OH, CRAP.
LANTERN!

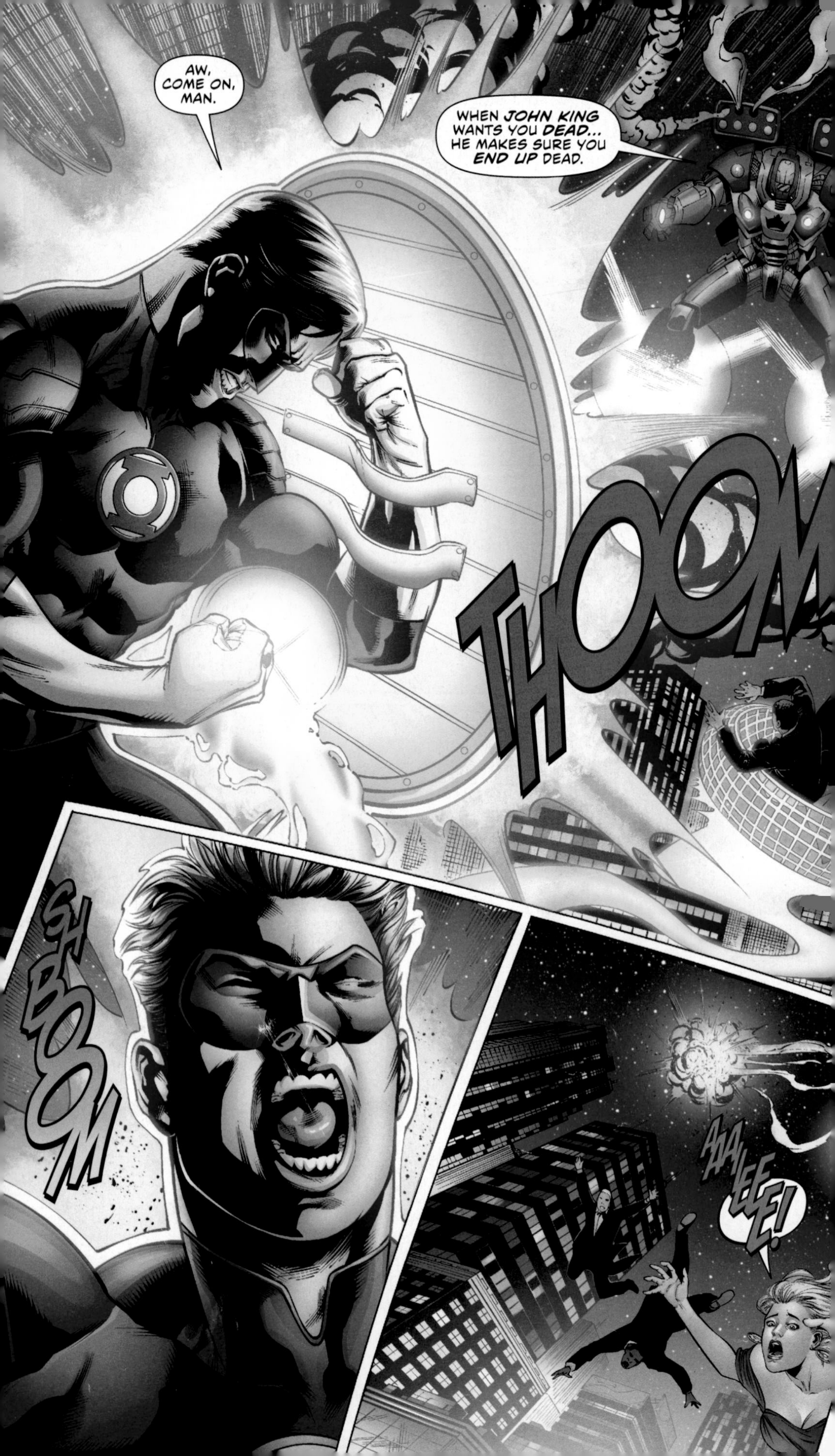
AW, COME ON, MAN.
WHEN JOHN KING WANTS YOU DEAD... HE MAKES SURE YOU END UP DEAD.
THOOM
SHBOOM
AAAIEEE!

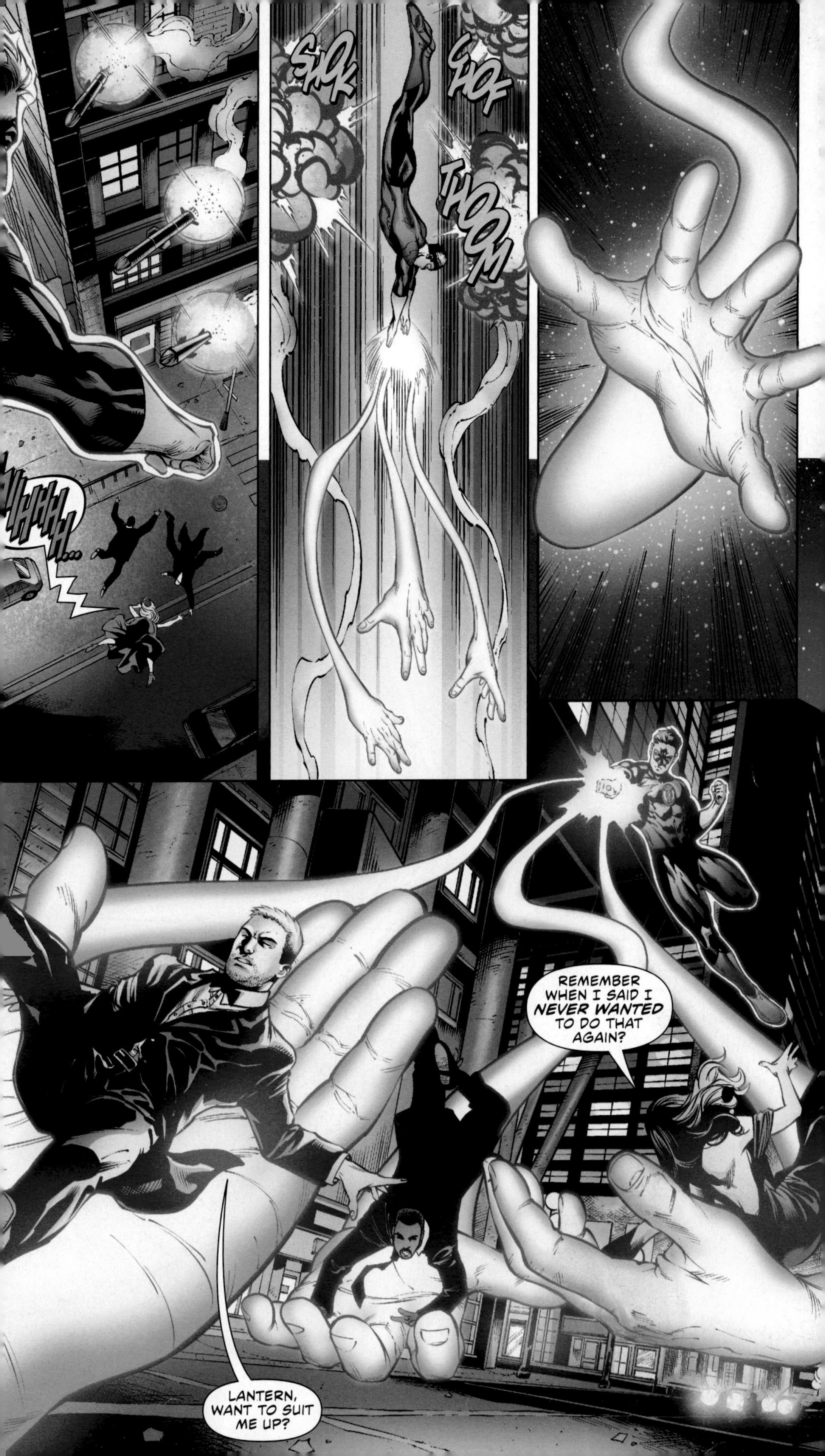
HHHHH...
SHOK
SHOK
THOOM
REMEMBER WHEN I SAID I *NEVER WANTED* TO DO THAT AGAIN?
LANTERN, WANT TO SUIT ME UP?

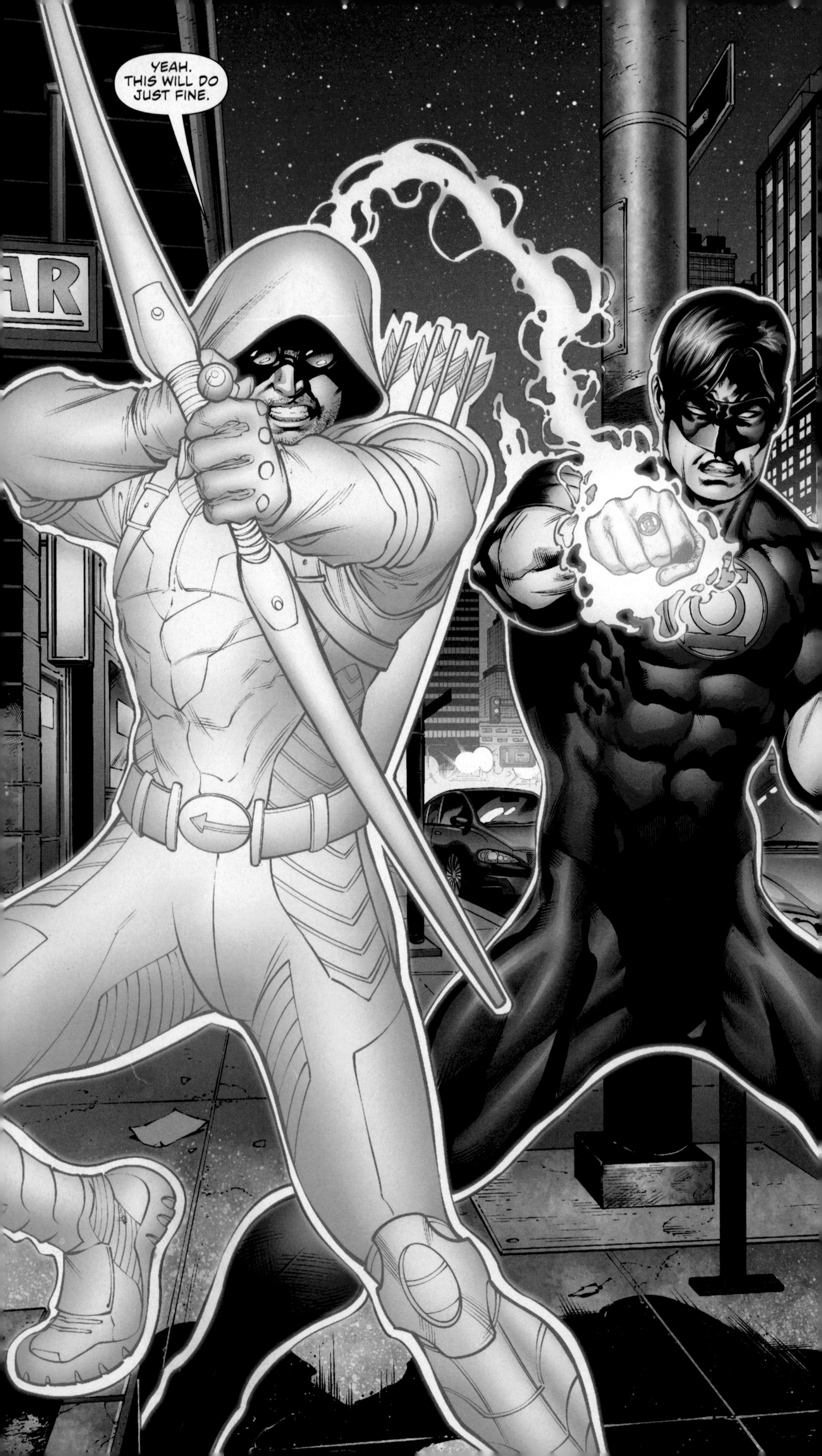
YEAH. THIS WILL DO JUST FINE.
AR

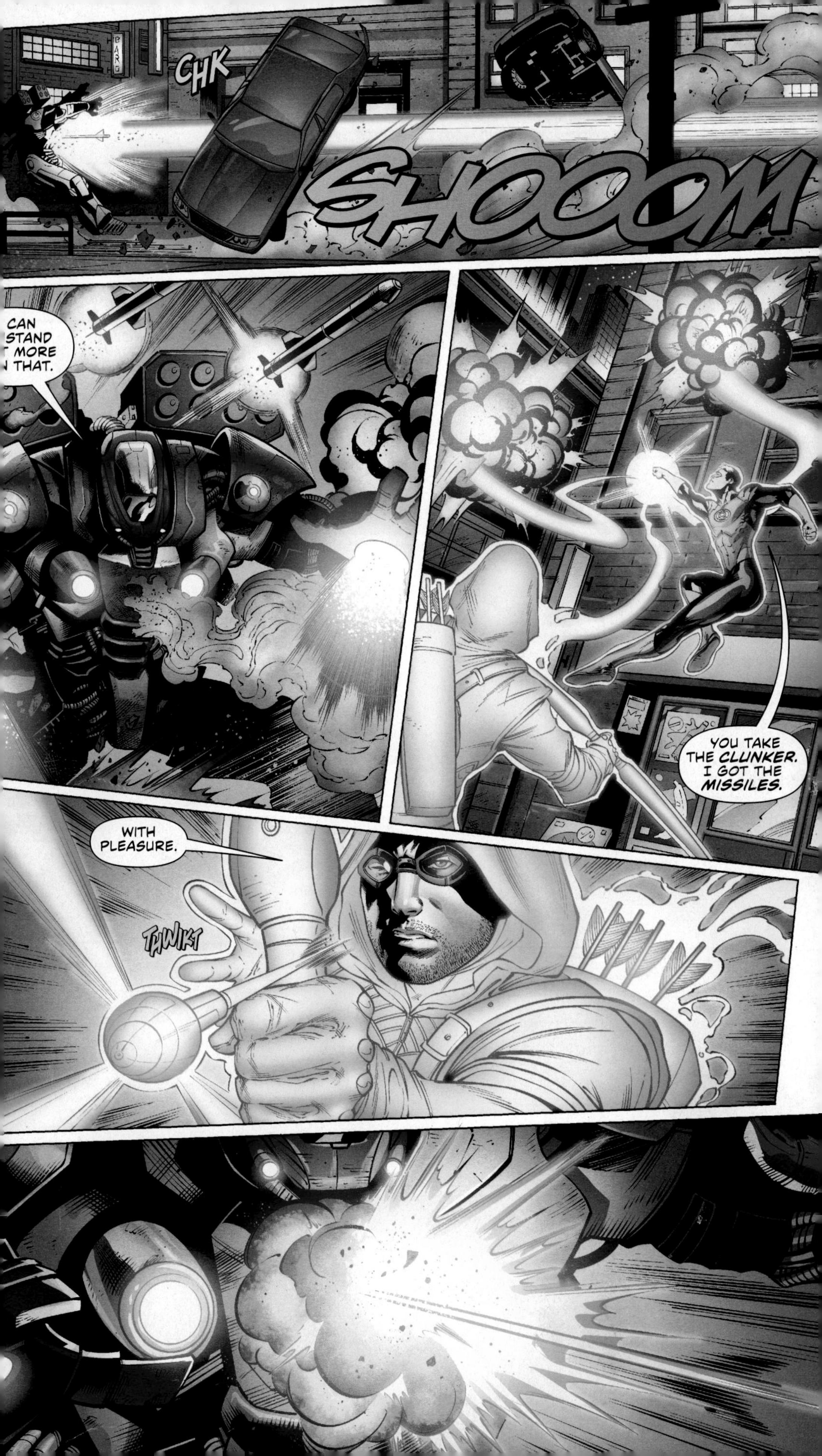
BAR
CHK
SHOOOM
CAN
STAND
T MORE
N THAT.
YOU TAKE THE CLUNKER. I GOT THE MISSILES.
WITH PLEASURE.
THWIKT

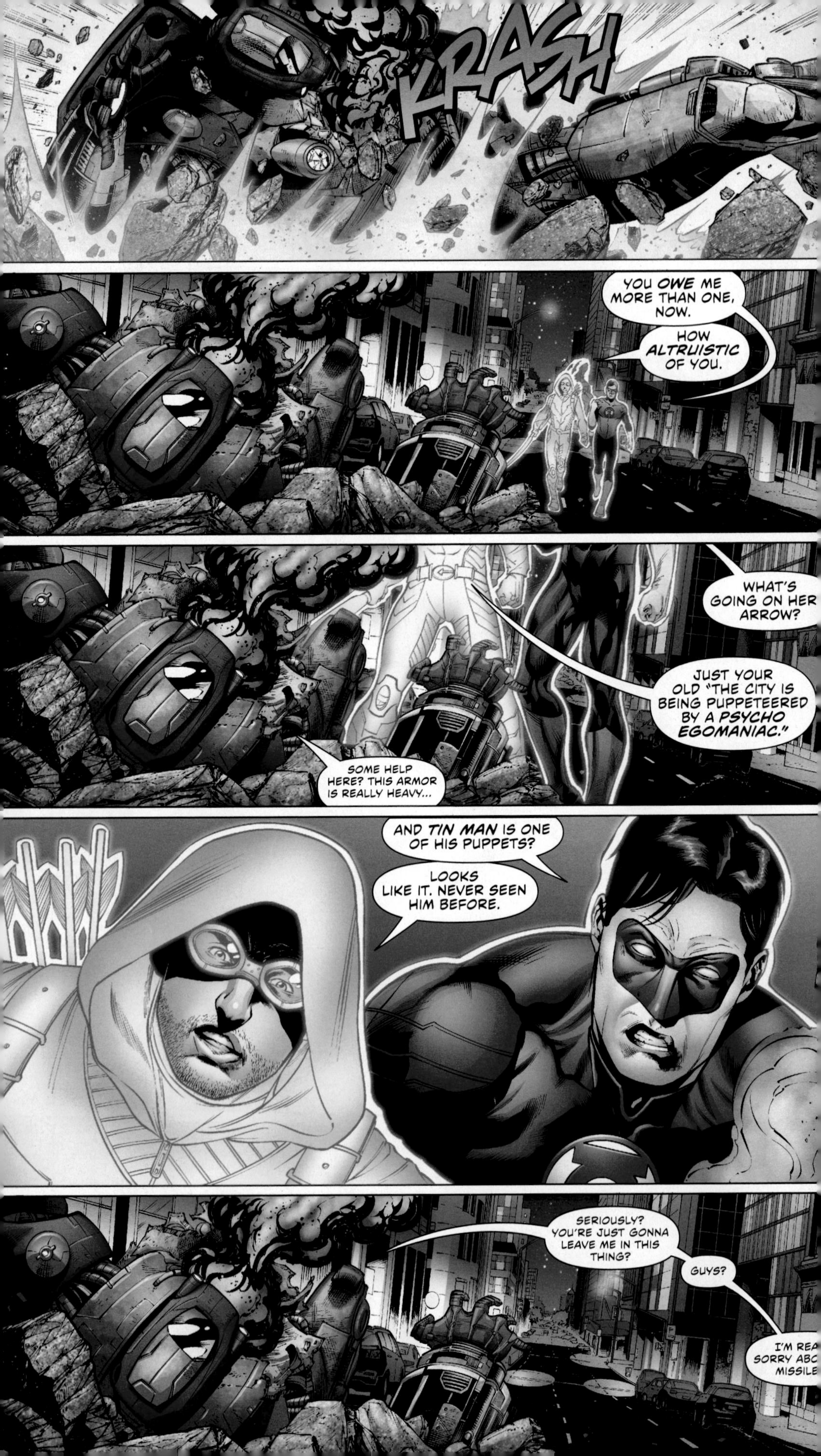
KRASH
YOU OWE ME MORE THAN ONE, NOW.
HOW ALTRUISTIC OF YOU.
WHAT'S GOING ON HER ARROW?
JUST YOUR OLD "THE CITY IS BEING PUPPETEERED BY A PSYCHO EGOMANIAC."
SOME HELP HERE? THIS ARMOR IS REALLY HEAVY...
AND TIN MAN IS ONE OF HIS PUPPETS?
LOOKS LIKE IT. NEVER SEEN HIM BEFORE.
SERIOUSLY? YOU'RE JUST GONNA LEAVE ME IN THIS THING?
GUYS?

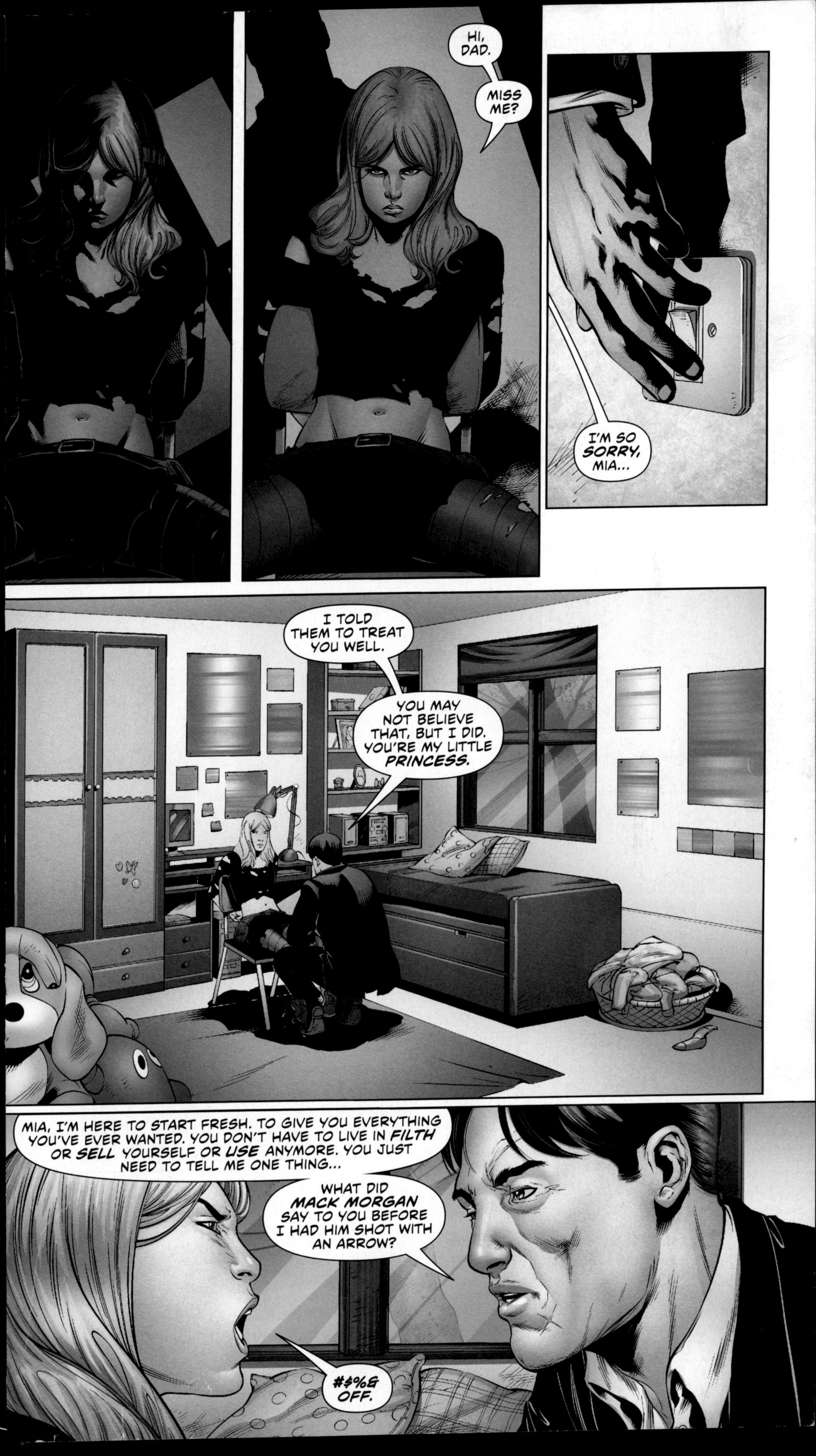
HI, DAD.
MISS ME?
I'M SO SORRY, MIA...
I TOLD THEM TO TREAT YOU WELL.
YOU MAY NOT BELIEVE THAT, BUT I DID. YOU'RE MY LITTLE PRINCESS.
MIA, I'M HERE TO START FRESH. TO GIVE YOU EVERYTHING YOU'VE EVER WANTED. YOU DON'T HAVE TO LIVE IN FILTH OR SELL YOURSELF OR USE ANYMORE. YOU JUST NEED TO TELL ME ONE THING...
WHAT DID MACK MORGAN SAY TO YOU BEFORE I HAD HIM SHOT WITH AN ARROW?
#$%& OFF.

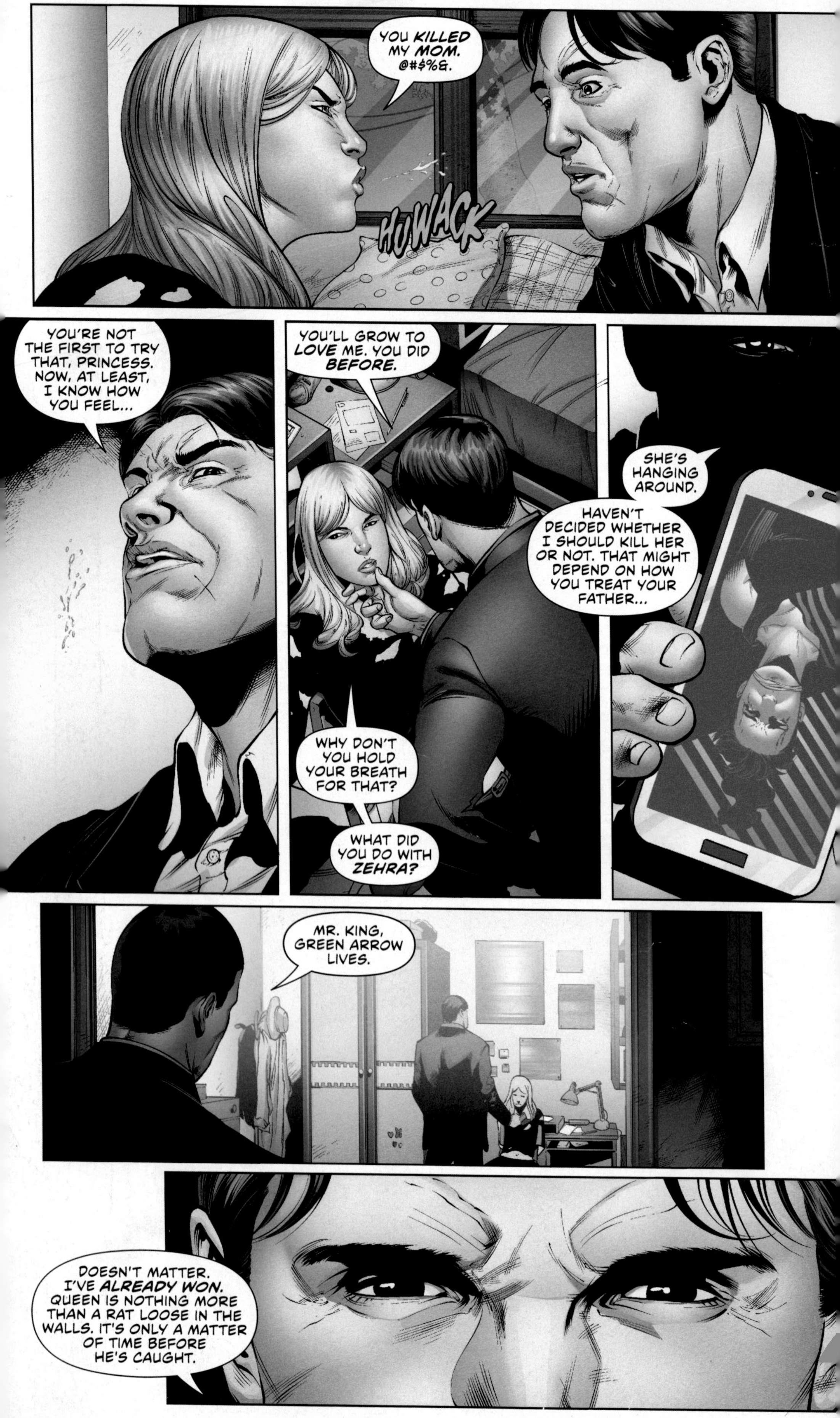
YOU KILLED MY MOM. @#$%&.
HUWACK
YOU'RE NOT THE FIRST TO TRY THAT, PRINCESS. NOW, AT LEAST, I KNOW HOW YOU FEEL...
YOU'LL GROW TO LOVE ME. YOU DID BEFORE.
WHY DON'T YOU HOLD YOUR BREATH FOR THAT?
WHAT DID YOU DO WITH ZEHRA?
SHE'S HANGING AROUND.
HAVEN'T DECIDED WHETHER I SHOULD KILL HER OR NOT. THAT MIGHT DEPEND ON HOW YOU TREAT YOUR FATHER...
MR. KING, GREEN ARROW LIVES.
DOESN'T MATTER. I'VE ALREADY WON. QUEEN IS NOTHING MORE THAN A RAT LOOSE IN THE WALLS. IT'S ONLY A MATTER OF TIME BEFORE HE'S CAUGHT.

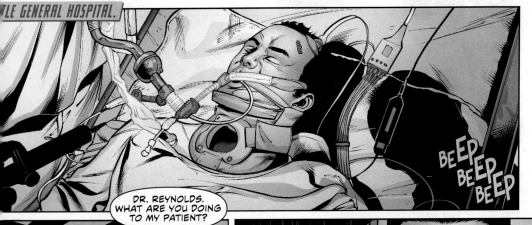

BEEP BEEP BEEP

BEEP BEEP BEEP

DR. REYNOLDS. WHAT ARE YOU DOING TO MY PATIENT?

STEVE, I ASKED YOU A QUESTION.

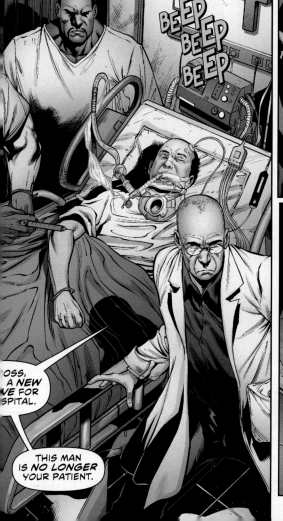

BEEP BEEP BEEP

OSS, A NEW VE FOR SPITAL.

THIS MAN IS *NO LONGER* YOUR PATIENT.

WE WON'T BE *WASTING RESOURCES* ON THE *DYING* ANY LONGER...

...FOR THE *GREATER GOOD* OF OUR *SAVABLE* PATIENTS.

BEEP BEEP BEEP

THE DIRECTIVE IS BEING IMPLEMENTED *IMMEDIATELY*.

YOU'RE *CULLING THE HERD.* YOU CAN'T DO THIS.

DR. CROSS IS *NOT COOPERATING.* THAT MEANS HE WON'T BE NECESSARY ANYMORE...

BEEEEEEEEEEEEEEE✳

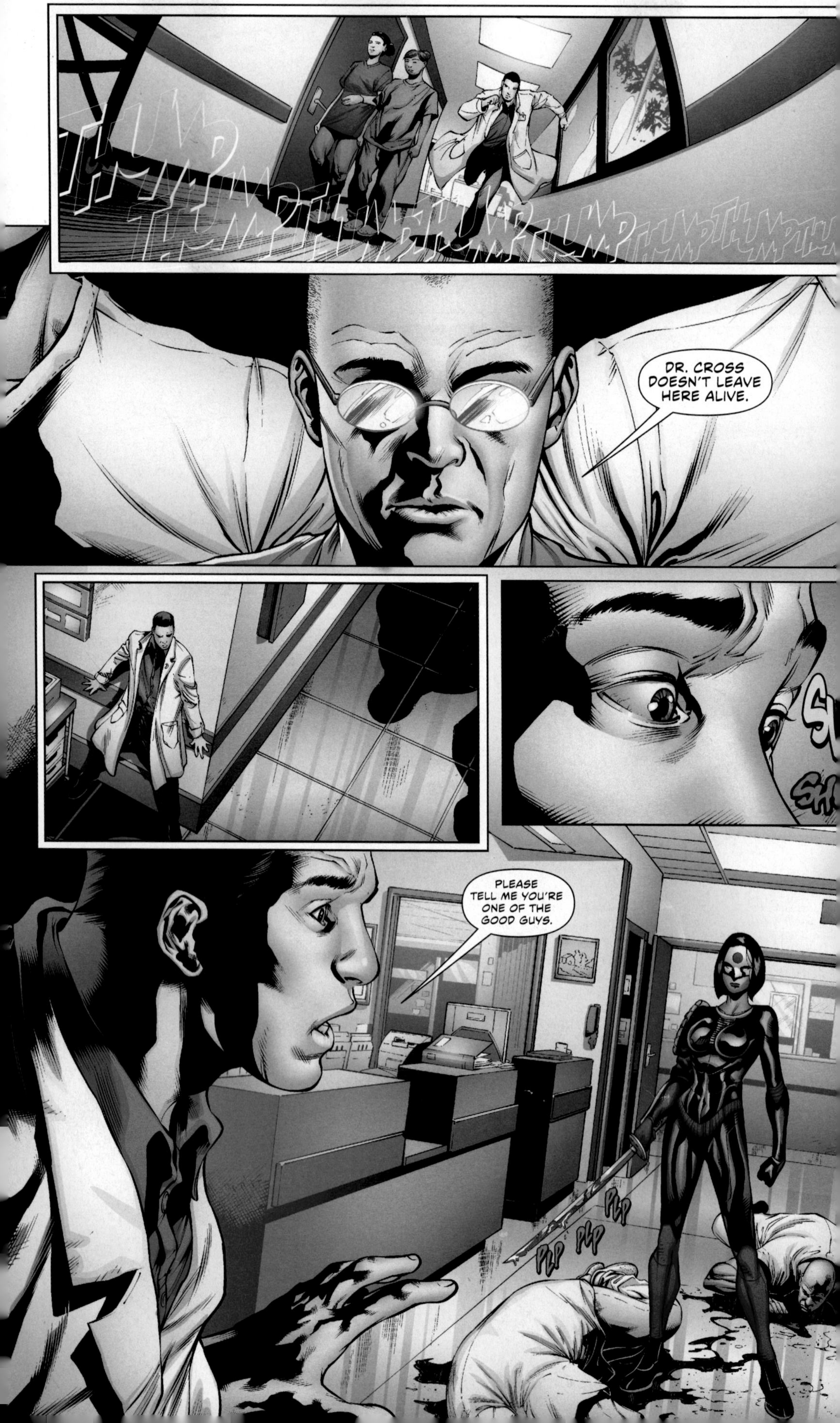
THUMP THUMP THUMP THUMP THUMP THUMP THUMP
DR. CROSS DOESN'T LEAVE HERE ALIVE.
PLEASE TELL ME YOU'RE ONE OF THE GOOD GUYS.
PLIP PLIP PLIP

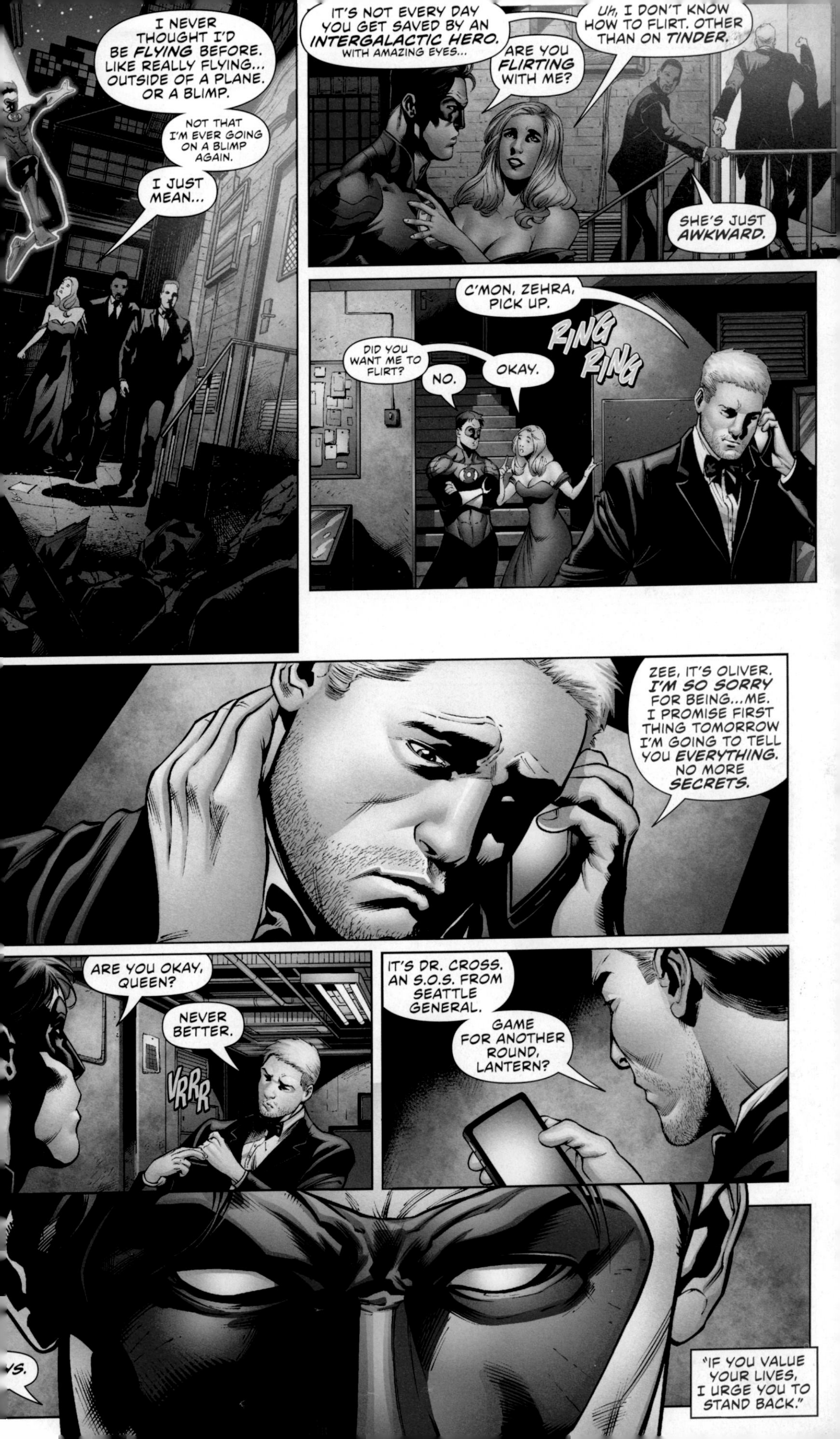
I NEVER THOUGHT I'D BE FLYING BEFORE. LIKE REALLY FLYING... OUTSIDE OF A PLANE. OR A BLIMP.
NOT THAT I'M EVER GOING ON A BLIMP AGAIN.
I JUST MEAN...
IT'S NOT EVERY DAY YOU GET SAVED BY AN INTERGALACTIC HERO. WITH AMAZING EYES...
ARE YOU FLIRTING WITH ME?
Uh, I DON'T KNOW HOW TO FLIRT. OTHER THAN ON TINDER.
SHE'S JUST AWKWARD.
C'MON, ZEHRA, PICK UP.
RING RING
DID YOU WANT ME TO FLIRT?
NO.
OKAY.
ZEE, IT'S OLIVER. I'M SO SORRY FOR BEING...ME. I PROMISE FIRST THING TOMORROW I'M GOING TO TELL YOU EVERYTHING. NO MORE SECRETS.
ARE YOU OKAY, QUEEN?
NEVER BETTER.
VRRR
IT'S DR. CROSS. AN S.O.S. FROM SEATTLE GENERAL.
GAME FOR ANOTHER ROUND, LANTERN?
"IF YOU VALUE YOUR LIVES, I URGE YOU TO STAND BACK."

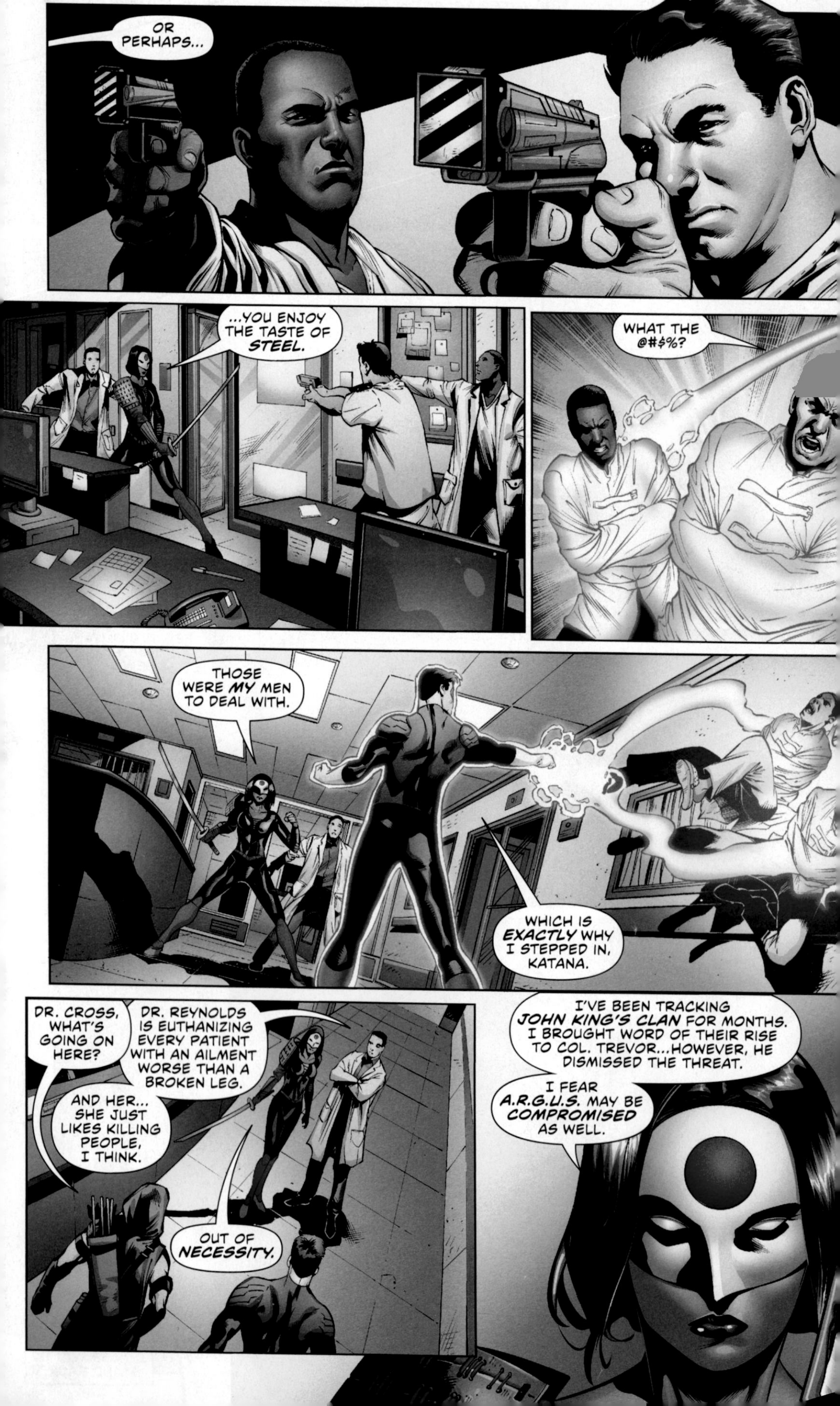
OR PERHAPS...
...YOU ENJOY THE TASTE OF STEEL.
WHAT THE @#$%?
THOSE WERE MY MEN TO DEAL WITH.
WHICH IS EXACTLY WHY I STEPPED IN, KATANA.
DR. CROSS, WHAT'S GOING ON HERE?
DR. REYNOLDS IS EUTHANIZING EVERY PATIENT WITH AN AILMENT WORSE THAN A BROKEN LEG.
AND HER... SHE JUST LIKES KILLING PEOPLE, I THINK.
OUT OF NECESSITY.
I'VE BEEN TRACKING JOHN KING'S CLAN FOR MONTHS. I BROUGHT WORD OF THEIR RISE TO COL. TREVOR...HOWEVER, HE DISMISSED THE THREAT.
I FEAR A.R.G.U.S. MAY BE COMPROMISED AS WELL.

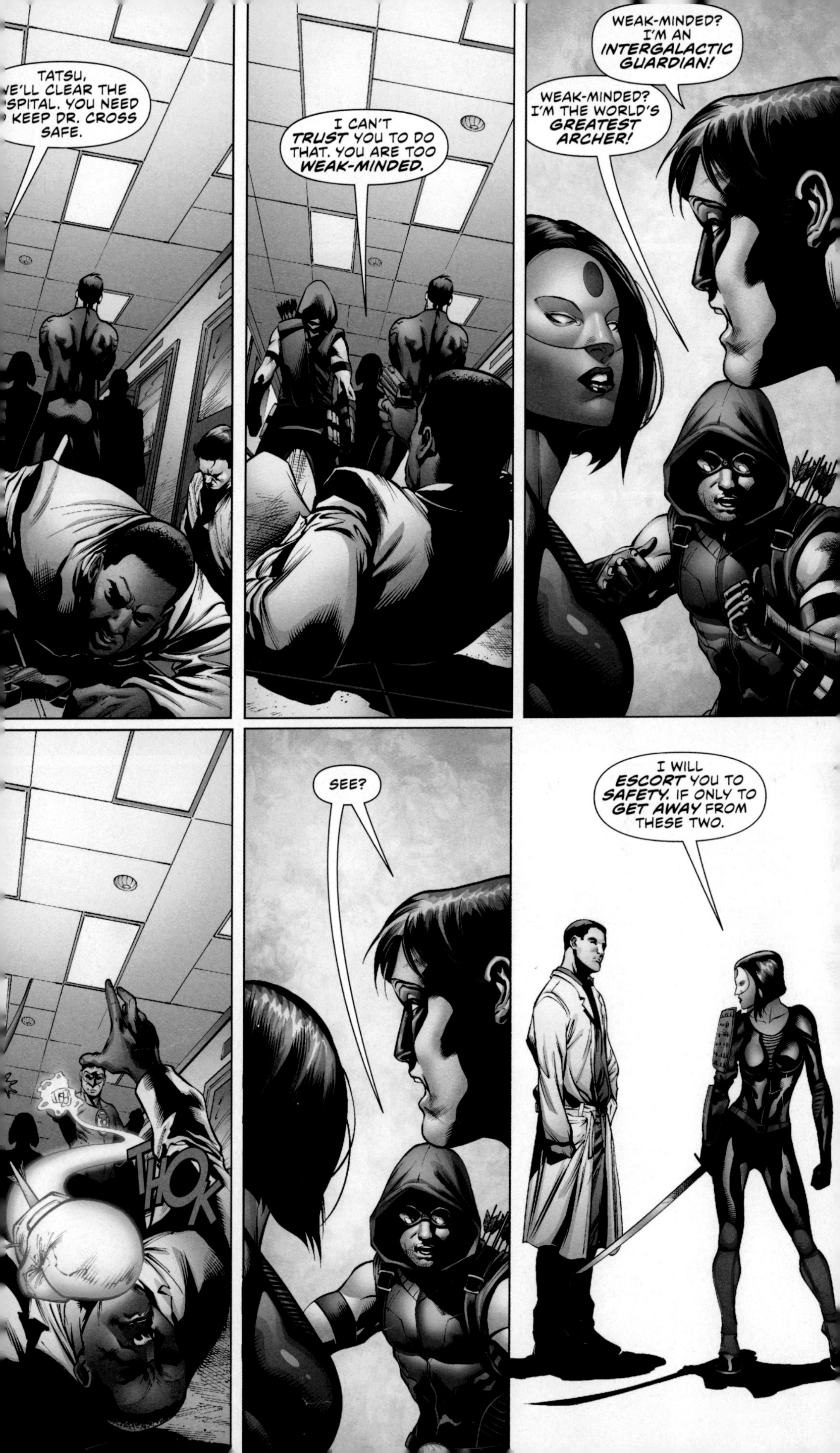
TATSU, E'LL CLEAR THE SPITAL. YOU NEED KEEP DR. CROSS SAFE.
I CAN'T TRUST YOU TO DO THAT. YOU ARE TOO WEAK-MINDED.
WEAK-MINDED? I'M AN INTERGALACTIC GUARDIAN!
WEAK-MINDED? I'M THE WORLD'S GREATEST ARCHER!
THOK
SEE?
I WILL ESCORT YOU TO SAFETY. IF ONLY TO GET AWAY FROM THESE TWO.

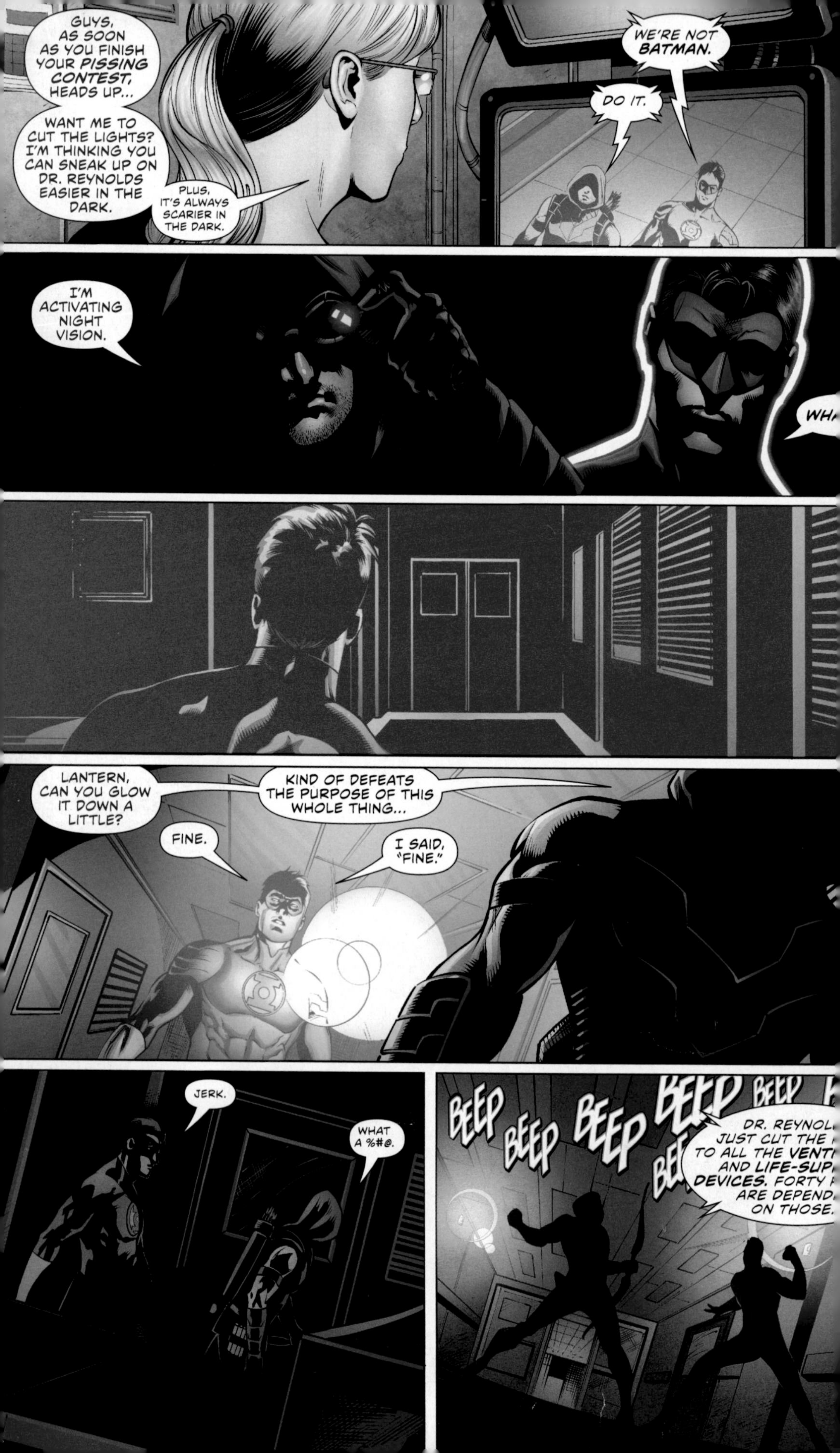
GUYS, AS SOON AS YOU FINISH YOUR PISSING CONTEST, HEADS UP...
WANT ME TO CUT THE LIGHTS? I'M THINKING YOU CAN SNEAK UP ON DR. REYNOLDS EASIER IN THE DARK.
PLUS, IT'S ALWAYS SCARIER IN THE DARK.
DO IT.
WE'RE NOT BATMAN.
I'M ACTIVATING NIGHT VISION.
LANTERN, CAN YOU GLOW IT DOWN A LITTLE?
KIND OF DEFEATS THE PURPOSE OF THIS WHOLE THING...
FINE.
I SAID, "FINE."
JERK.
WHAT A %#@.
BEEP BEEP BEEP BEEP

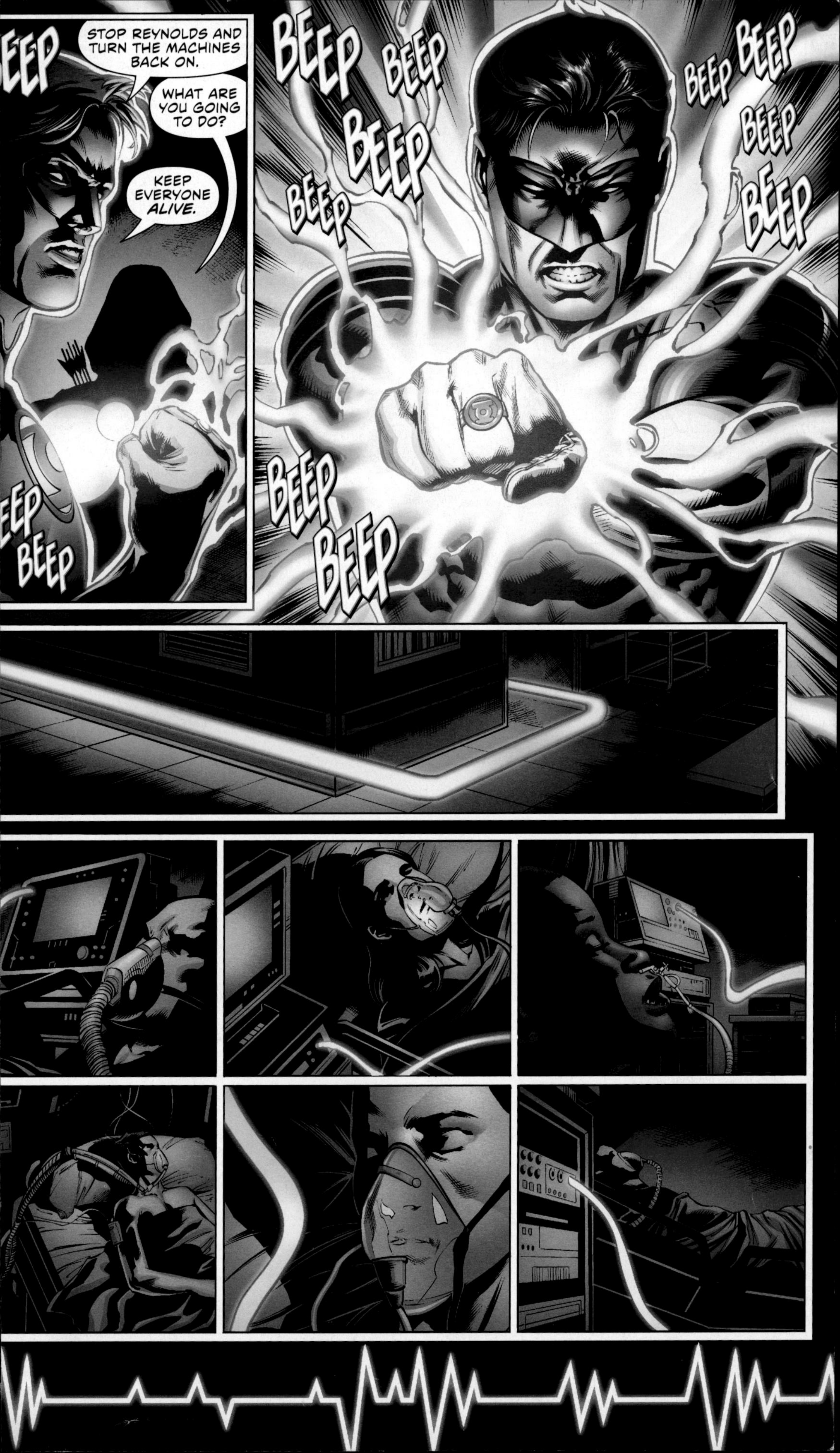
BEEP
STOP REYNOLDS AND TURN THE MACHINES BACK ON.
WHAT ARE YOU GOING TO DO?
KEEP EVERYONE ALIVE.
BEEP
BEEP
BEEP
BEEP
BEEP
BEEP
BEEP
BEEP
BEEP
BEEP
BEEP
BEEP
BEEP

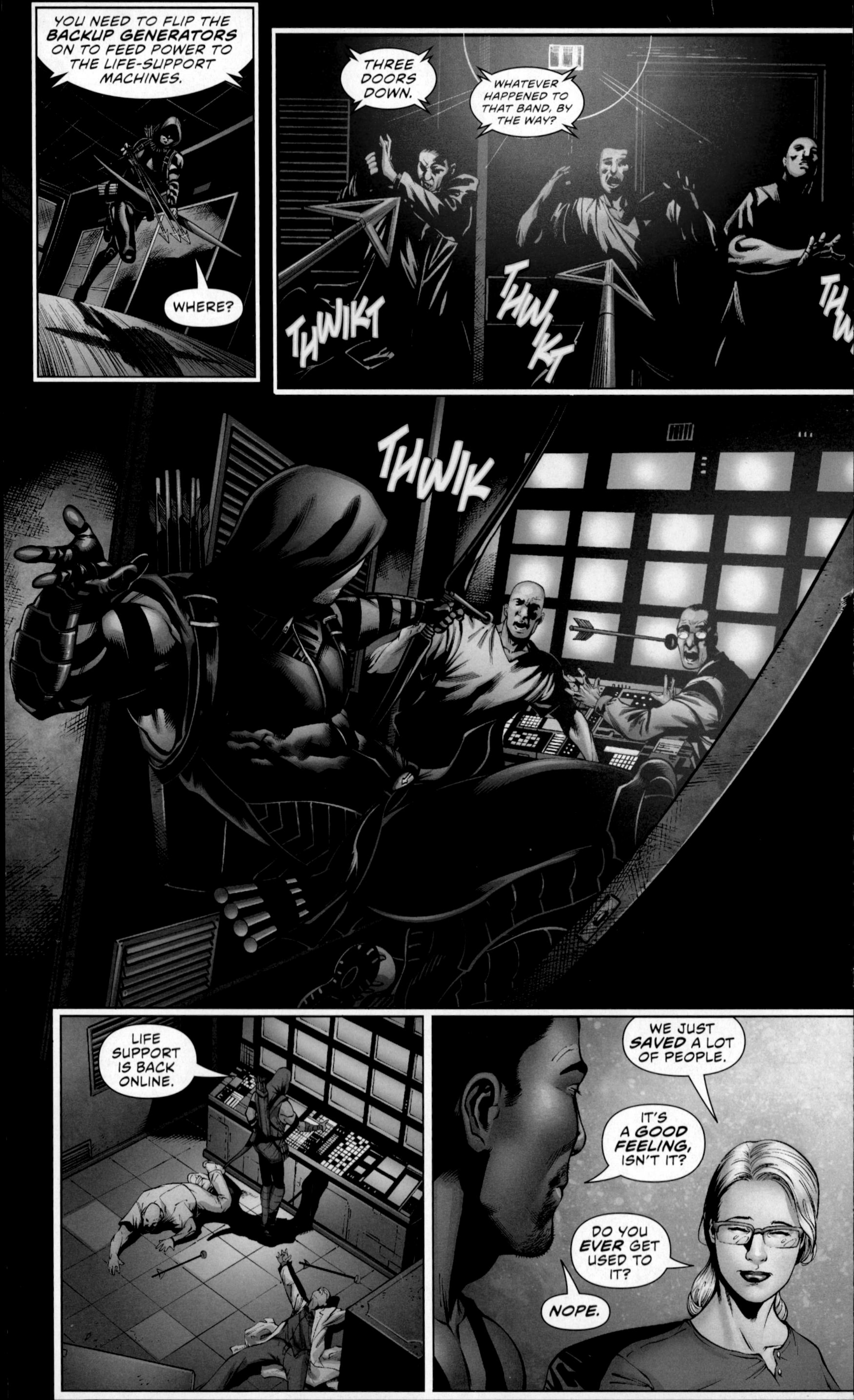
YOU NEED TO FLIP THE BACKUP GENERATORS ON TO FEED POWER TO THE LIFE-SUPPORT MACHINES.
WHERE?
THREE DOORS DOWN.
WHATEVER HAPPENED TO THAT BAND, BY THE WAY?
THWIKT
THWIKT
THWIK
LIFE SUPPORT IS BACK ONLINE.
WE JUST SAVED A LOT OF PEOPLE.
IT'S A GOOD FEELING, ISN'T IT?
DO YOU EVER GET USED TO IT?
NOPE.

FOR
G ME,
OUSLY.
SE ALL
PORT
GET
NOW.

YOU'RE AN **ASS**. BUT **ANYTIME**.

GOOD LUCK WITH **KING**. YOU'LL NEED IT.

WAIT. YOU'RE... **LEAVING**?

WE MAY HAVE WON THIS **BATTLE**, BUT THE WAR'S NOT OVER. NOT EVEN CLOSE.

I'M NOT ALLOWED TO USE **MY RING** ON **EARTH**, QUEEN.

I HELPED AS MUCH AS I CAN, BUT **OTHERS NEED** ME, TOO.

FIGURES. YOU'VE FORGOTTEN WHERE OU CAME FROM, HAL. W MANY **DAYS** HAVE U SPENT ON **EARTH** THIS YEAR?

THESE PEOPLE NEED YOU. YOU HAVE RESPONSIBILITIES **HERE**, NOT JUST **EIGHTY MILLION LIGHT YEARS** AWAY.

IT'S A **BIG UNIVERSE**, QUEEN. AND OF COURSE, YOU'RE A SPOILED RICH KID WHO BELIEVES IT REVOLVES AROUND YOU.

AND **I'M** THE ASS?

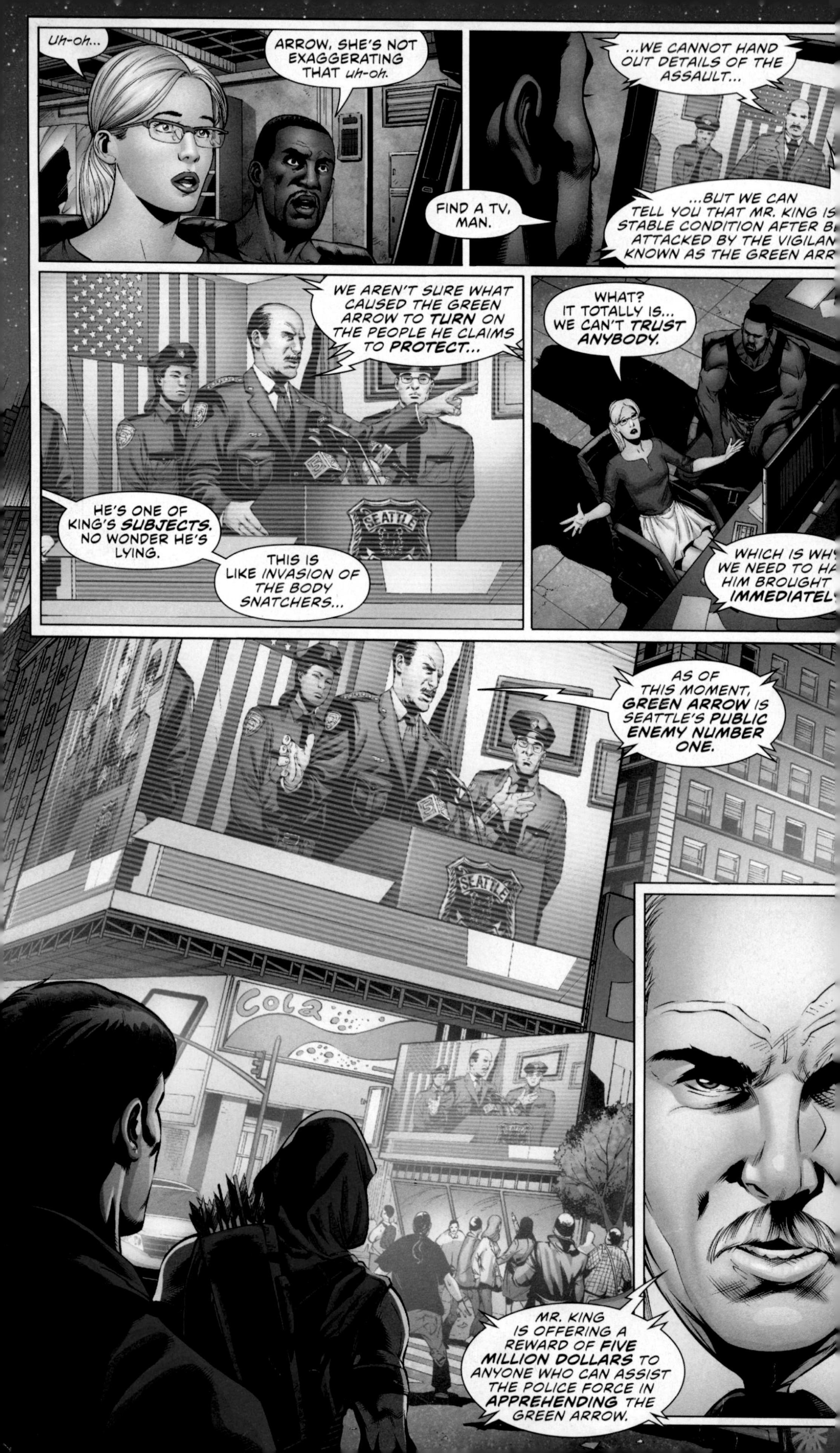
Uh-oh...
ARROW, SHE'S NOT EXAGGERATING THAT uh-oh.
FIND A TV, MAN.
...WE CANNOT HAND OUT DETAILS OF THE ASSAULT...
...BUT WE CAN TELL YOU THAT MR. KING IS STABLE CONDITION AFTER B ATTACKED BY THE VIGILAN KNOWN AS THE GREEN ARR
WE AREN'T SURE WHAT CAUSED THE GREEN ARROW TO TURN ON THE PEOPLE HE CLAIMS TO PROTECT...
HE'S ONE OF KING'S SUBJECTS. NO WONDER HE'S LYING.
THIS IS LIKE INVASION OF THE BODY SNATCHERS...
WHAT? IT TOTALLY IS... WE CAN'T TRUST ANYBODY.
WHICH IS WHY WE NEED TO HA HIM BROUGHT IMMEDIATEL
AS OF THIS MOMENT, GREEN ARROW IS SEATTLE'S PUBLIC ENEMY NUMBER ONE.
SEATTLE
Cola
MR. KING IS OFFERING A REWARD OF FIVE MILLION DOLLARS TO ANYONE WHO CAN ASSIST THE POLICE FORCE IN APPREHENDING THE GREEN ARROW.

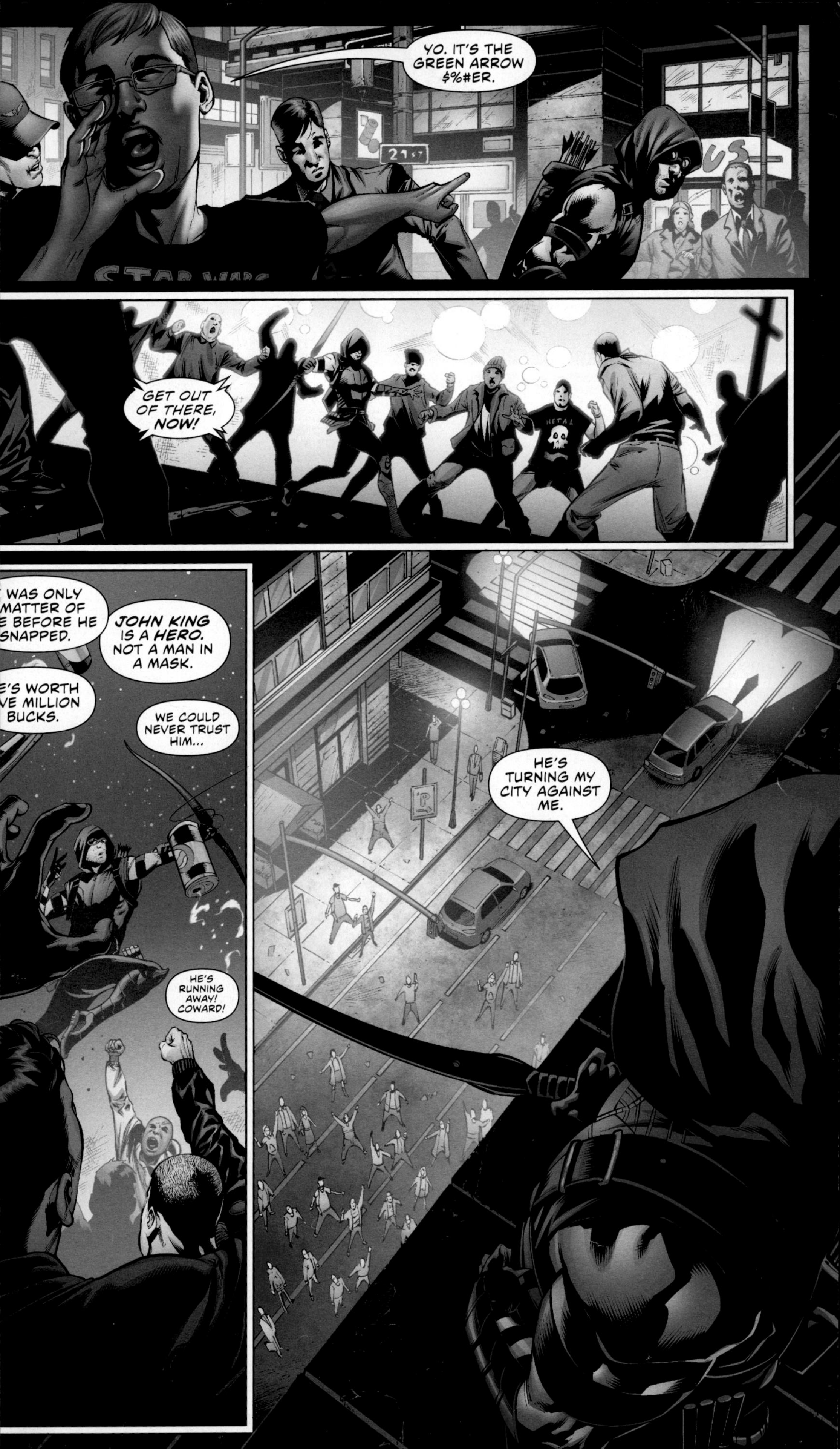
YO. IT'S THE GREEN ARROW $%#ER.
STAR WARS
21ST
GET OUT OF THERE, NOW!
METAL
WAS ONLY MATTER OF E BEFORE HE SNAPPED.
JOHN KING IS A HERO. NOT A MAN IN A MASK.
E'S WORTH VE MILLION BUCKS.
WE COULD NEVER TRUST HIM...
HE'S TURNING MY CITY AGAINST ME.
HE'S RUNNING AWAY! COWARD!

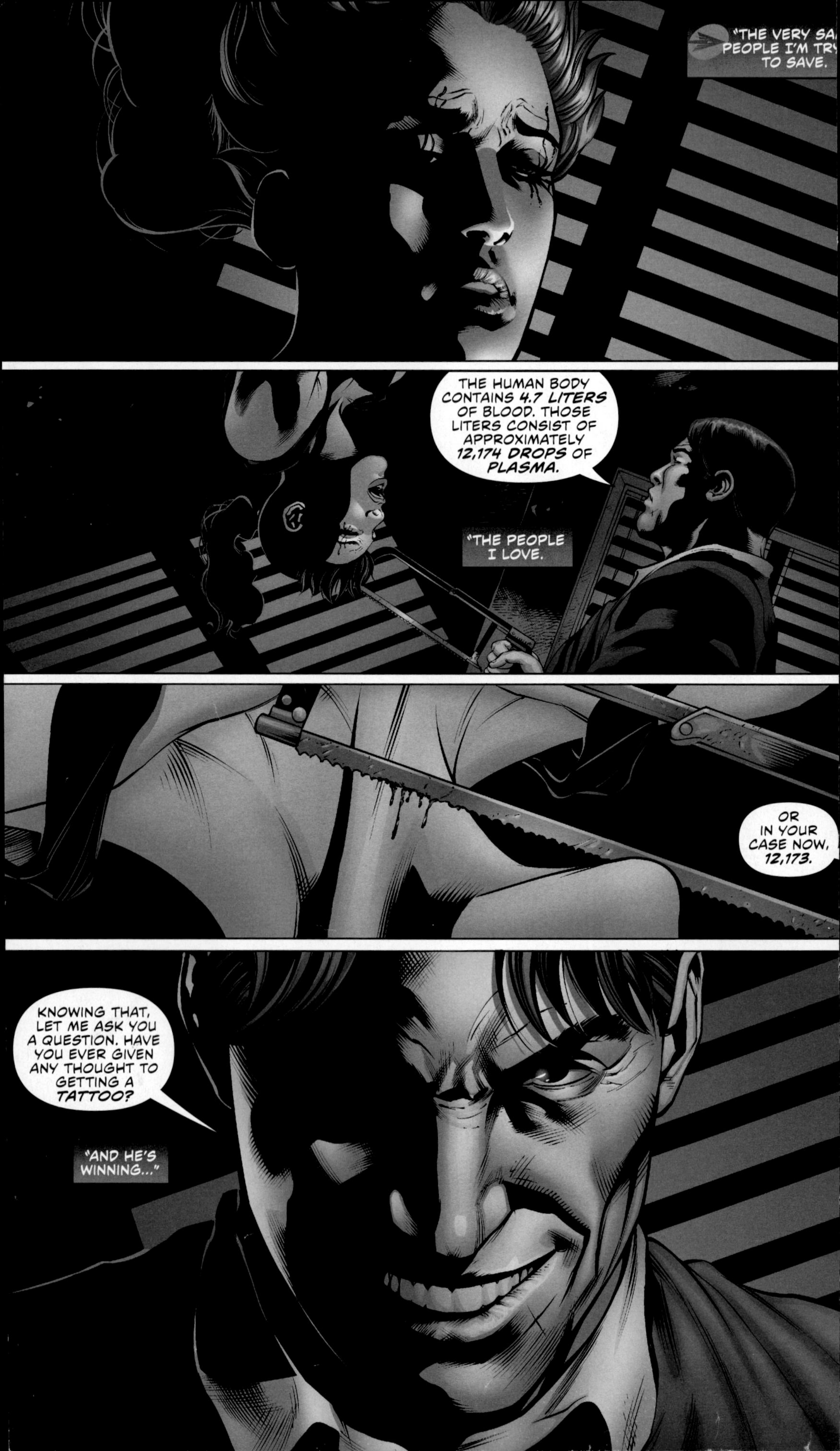
"THE VERY SA
PEOPLE I'M TRY
TO SAVE.
THE HUMAN BODY CONTAINS 4.7 LITERS OF BLOOD. THOSE LITERS CONSIST OF APPROXIMATELY 12,174 DROPS OF PLASMA.
"THE PEOPLE I LOVE.
OR IN YOUR CASE NOW, 12,173.
KNOWING THAT, LET ME ASK YOU A QUESTION. HAVE YOU EVER GIVEN ANY THOUGHT TO GETTING A TATTOO?
"AND HE'S WINNING..."

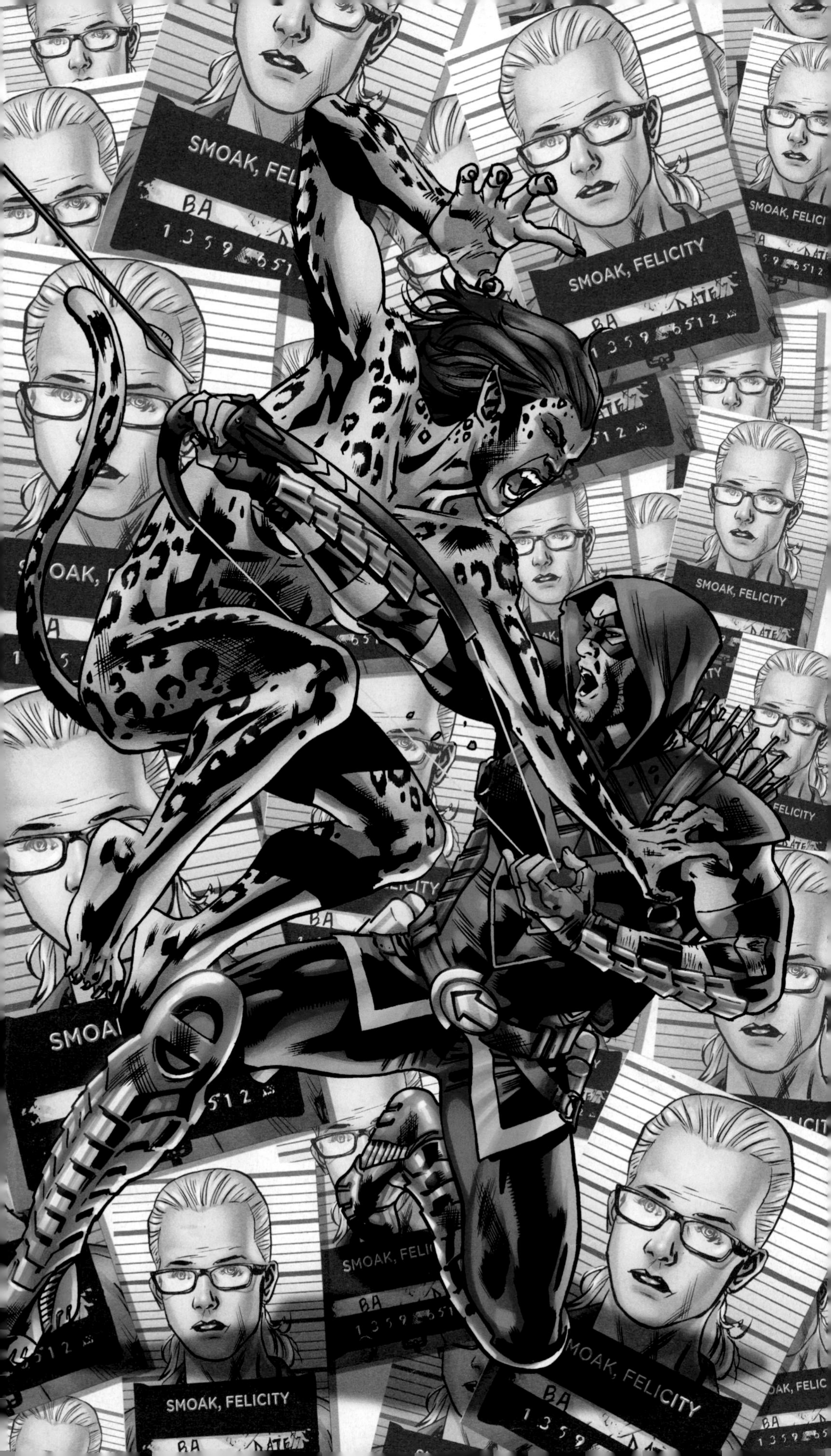
SMOAK, FELICITY
SMOAK, FELICITY
SMOAK, FELICITY
SMOAK, FELICITY

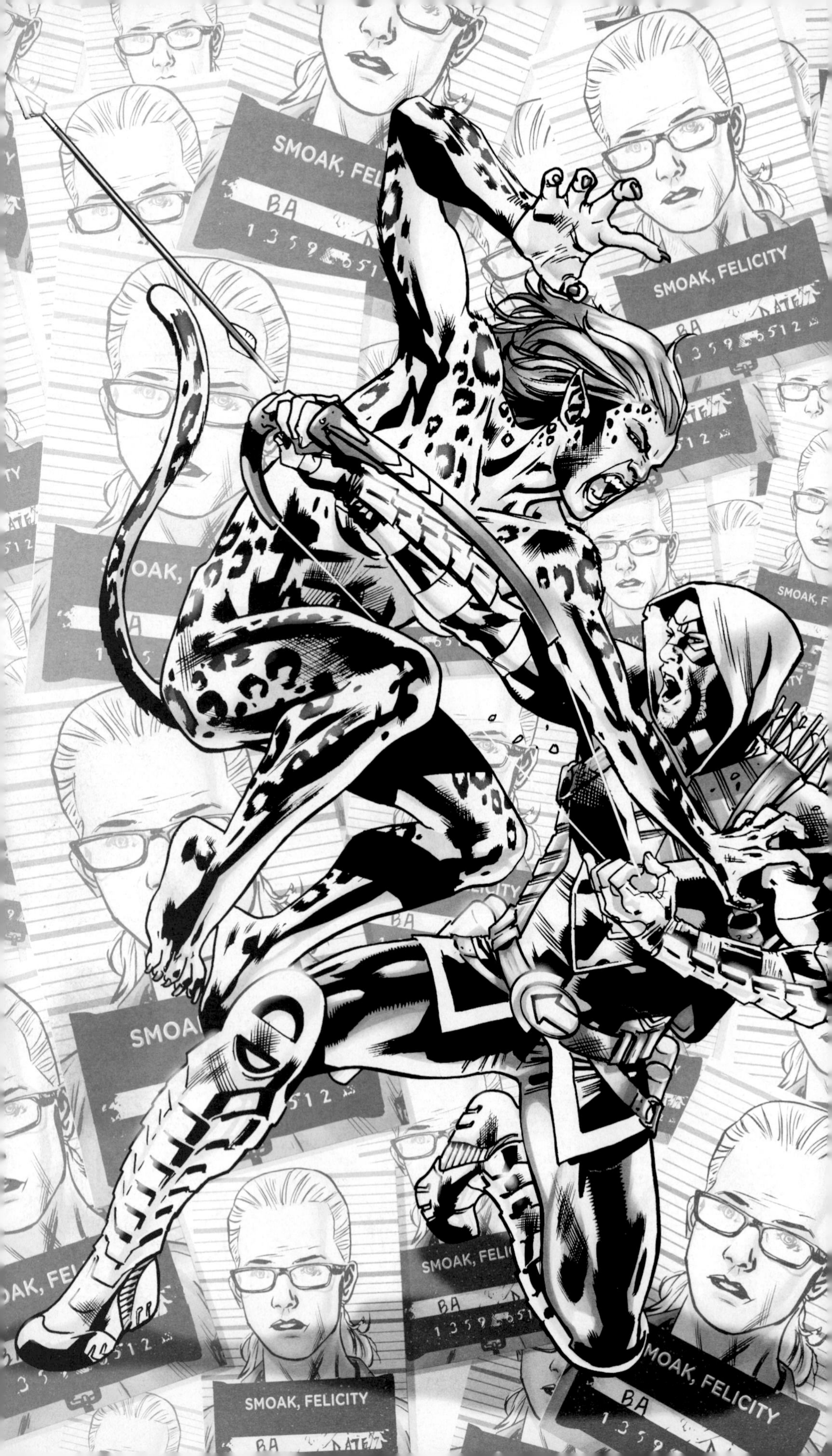
SMOAK, FELICITY
SMOAK, FELICITY
SMOAK, FELICITY

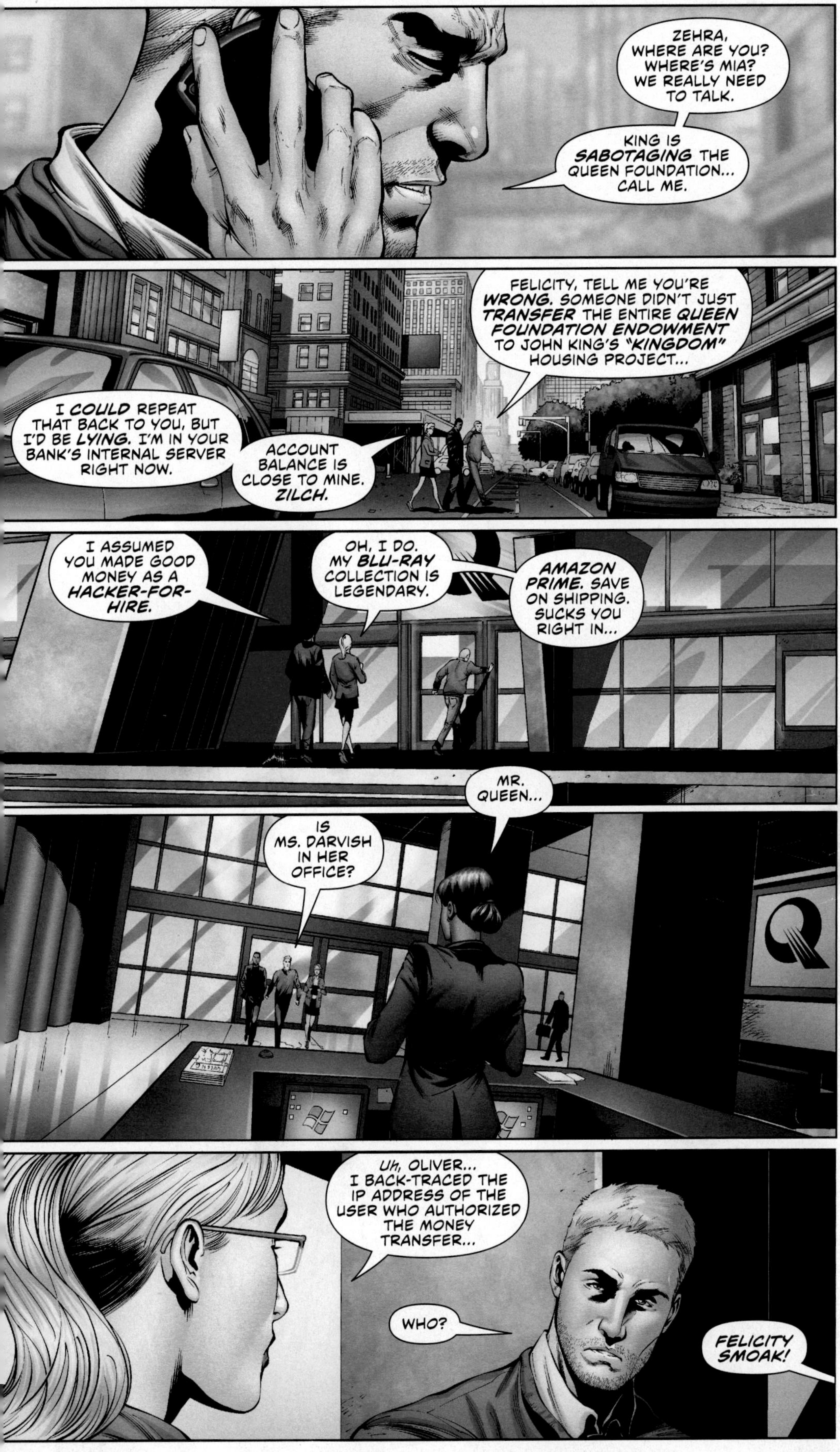
ZEHRA, WHERE ARE YOU? WHERE'S MIA? WE REALLY NEED TO TALK.
KING IS SABOTAGING THE QUEEN FOUNDATION... CALL ME.
FELICITY, TELL ME YOU'RE WRONG. SOMEONE DIDN'T JUST TRANSFER THE ENTIRE QUEEN FOUNDATION ENDOWMENT TO JOHN KING'S "KINGDOM" HOUSING PROJECT...
I COULD REPEAT THAT BACK TO YOU, BUT I'D BE LYING. I'M IN YOUR BANK'S INTERNAL SERVER RIGHT NOW.
ACCOUNT BALANCE IS CLOSE TO MINE. ZILCH.
I ASSUMED YOU MADE GOOD MONEY AS A HACKER-FOR-HIRE.
OH, I DO. MY BLU-RAY COLLECTION IS LEGENDARY.
AMAZON PRIME. SAVE ON SHIPPING. SUCKS YOU RIGHT IN...
MR. QUEEN...
IS MS. DARVISH IN HER OFFICE?
Uh, OLIVER... I BACK-TRACED THE IP ADDRESS OF THE USER WHO AUTHORIZED THE MONEY TRANSFER...
WHO?
FELICITY SMOAK!

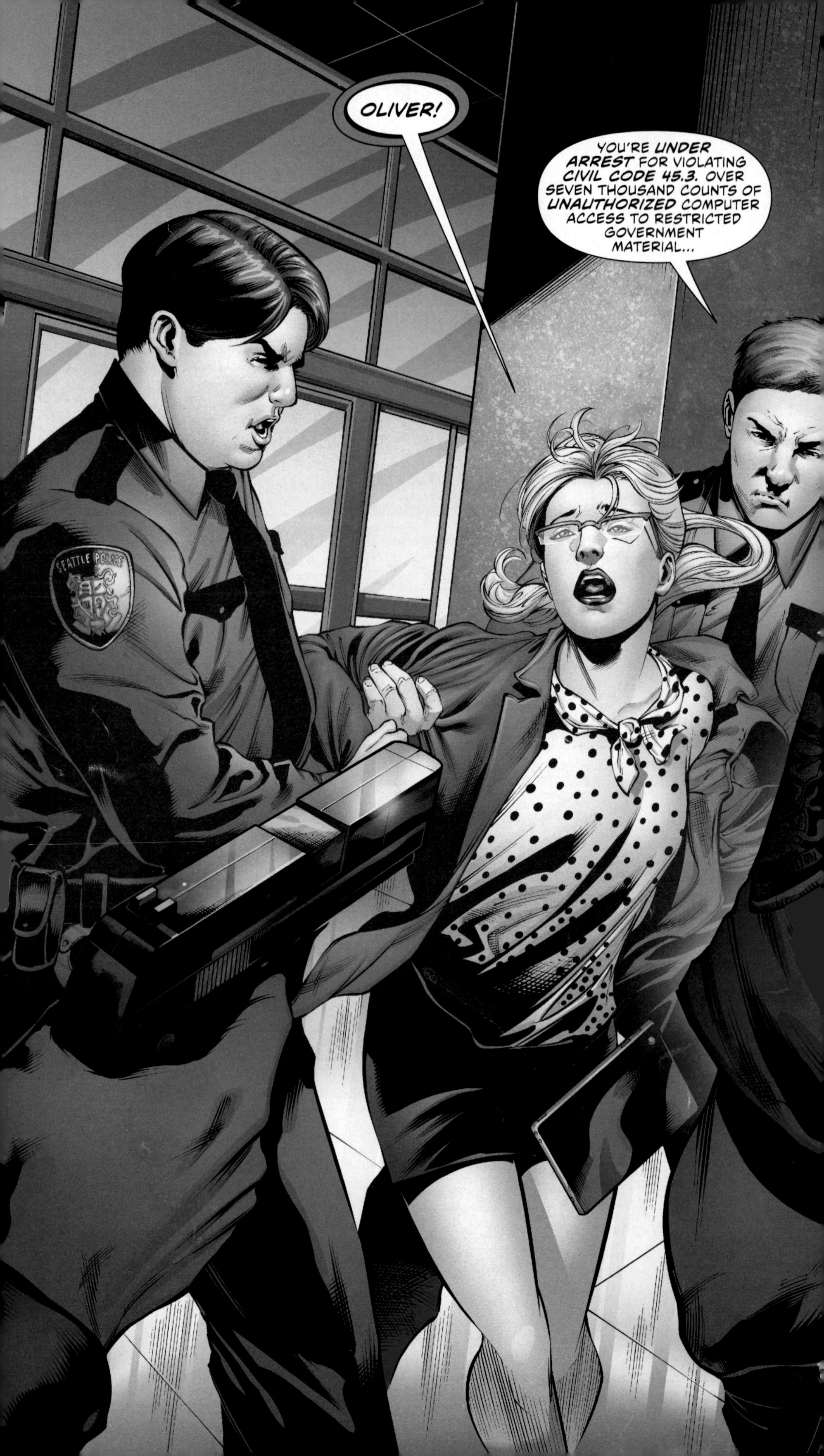
OLIVER!
YOU'RE UNDER ARREST FOR VIOLATING CIVIL CODE 45.3. OVER SEVEN THOUSAND COUNTS OF UNAUTHORIZED COMPUTER ACCESS TO RESTRICTED GOVERNMENT MATERIAL...
SEATTLE POLICE

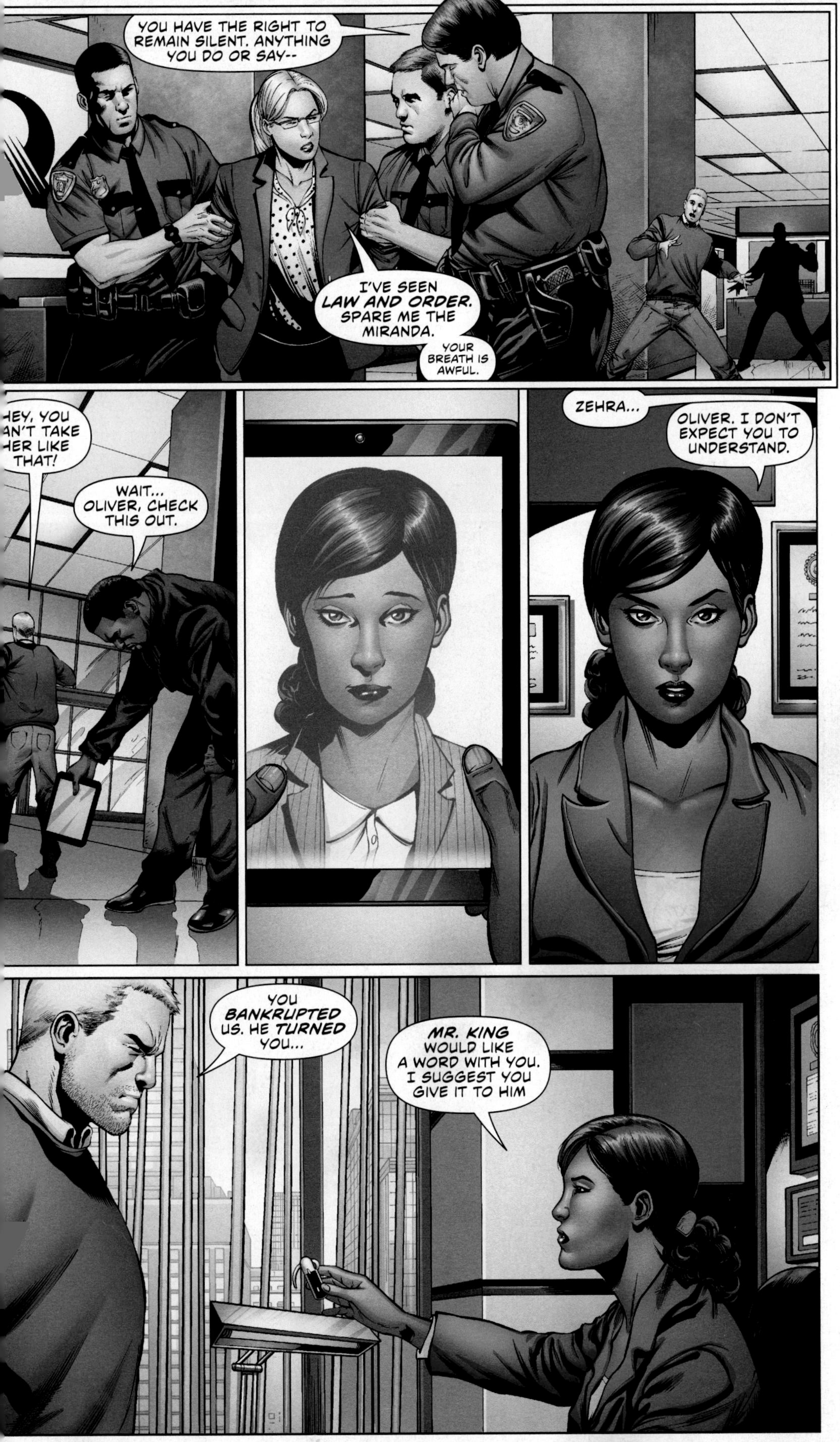
YOU HAVE THE RIGHT TO REMAIN SILENT. ANYTHING YOU DO OR SAY--
I'VE SEEN LAW AND ORDER. SPARE ME THE MIRANDA.
YOUR BREATH IS AWFUL.
HEY, YOU CAN'T TAKE HER LIKE THAT!
WAIT... OLIVER, CHECK THIS OUT.
ZEHRA...
OLIVER. I DON'T EXPECT YOU TO UNDERSTAND.
YOU BANKRUPTED US. HE TURNED YOU...
MR. KING WOULD LIKE A WORD WITH YOU. I SUGGEST YOU GIVE IT TO HIM

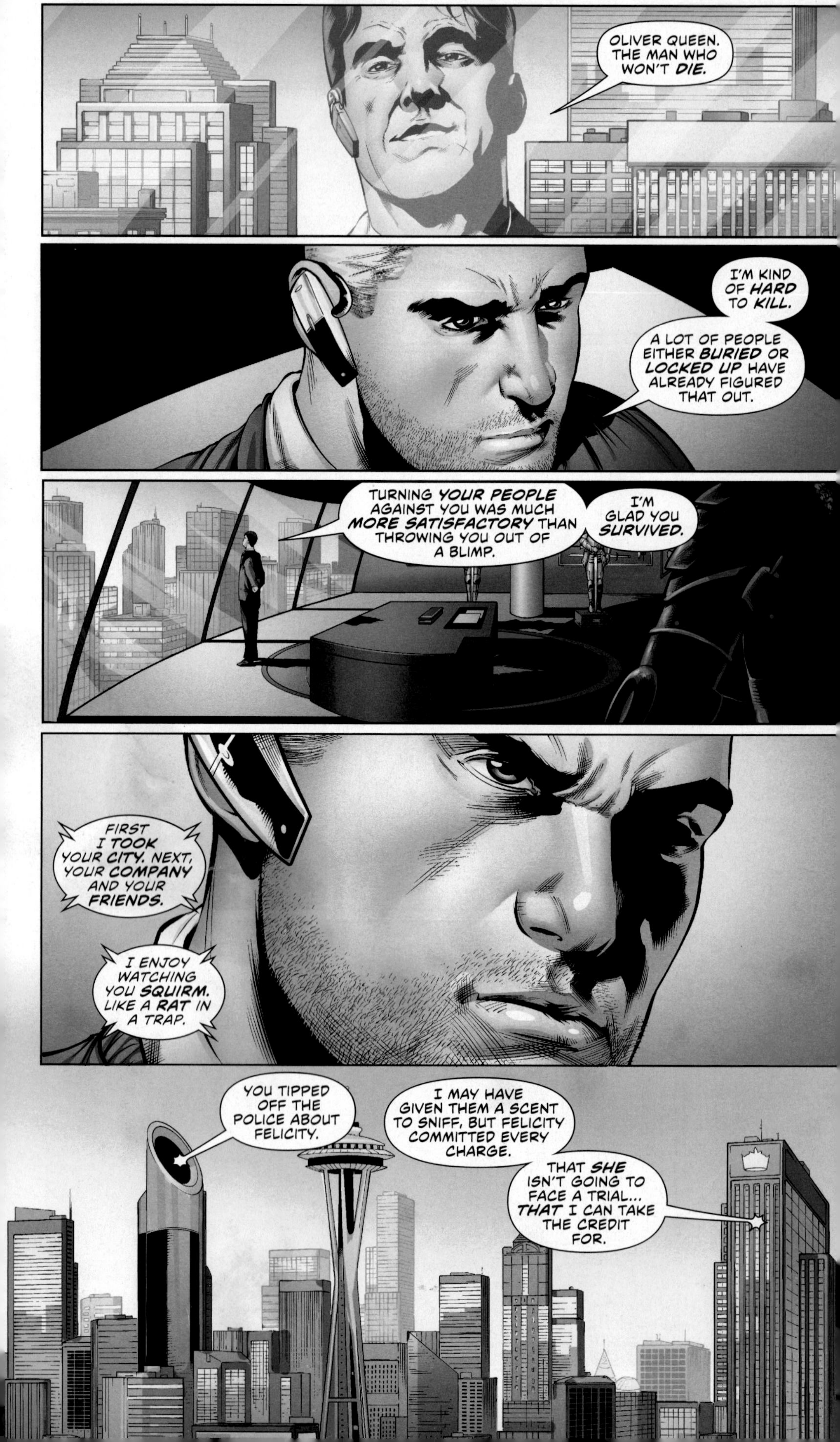
OLIVER QUEEN. THE MAN WHO WON'T DIE.
I'M KIND OF HARD TO KILL.
A LOT OF PEOPLE EITHER BURIED OR LOCKED UP HAVE ALREADY FIGURED THAT OUT.
TURNING YOUR PEOPLE AGAINST YOU WAS MUCH MORE SATISFACTORY THAN THROWING YOU OUT OF A BLIMP.
I'M GLAD YOU SURVIVED.
FIRST I TOOK YOUR CITY. NEXT, YOUR COMPANY AND YOUR FRIENDS.
I ENJOY WATCHING YOU SQUIRM. LIKE A RAT IN A TRAP.
YOU TIPPED OFF THE POLICE ABOUT FELICITY.
I MAY HAVE GIVEN THEM A SCENT TO SNIFF, BUT FELICITY COMMITTED EVERY CHARGE.
THAT SHE ISN'T GOING TO FACE A TRIAL... THAT I CAN TAKE THE CREDIT FOR.

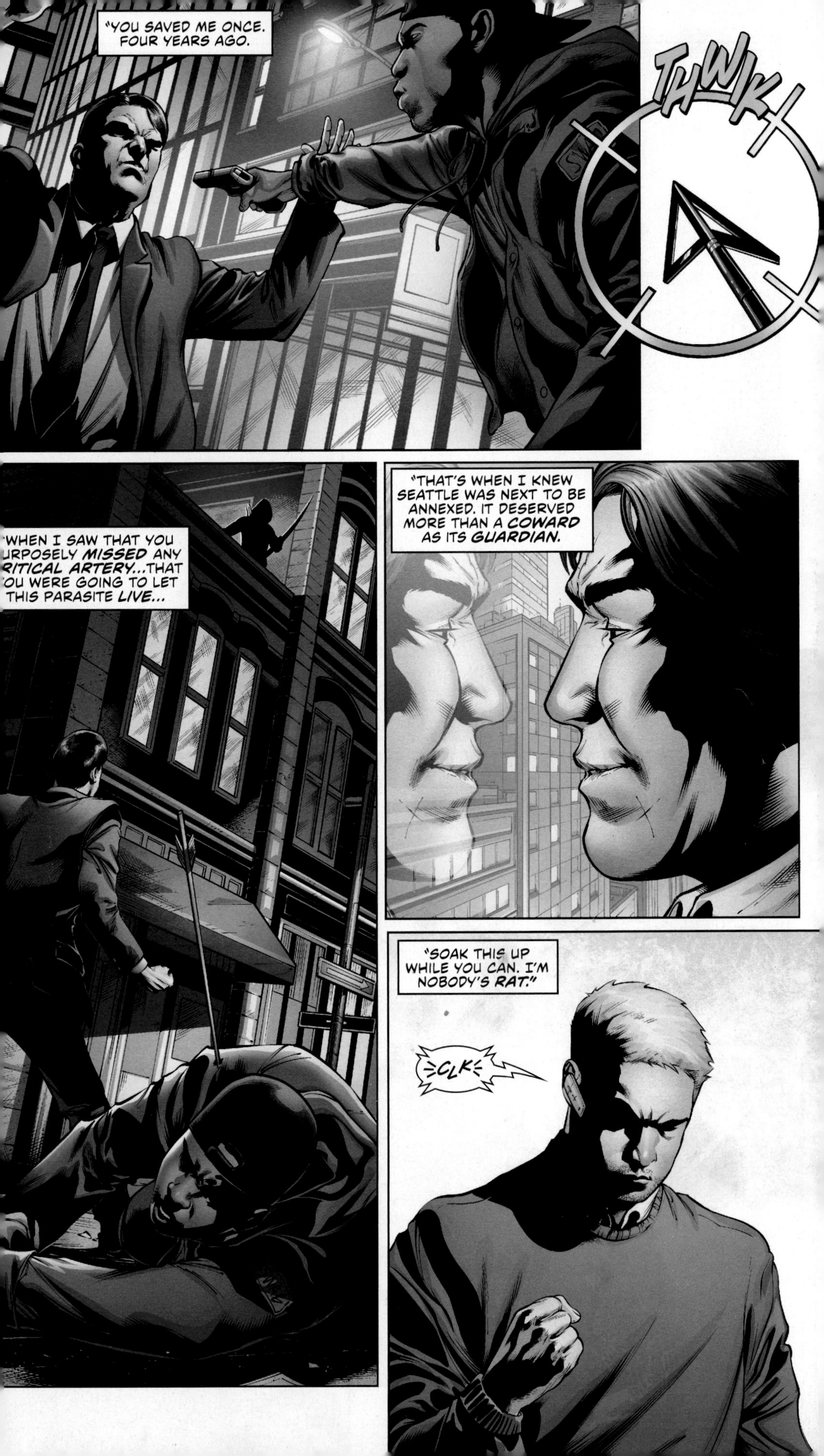
"YOU SAVED ME ONCE. FOUR YEARS AGO.
THWIK
"WHEN I SAW THAT YOU PURPOSELY MISSED ANY CRITICAL ARTERY... THAT YOU WERE GOING TO LET THIS PARASITE LIVE...
"THAT'S WHEN I KNEW SEATTLE WAS NEXT TO BE ANNEXED. IT DESERVED MORE THAN A COWARD AS ITS GUARDIAN.
"SOAK THIS UP WHILE YOU CAN. I'M NOBODY'S RAT."
CLK

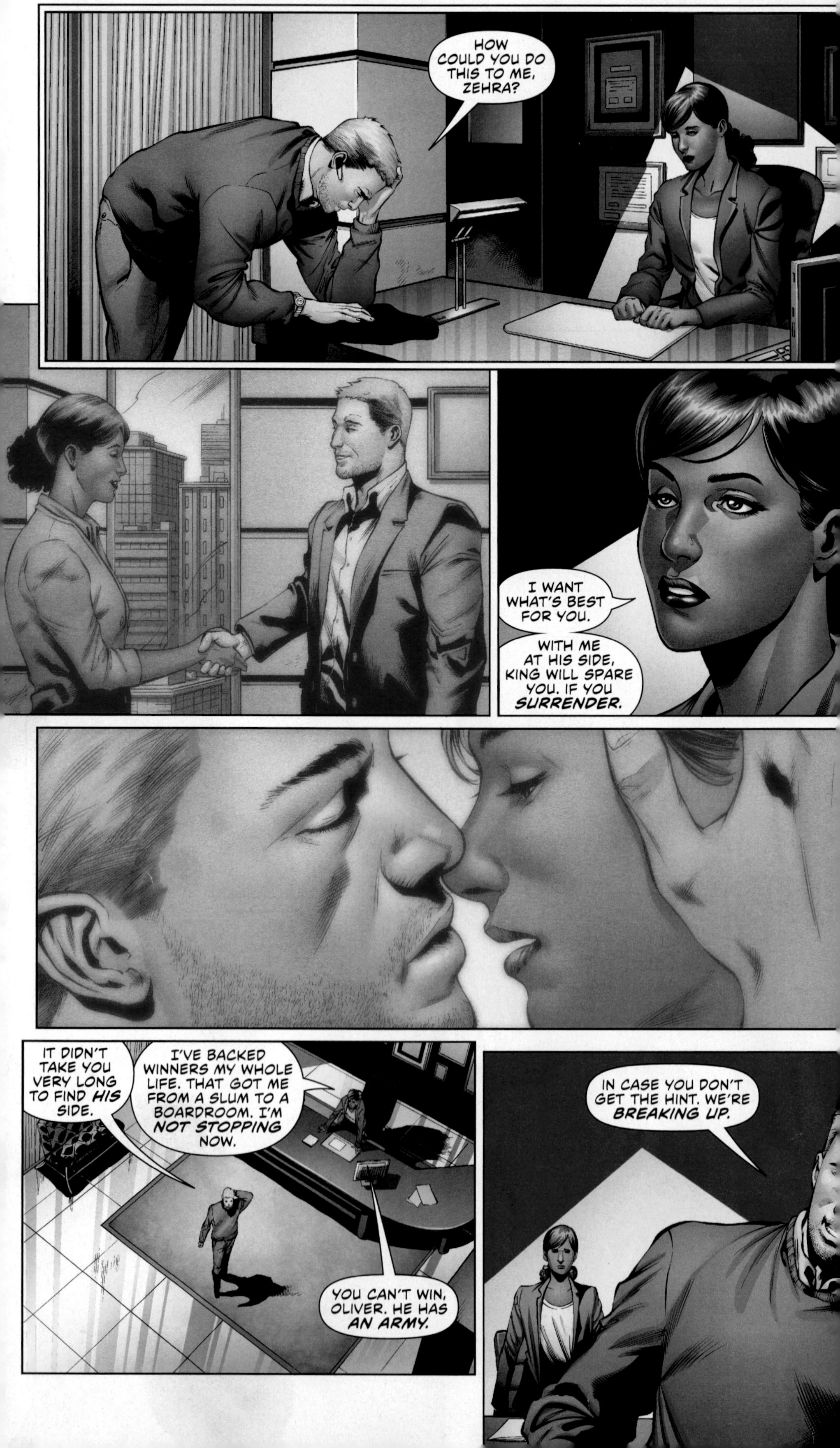
HOW COULD YOU DO THIS TO ME, ZEHRA?
I WANT WHAT'S BEST FOR YOU.
WITH ME AT HIS SIDE, KING WILL SPARE YOU. IF YOU *SURRENDER.*
IT DIDN'T TAKE YOU VERY LONG TO FIND *HIS* SIDE.
I'VE BACKED WINNERS MY WHOLE LIFE. THAT GOT ME FROM A SLUM TO A BOARDROOM. I'M *NOT STOPPING* NOW.
YOU CAN'T WIN, OLIVER. HE HAS *AN ARMY.*
IN CASE YOU DON'T GET THE HINT. WE'RE *BREAKING UP.*

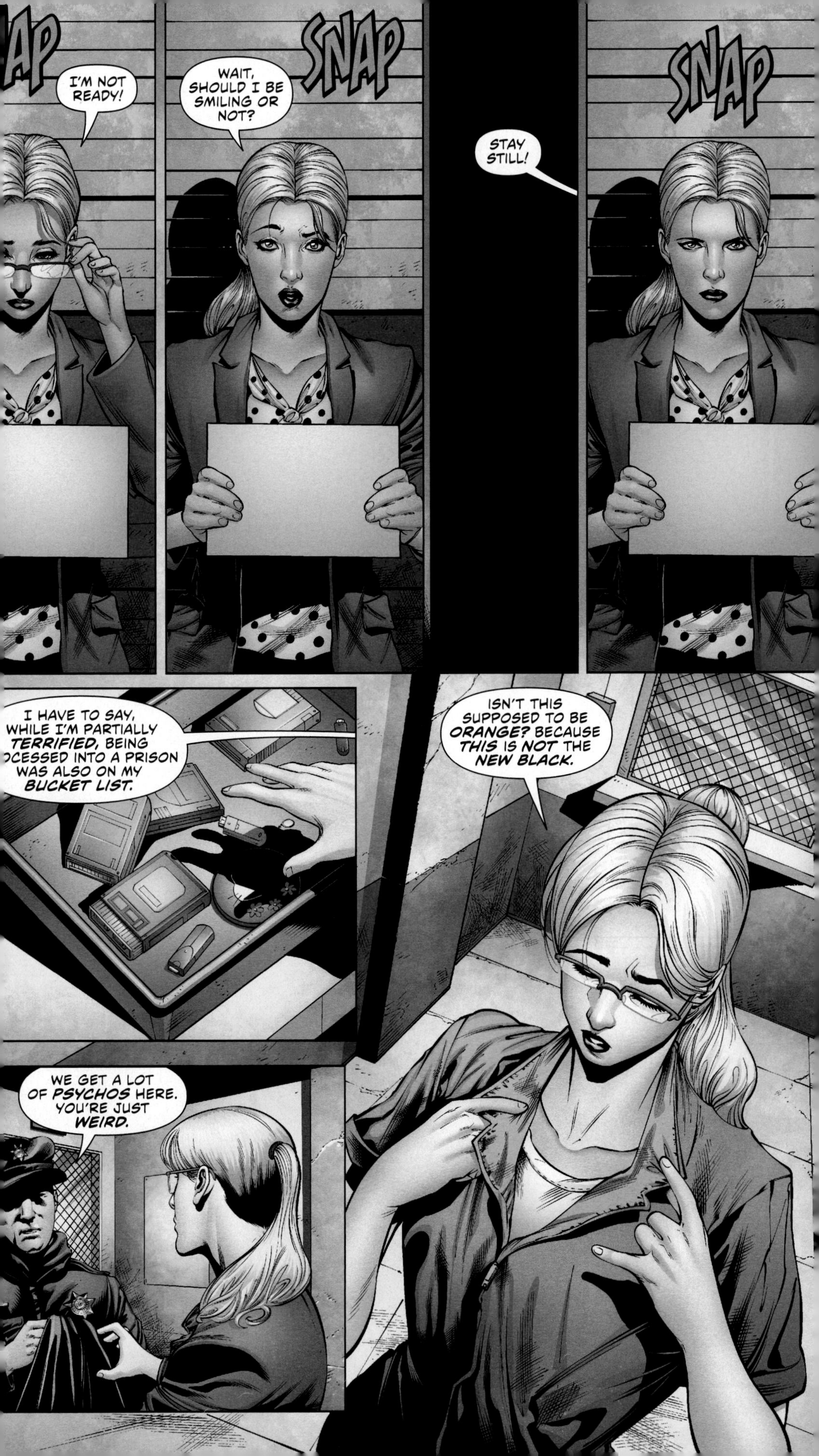
AP
I'M NOT READY!
WAIT, SHOULD I BE SMILING OR NOT?
SNAP
STAY STILL!
SNAP
I HAVE TO SAY, WHILE I'M PARTIALLY TERRIFIED, BEING OCESSED INTO A PRISON WAS ALSO ON MY BUCKET LIST.
WE GET A LOT OF PSYCHOS HERE. YOU'RE JUST WEIRD.
ISN'T THIS SUPPOSED TO BE ORANGE? BECAUSE THIS IS NOT THE NEW BLACK.

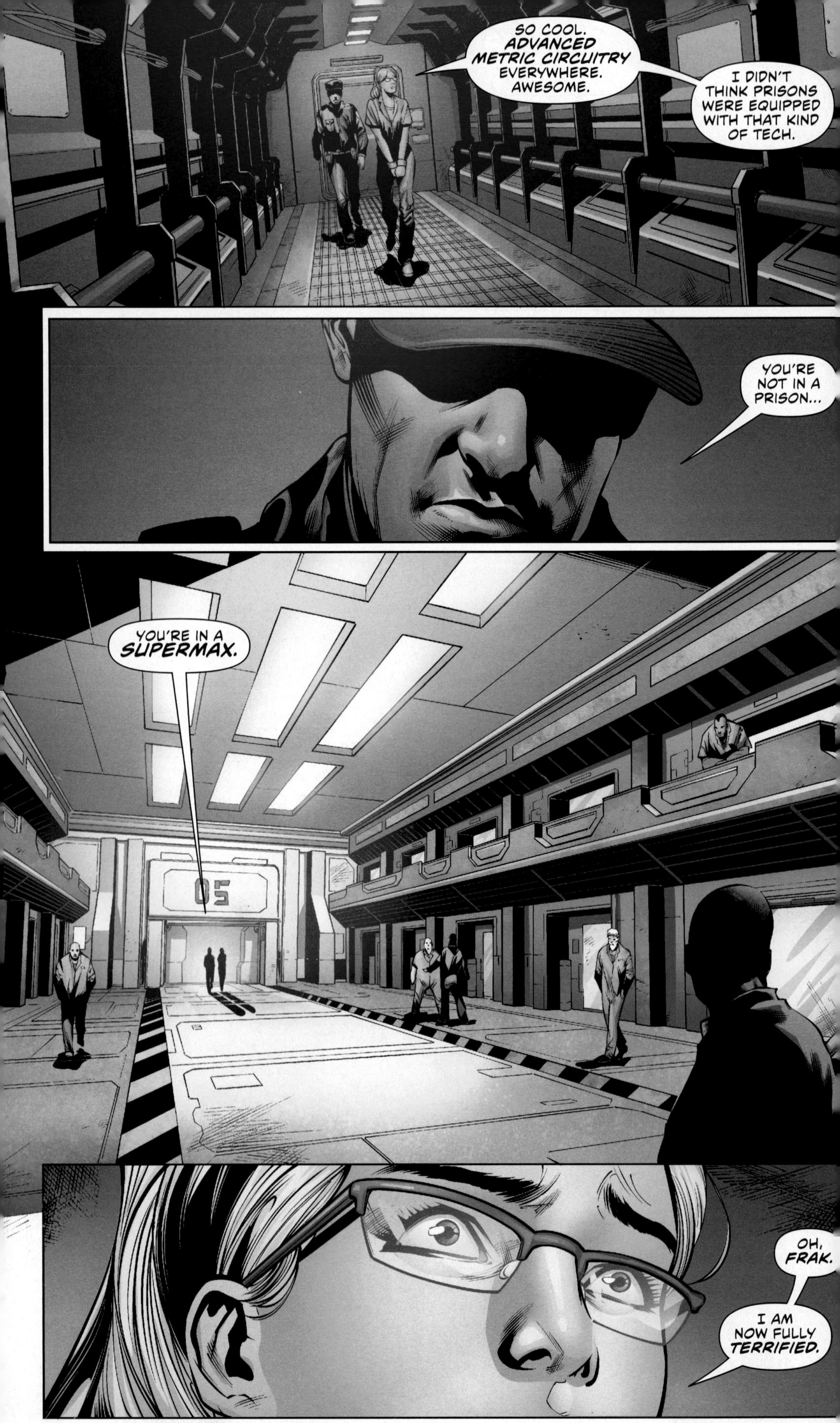

SO COOL. ADVANCED METRIC CIRCUITRY EVERYWHERE. AWESOME.
I DIDN'T THINK PRISONS WERE EQUIPPED WITH THAT KIND OF TECH.
YOU'RE NOT IN A PRISON...
YOU'RE IN A SUPERMAX.
05
OH, FRAK.
I AM NOW FULLY TERRIFIED.

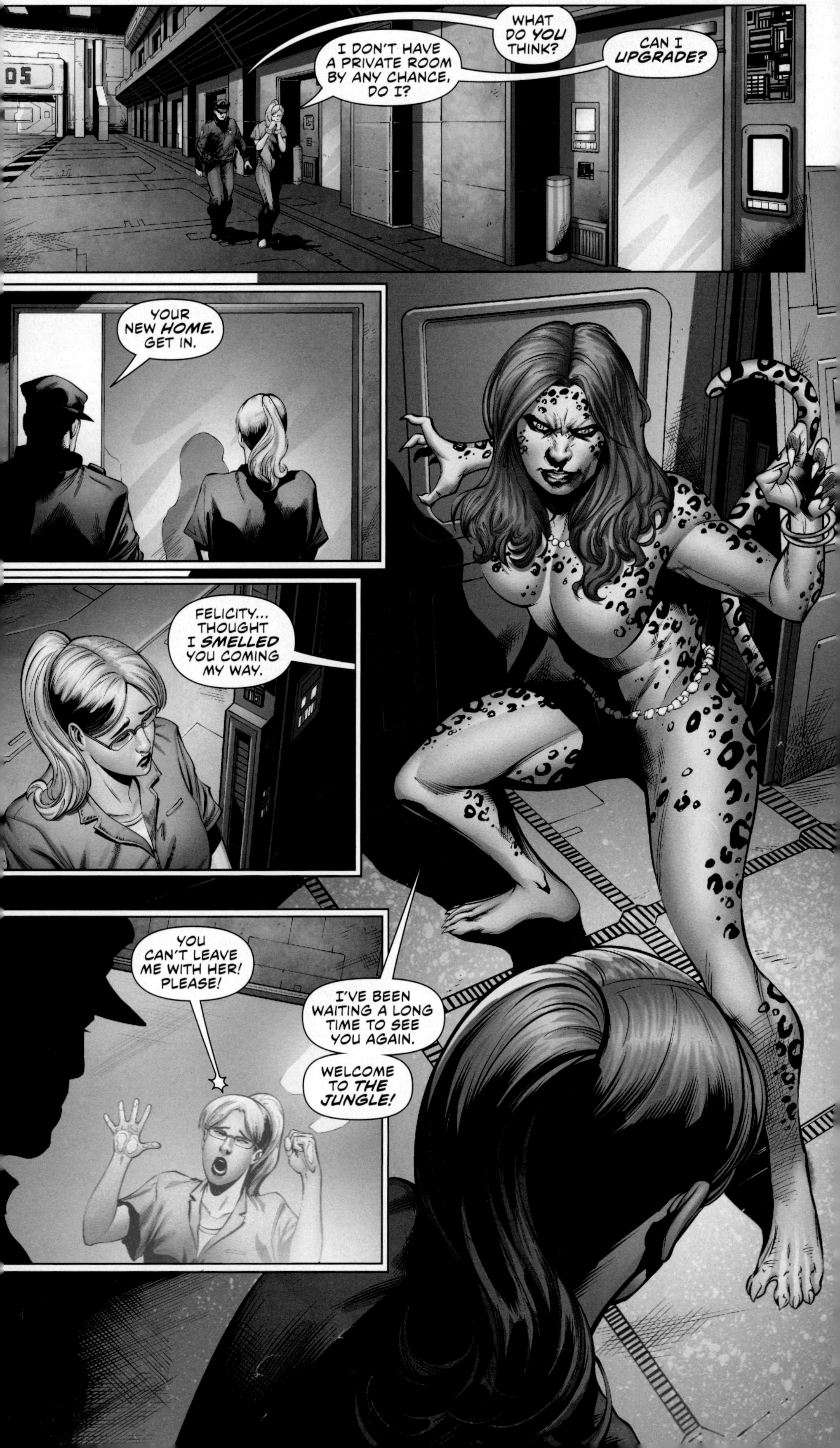
I DON'T HAVE A PRIVATE ROOM BY ANY CHANCE, DO I?
WHAT DO YOU THINK?
CAN I UPGRADE?
YOUR NEW HOME. GET IN.
FELICITY... THOUGHT I SMELLED YOU COMING MY WAY.
YOU CAN'T LEAVE ME WITH HER! PLEASE!
I'VE BEEN WAITING A LONG TIME TO SEE YOU AGAIN.
WELCOME TO THE JUNGLE!

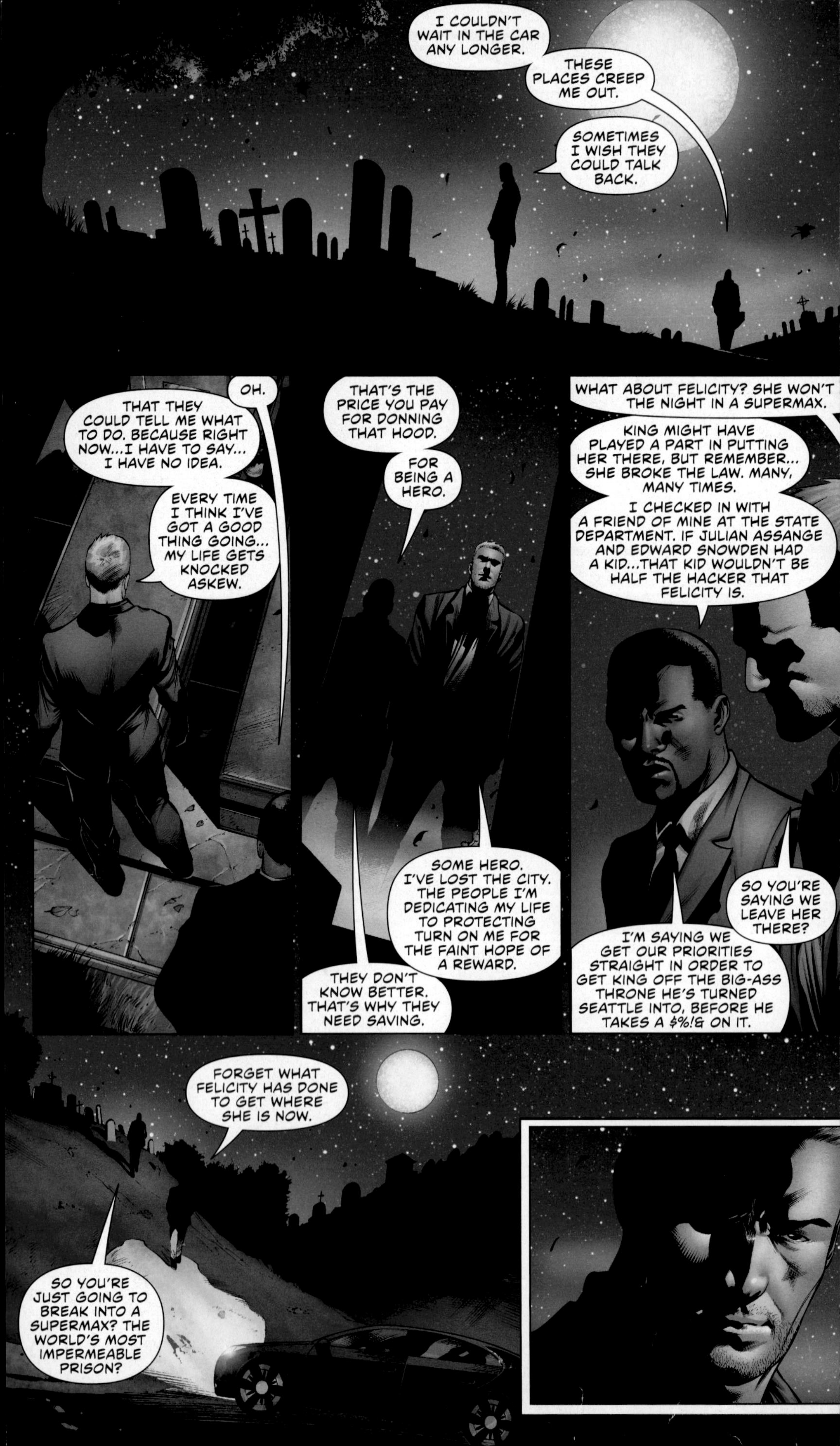
I COULDN'T WAIT IN THE CAR ANY LONGER.
THESE PLACES CREEP ME OUT.
SOMETIMES I WISH THEY COULD TALK BACK.
OH.
THAT THEY COULD TELL ME WHAT TO DO. BECAUSE RIGHT NOW...I HAVE TO SAY... I HAVE NO IDEA.
EVERY TIME I THINK I'VE GOT A GOOD THING GOING... MY LIFE GETS KNOCKED ASKEW.
THAT'S THE PRICE YOU PAY FOR DONNING THAT HOOD.
FOR BEING A HERO.
SOME HERO. I'VE LOST THE CITY. THE PEOPLE I'M DEDICATING MY LIFE TO PROTECTING TURN ON ME FOR THE FAINT HOPE OF A REWARD.
THEY DON'T KNOW BETTER. THAT'S WHY THEY NEED SAVING.
WHAT ABOUT FELICITY? SHE WON'T THE NIGHT IN A SUPERMAX.
KING MIGHT HAVE PLAYED A PART IN PUTTING HER THERE, BUT REMEMBER... SHE BROKE THE LAW. MANY, MANY TIMES.
I CHECKED IN WITH A FRIEND OF MINE AT THE STATE DEPARTMENT. IF JULIAN ASSANGE AND EDWARD SNOWDEN HAD A KID...THAT KID WOULDN'T BE HALF THE HACKER THAT FELICITY IS.
SO YOU'RE SAYING WE LEAVE HER THERE?
I'M SAYING WE GET OUR PRIORITIES STRAIGHT IN ORDER TO GET KING OFF THE BIG-ASS THRONE HE'S TURNED SEATTLE INTO, BEFORE HE TAKES A $%!& ON IT.
FORGET WHAT FELICITY HAS DONE TO GET WHERE SHE IS NOW.
SO YOU'RE JUST GOING TO BREAK INTO A SUPERMAX? THE WORLD'S MOST IMPERMEABLE PRISON?

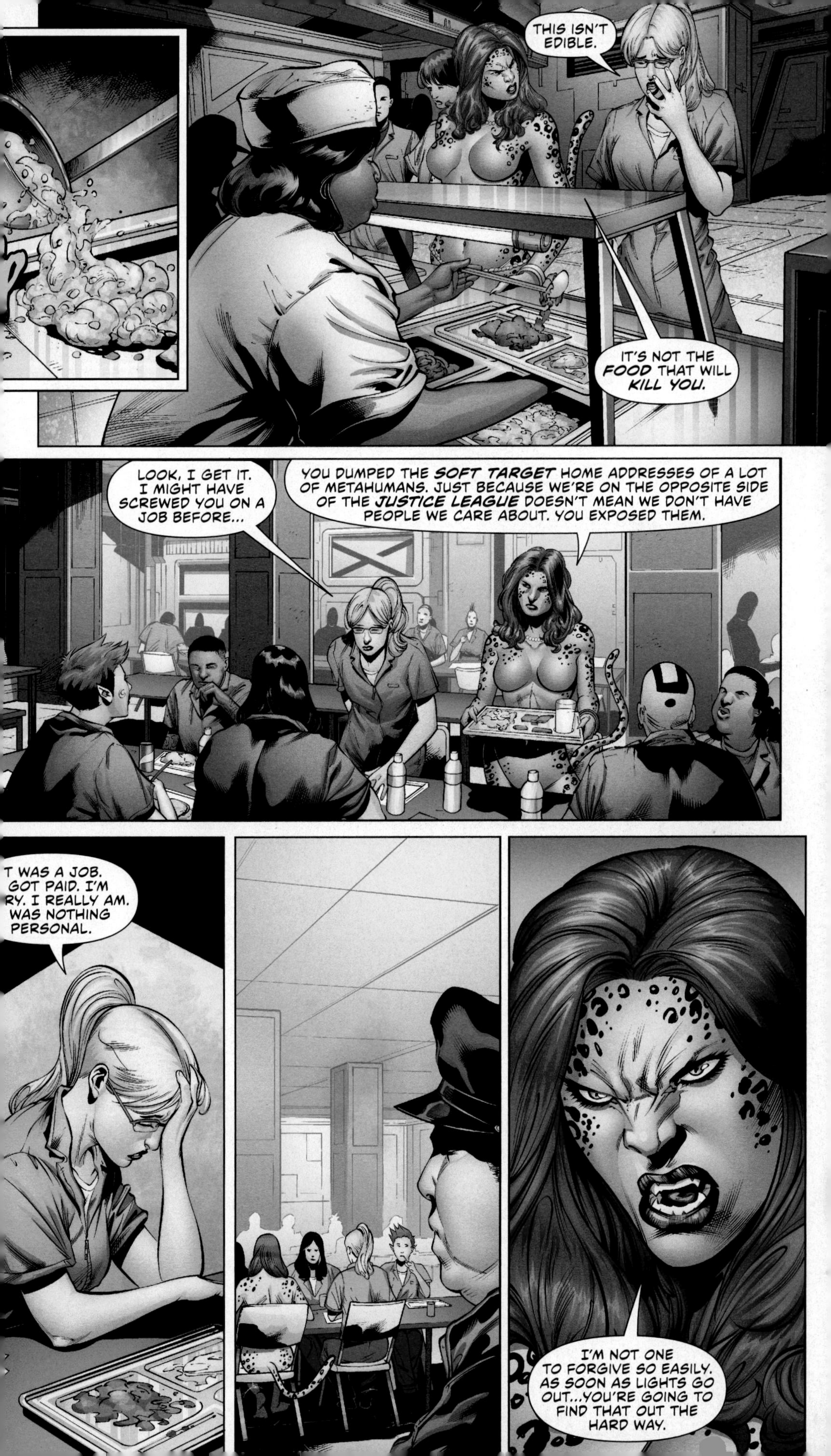
THIS ISN'T EDIBLE.
IT'S NOT THE FOOD THAT WILL KILL YOU.
LOOK, I GET IT. I MIGHT HAVE SCREWED YOU ON A JOB BEFORE...
YOU DUMPED THE SOFT TARGET HOME ADDRESSES OF A LOT OF METAHUMANS. JUST BECAUSE WE'RE ON THE OPPOSITE SIDE OF THE JUSTICE LEAGUE DOESN'T MEAN WE DON'T HAVE PEOPLE WE CARE ABOUT. YOU EXPOSED THEM.
T WAS A JOB. GOT PAID. I'M RY. I REALLY AM. WAS NOTHING PERSONAL.
I'M NOT ONE TO FORGIVE SO EASILY. AS SOON AS LIGHTS GO OUT...YOU'RE GOING TO FIND THAT OUT THE HARD WAY.

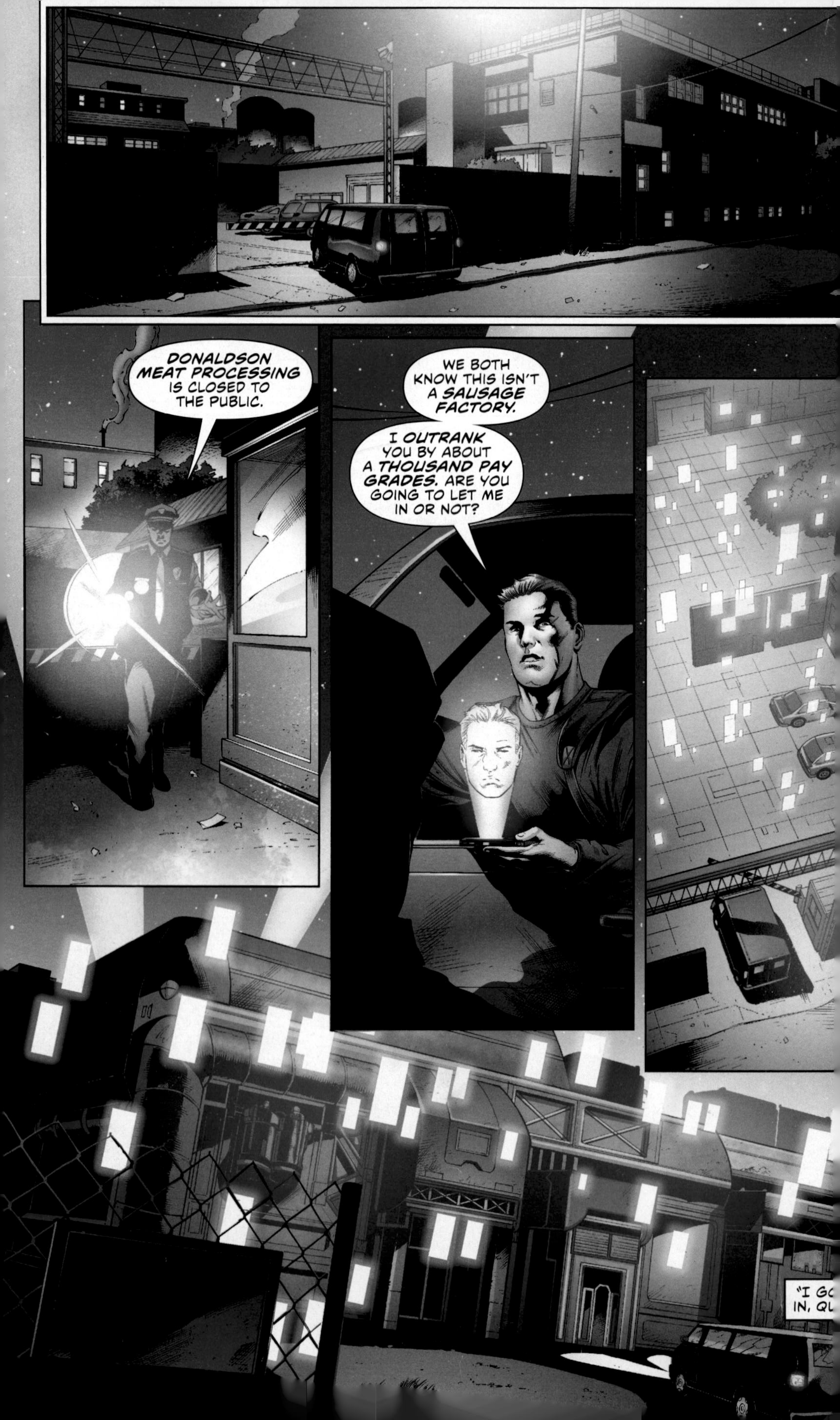
DONALDSON MEAT PROCESSING IS CLOSED TO THE PUBLIC.
WE BOTH KNOW THIS ISN'T A SAUSAGE FACTORY.
I OUTRANK YOU BY ABOUT A THOUSAND PAY GRADES. ARE YOU GOING TO LET ME IN OR NOT?

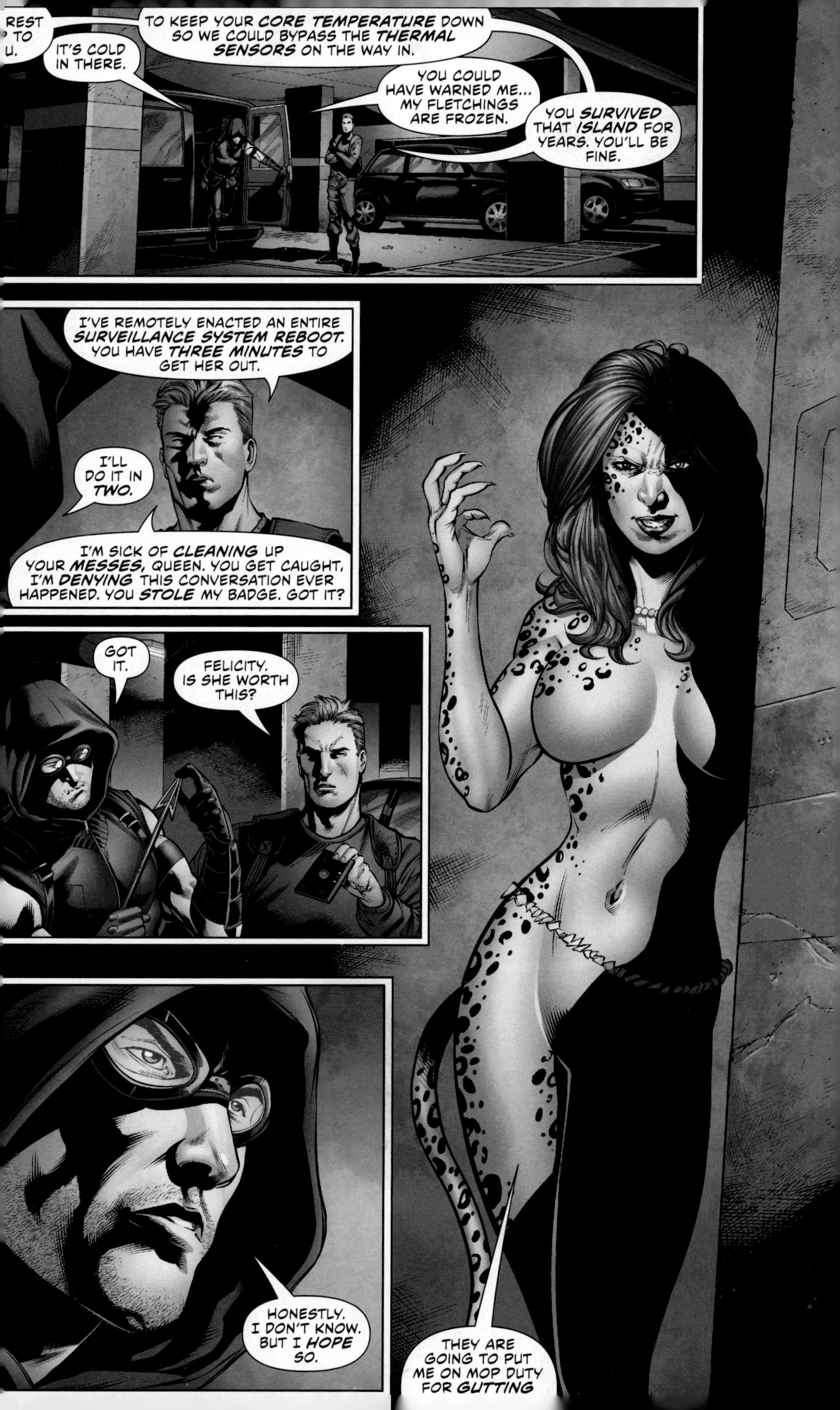

IT'S COLD IN THERE.
TO KEEP YOUR CORE TEMPERATURE DOWN SO WE COULD BYPASS THE THERMAL SENSORS ON THE WAY IN.
YOU COULD HAVE WARNED ME... MY FLETCHINGS ARE FROZEN.
YOU SURVIVED THAT ISLAND FOR YEARS. YOU'LL BE FINE.
I'VE REMOTELY ENACTED AN ENTIRE SURVEILLANCE SYSTEM REBOOT. YOU HAVE THREE MINUTES TO GET HER OUT.
I'LL DO IT IN TWO.
I'M SICK OF CLEANING UP YOUR MESSES, QUEEN. YOU GET CAUGHT, I'M DENYING THIS CONVERSATION EVER HAPPENED. YOU STOLE MY BADGE. GOT IT?
GOT IT.
FELICITY. IS SHE WORTH THIS?
HONESTLY. I DON'T KNOW. BUT I HOPE SO.
THEY ARE GOING TO PUT ME ON MOP DUTY FOR GUTTING

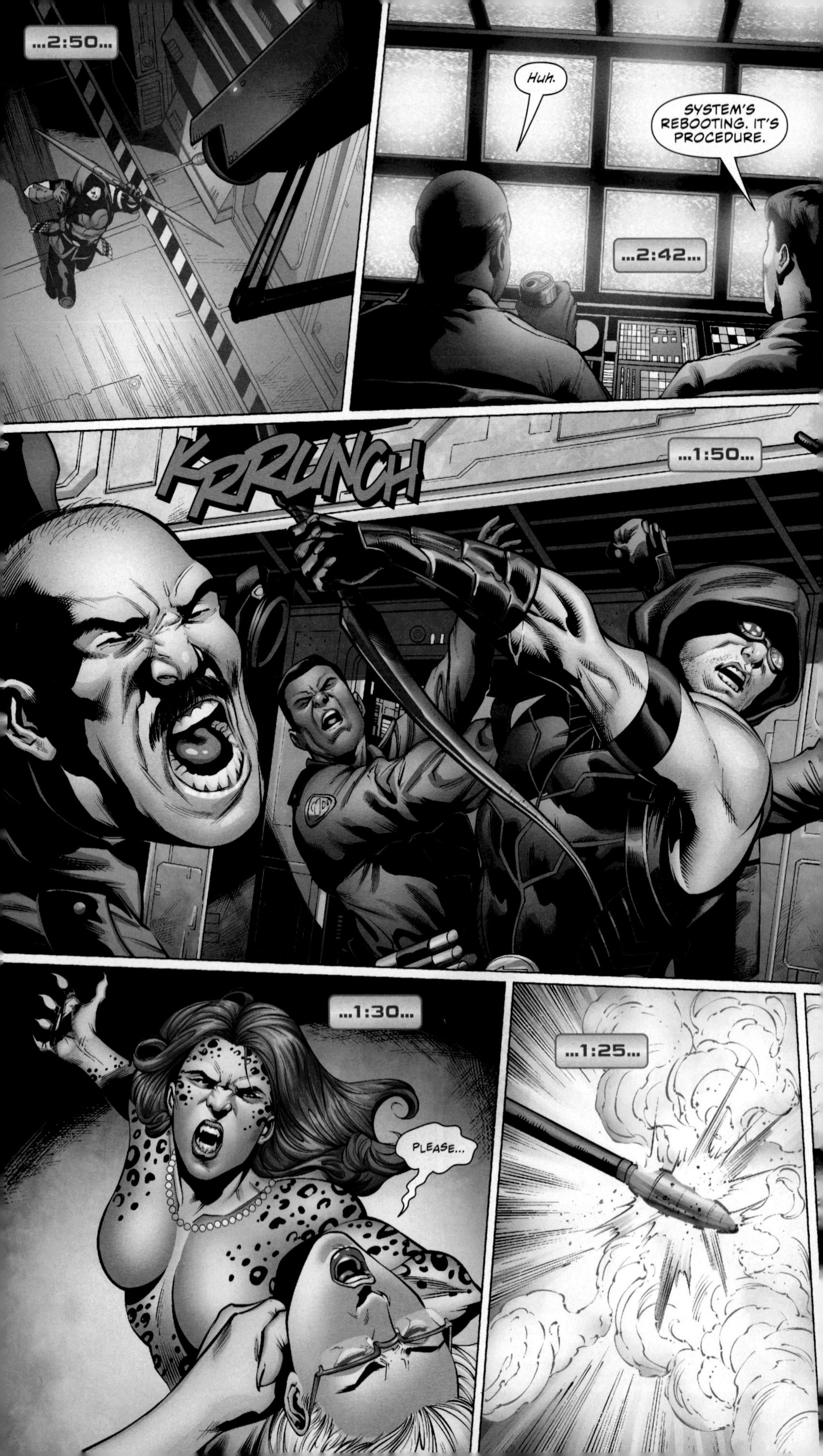
...2:50...
Huh.
SYSTEM'S REBOOTING. IT'S PROCEDURE.
...2:42...
KRRUNCH
...1:50...
...1:30...
PLEASE...
...1:25...

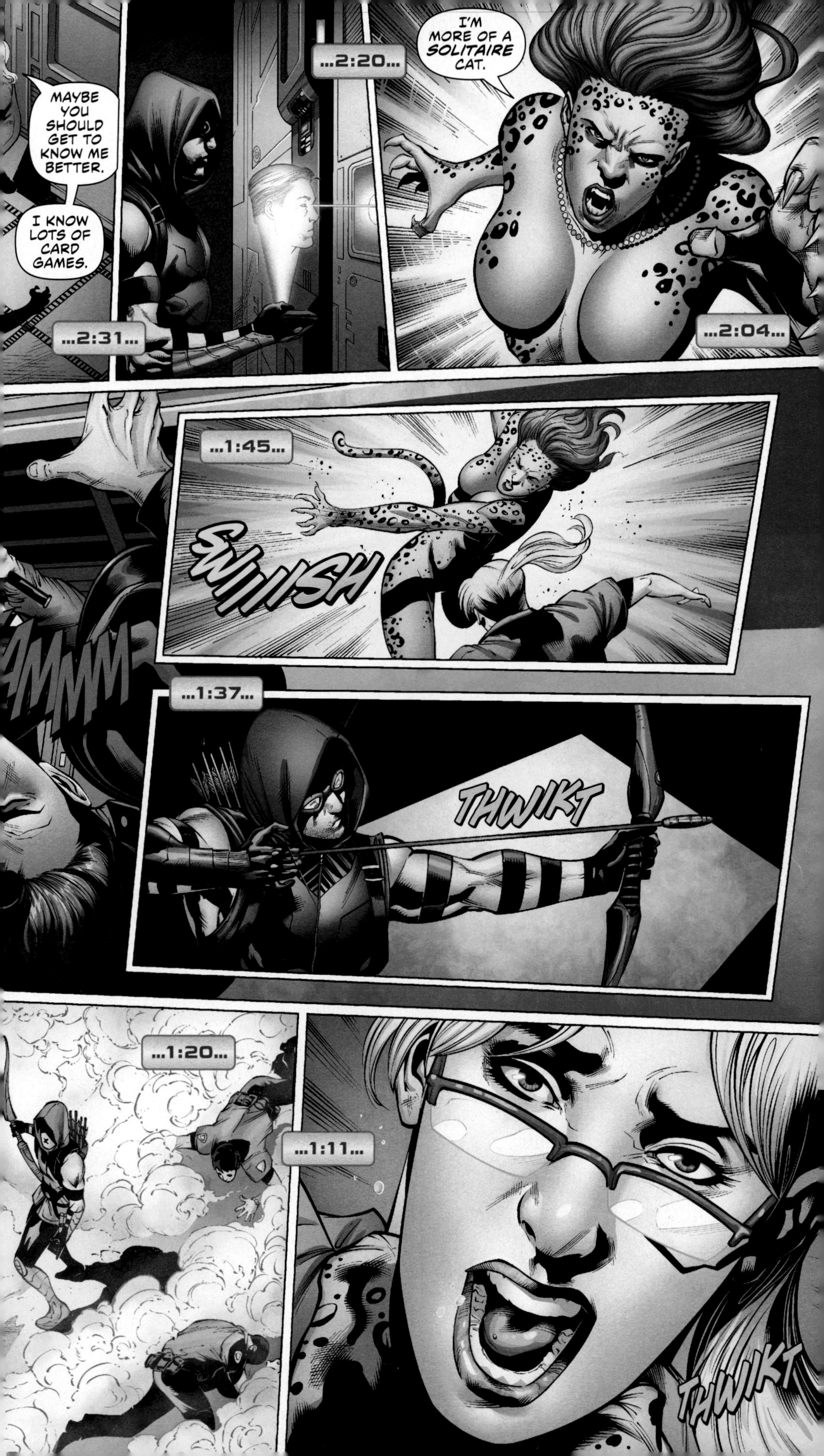

MAYBE YOU SHOULD GET TO KNOW ME BETTER.
I KNOW LOTS OF CARD GAMES.
...2:31...
...2:20...
I'M MORE OF A SOLITAIRE CAT.
...2:04...
...1:45...
SWIIISH
...1:37...
THWIKT
...1:20...
...1:11...
THWIKT

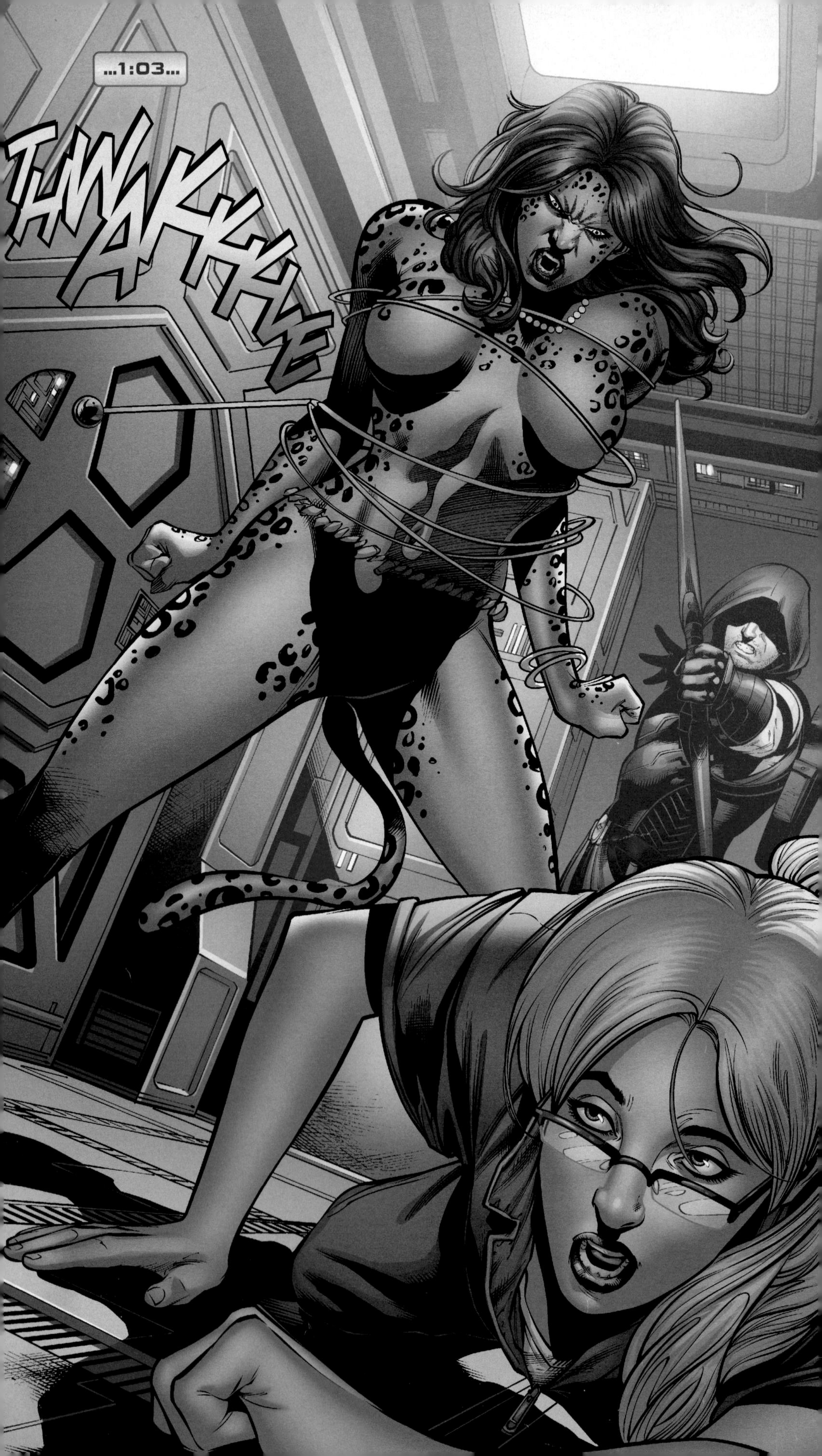
...1:03...
THWAKKLE

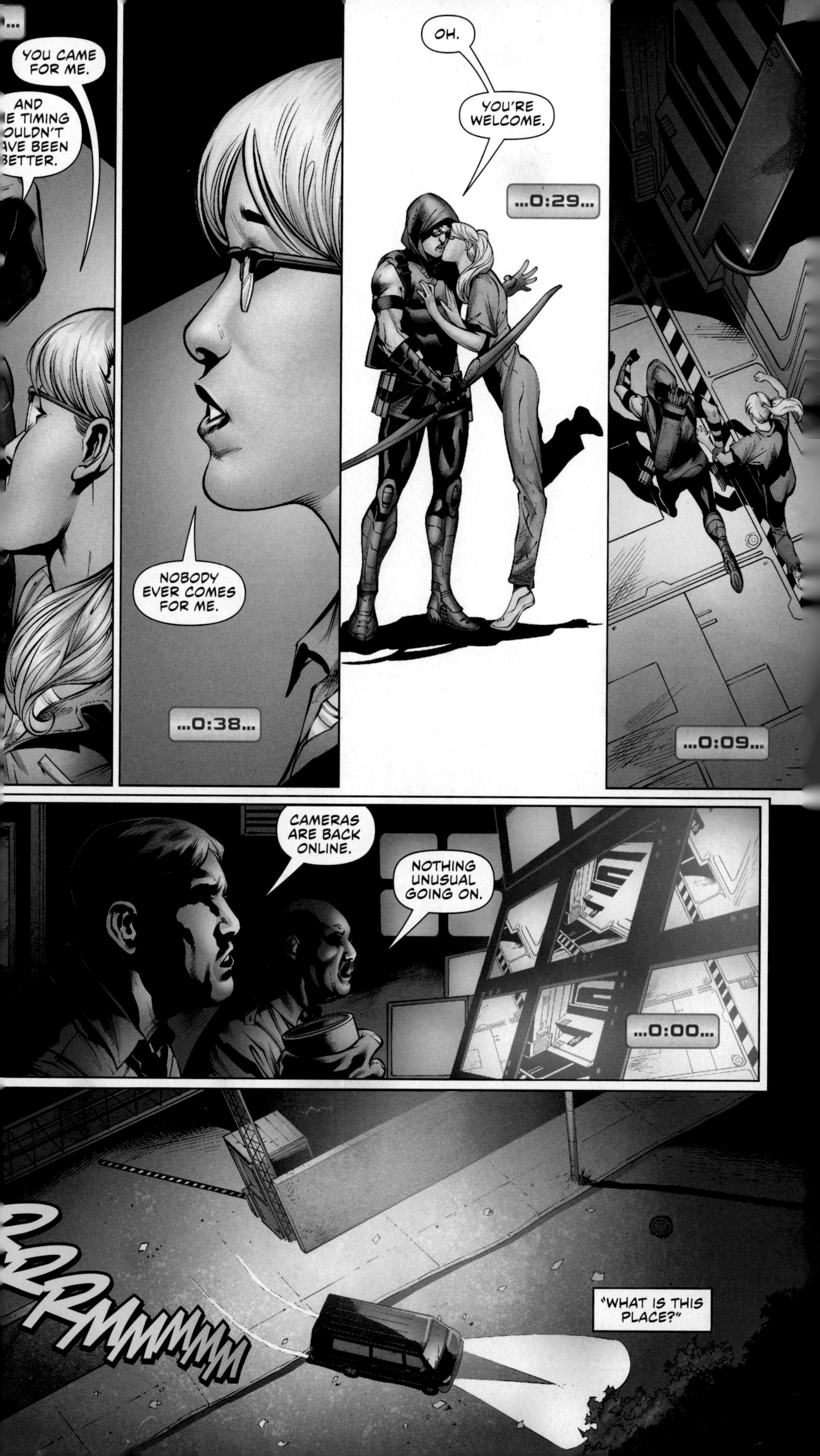

...
YOU CAME FOR ME.
AND
E TIMING
OULDN'T
AVE BEEN
BETTER.
NOBODY EVER COMES FOR ME.
...0:38...
OH.
YOU'RE WELCOME.
...0:29...
...0:09...
CAMERAS ARE BACK ONLINE.
NOTHING UNUSUAL GOING ON.
...0:00...
RRRMMMMM
"WHAT IS THIS PLACE?"

WHAT ARE WE DOING HERE?

I'M BUILDING THIS *FOR YOU*. AND THE OTHERS LIKE *YOU*.

WE DON'T *WANT* IT.

I BET THE OTHER *STREET KIDS* WILL. THEY NEED THE SHELTER, FOOD, JOBS I WILL BE PROVIDING. AND IN RETURN, THEY WILL *LOVE* ME.

YOU MEAN, THEY'LL BE YOUR SUBJECTS. AND THE CITY WILL BE *BETTER OFF*. THAT'S WHAT THIS IS ALL ABOUT. THE *GREATER GOOD*.

PRETTY SURE THAT'S WHAT HITLER KEPT TELLING HIMSELF.

I KNOW WHAT YOU DID AT THE HOSPITAL. YOU TRIED TO KILL THOSE PATIENTS...

I'LL TRY AGAIN TOMORROW. AND THE DAY AFTER THAT.

THE SICK AND DISEASED ARE AN ANCHOR. THEIR *EXPEDITED DEATHS* WILL HELP CURE THE REST OF *US*.

THEN WHAT D[o] THAT M[e] FOR M[e]

B[h] I'

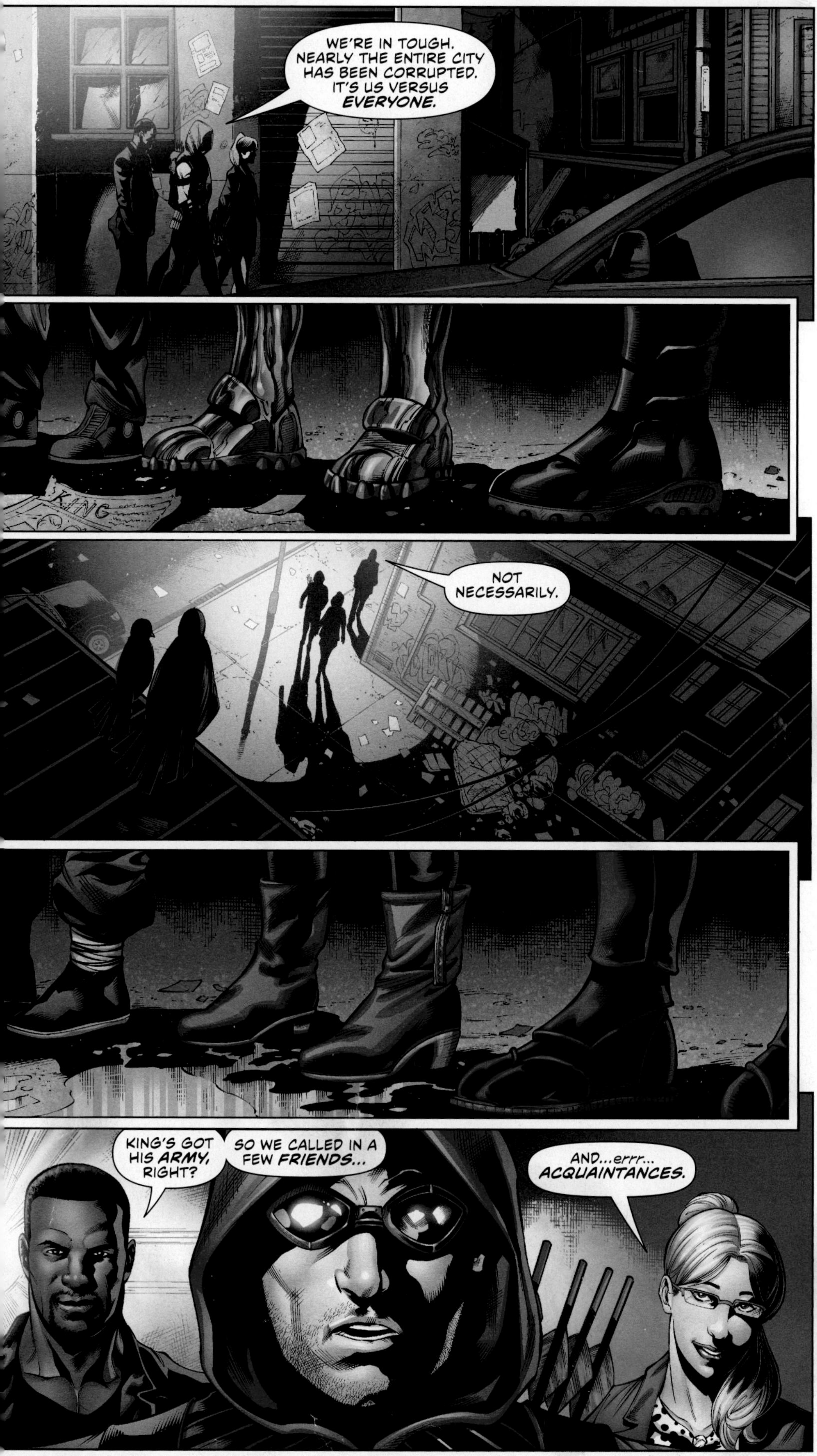
WE'RE IN TOUGH. NEARLY THE ENTIRE CITY HAS BEEN CORRUPTED. IT'S US VERSUS EVERYONE.
KING
NOT NECESSARILY.
KING'S GOT HIS ARMY, RIGHT?
SO WE CALLED IN A FEW FRIENDS...
AND...errr... ACQUAINTANCES.

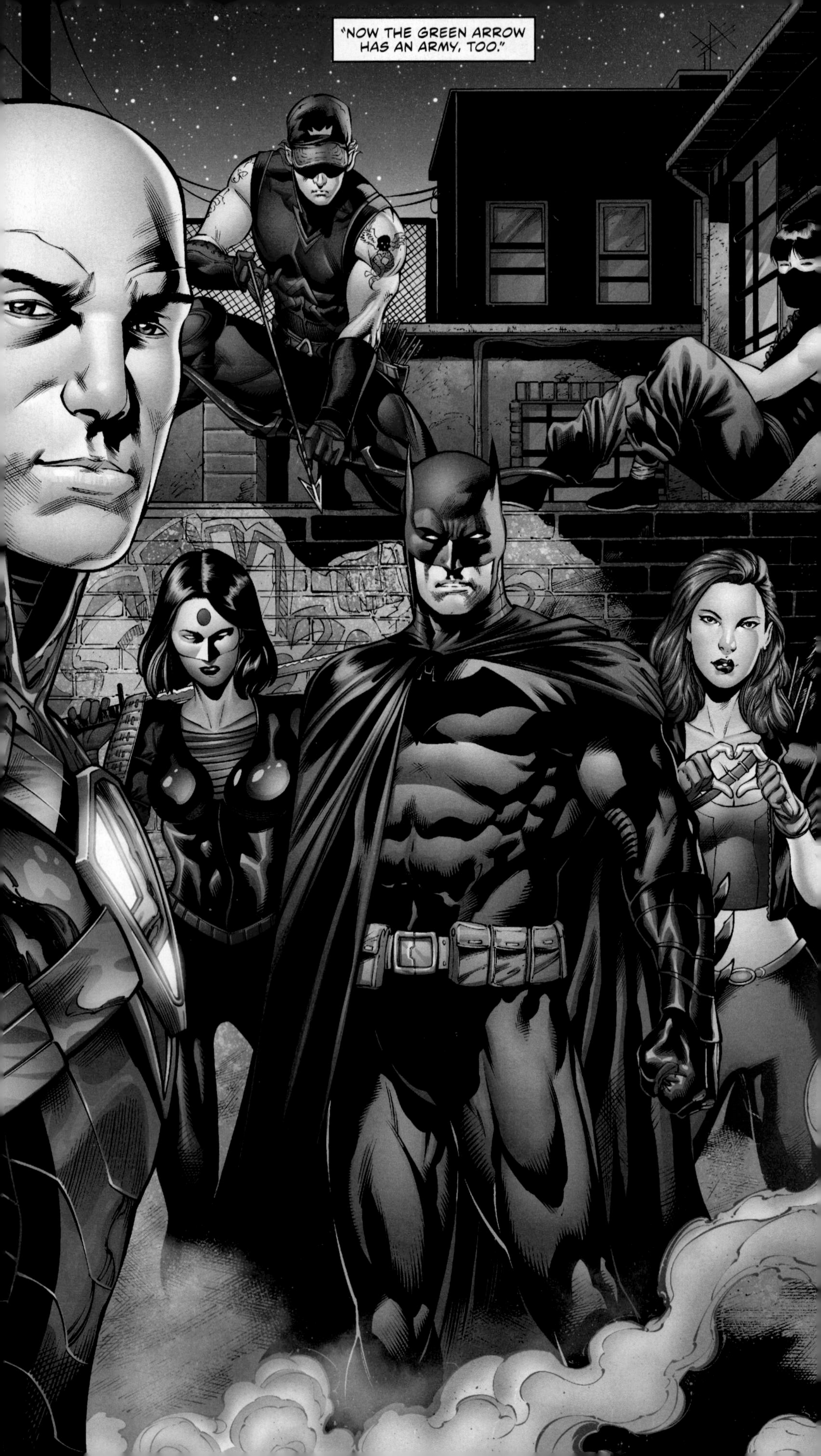
"NOW THE GREEN ARROW
HAS AN ARMY, TOO."

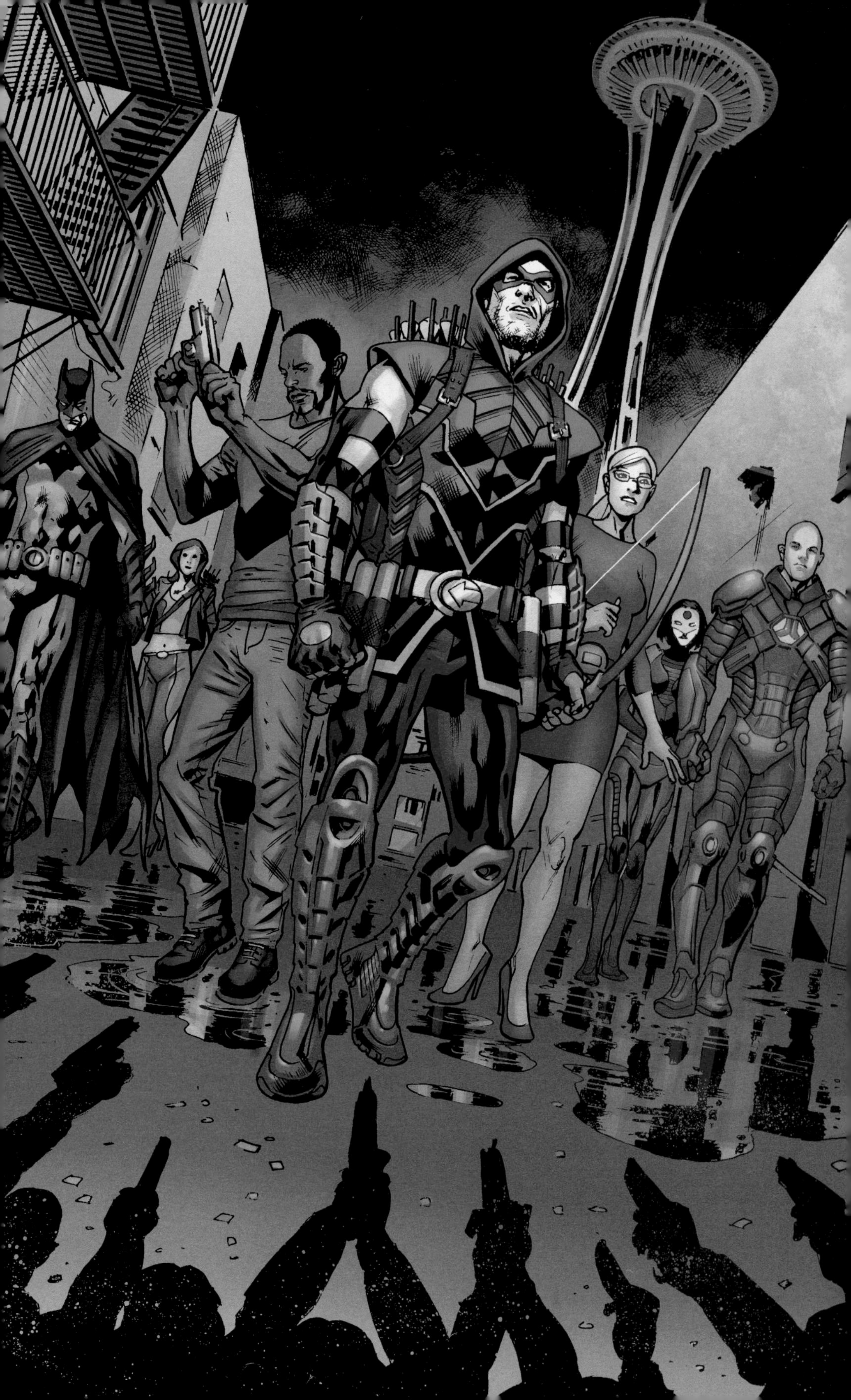

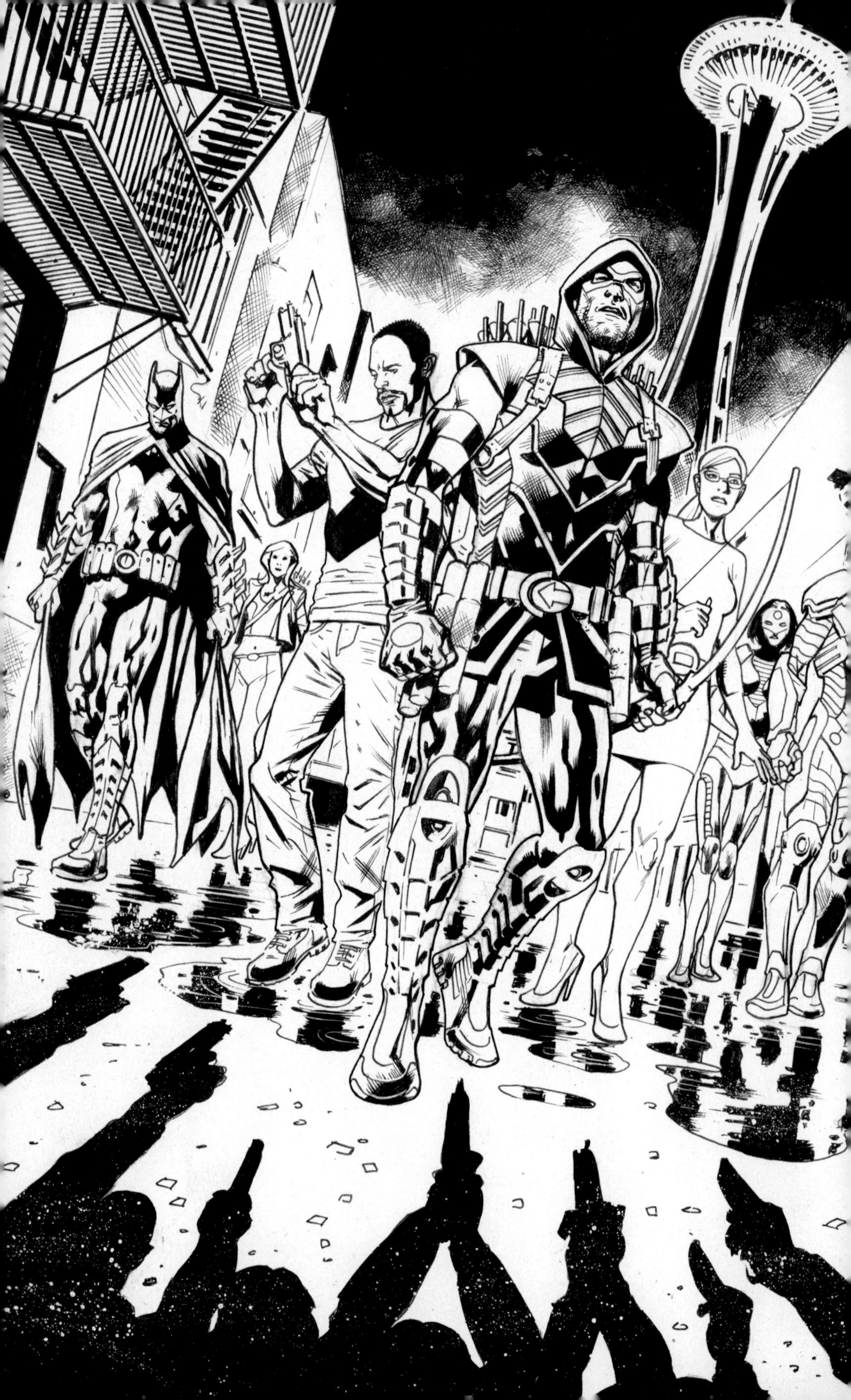

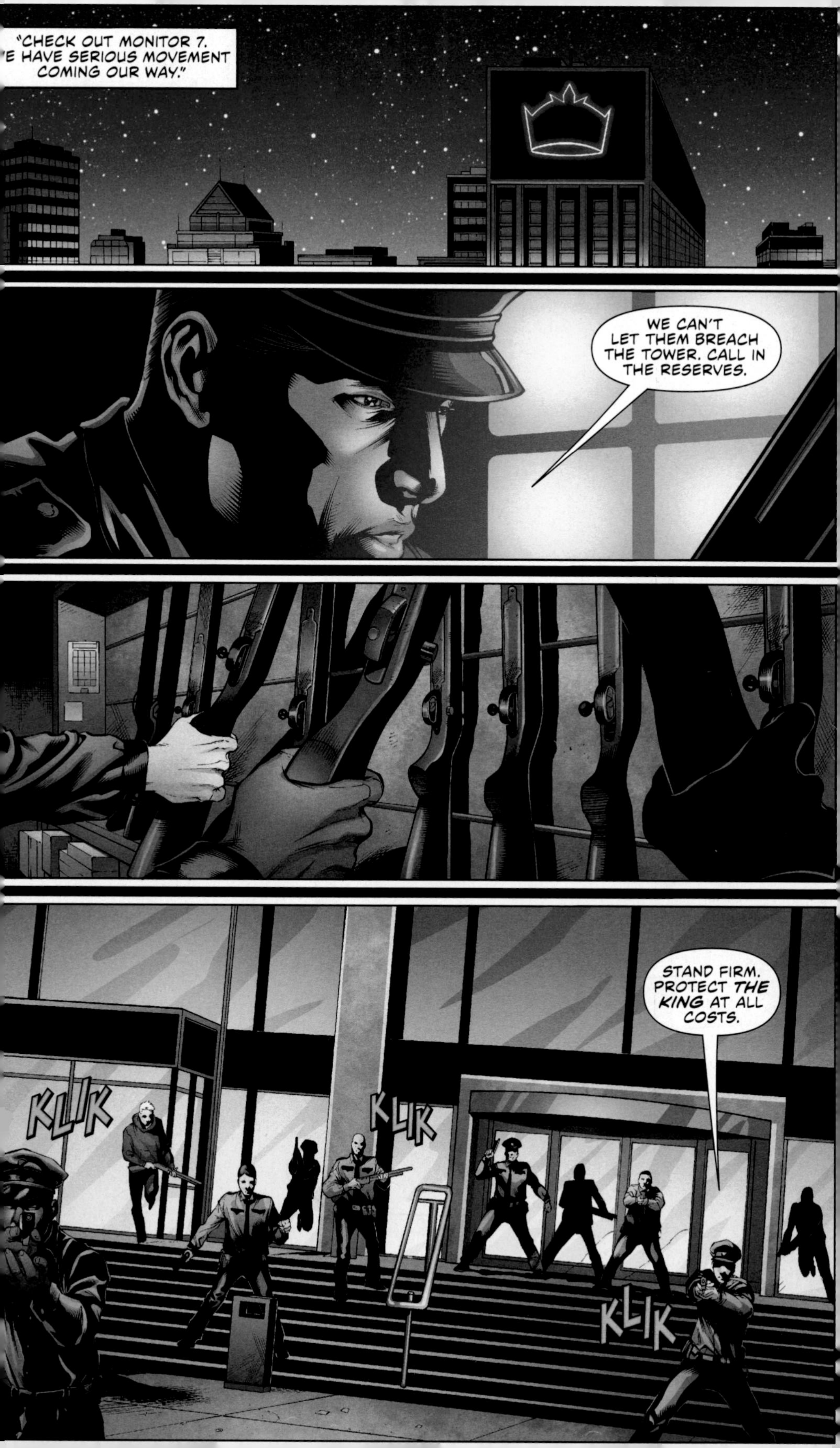
"CHECK OUT MONITOR 7.
'E HAVE SERIOUS MOVEMENT
COMING OUR WAY."
WE CAN'T LET THEM BREACH THE TOWER. CALL IN THE RESERVES.
STAND FIRM. PROTECT *THE KING* AT ALL COSTS.
KLIK
KLIK
KLIK

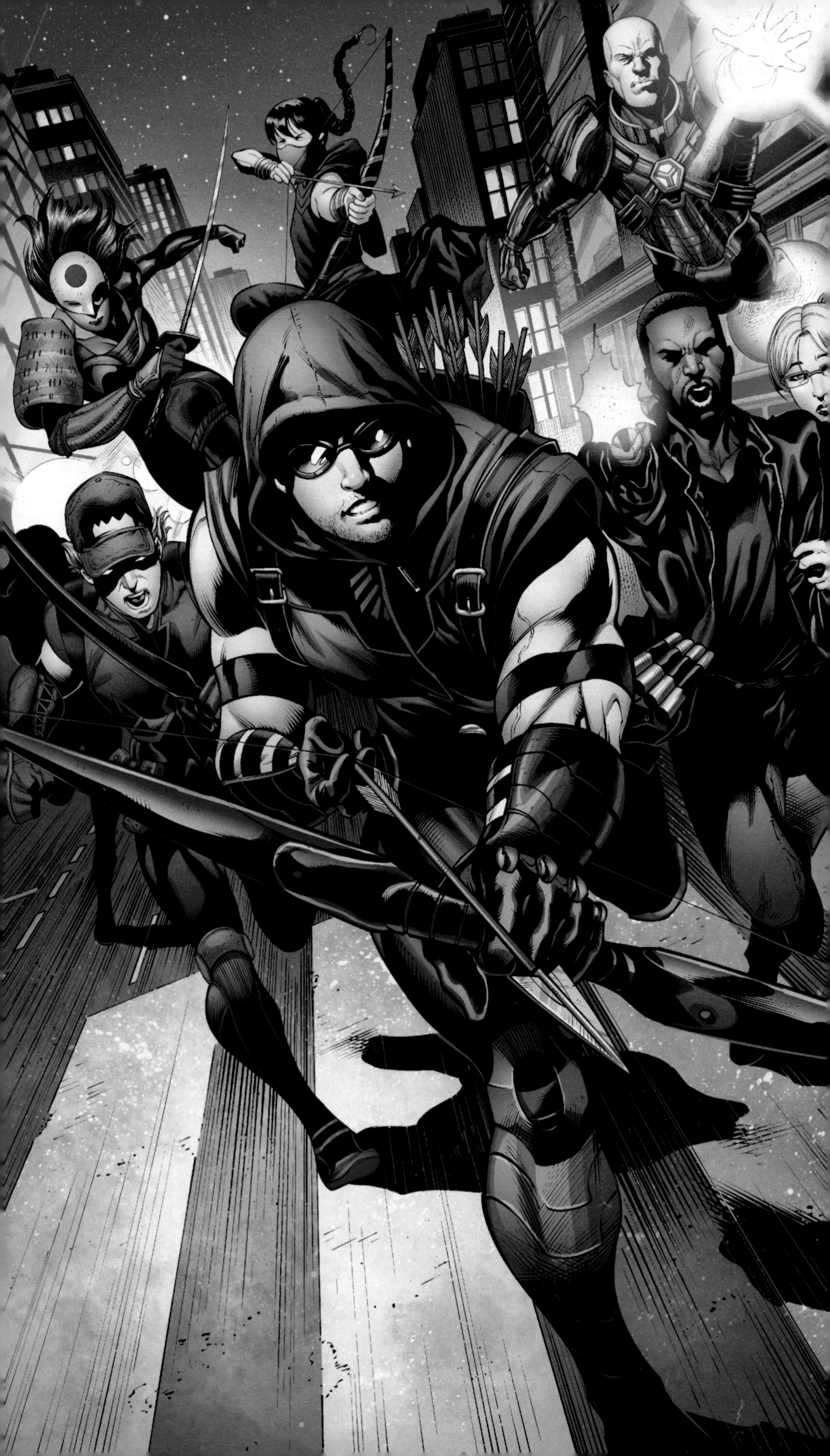

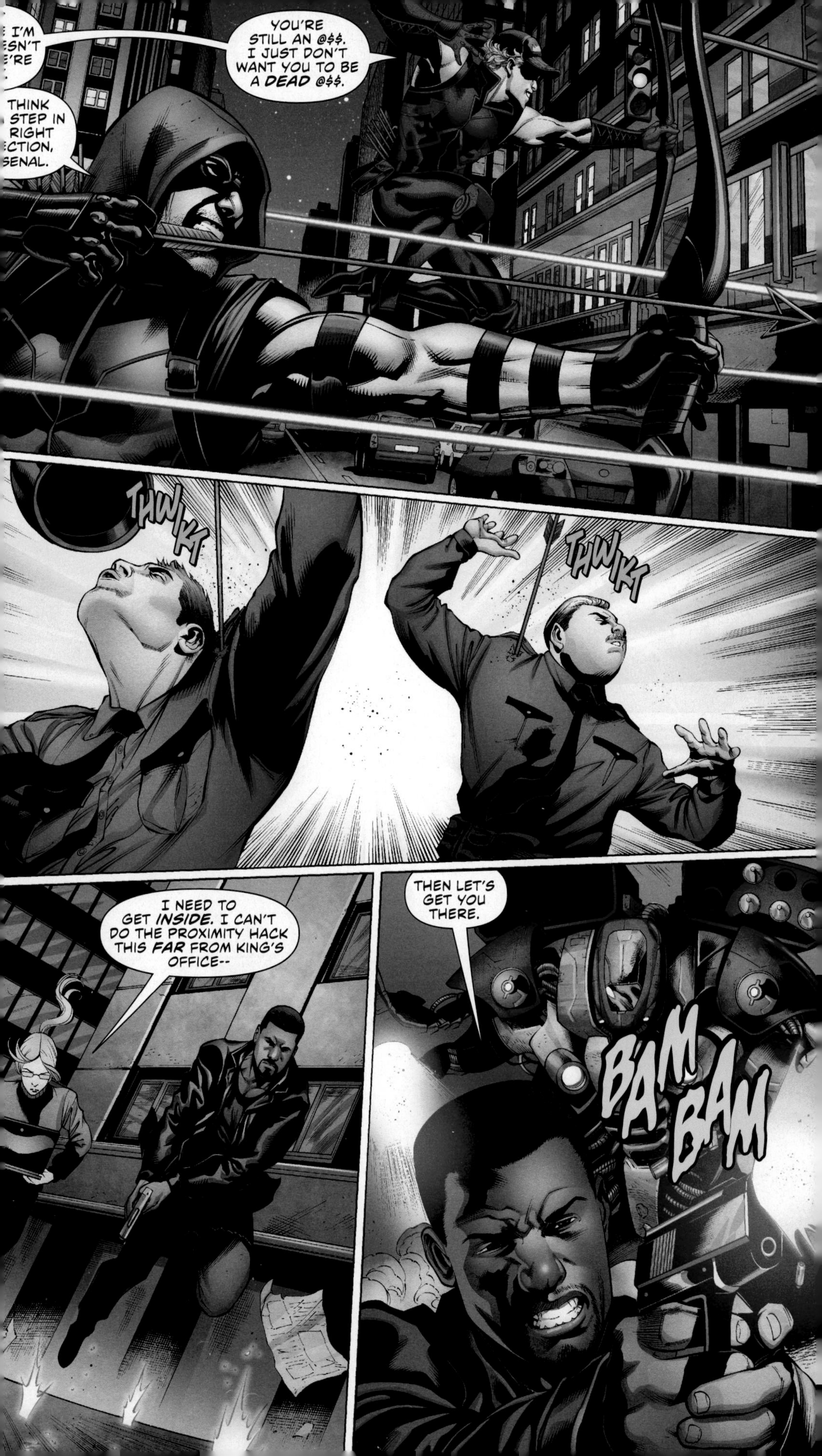
I'M
SN'T
'RE
YOU'RE STILL AN @$$. I JUST DON'T WANT YOU TO BE A DEAD @$$.
THINK STEP IN RIGHT CTION, SENAL.
THWIK!
THWIK!
I NEED TO GET INSIDE. I CAN'T DO THE PROXIMITY HACK THIS FAR FROM KING'S OFFICE--
THEN LET'S GET YOU THERE.
BAM BAM BAM

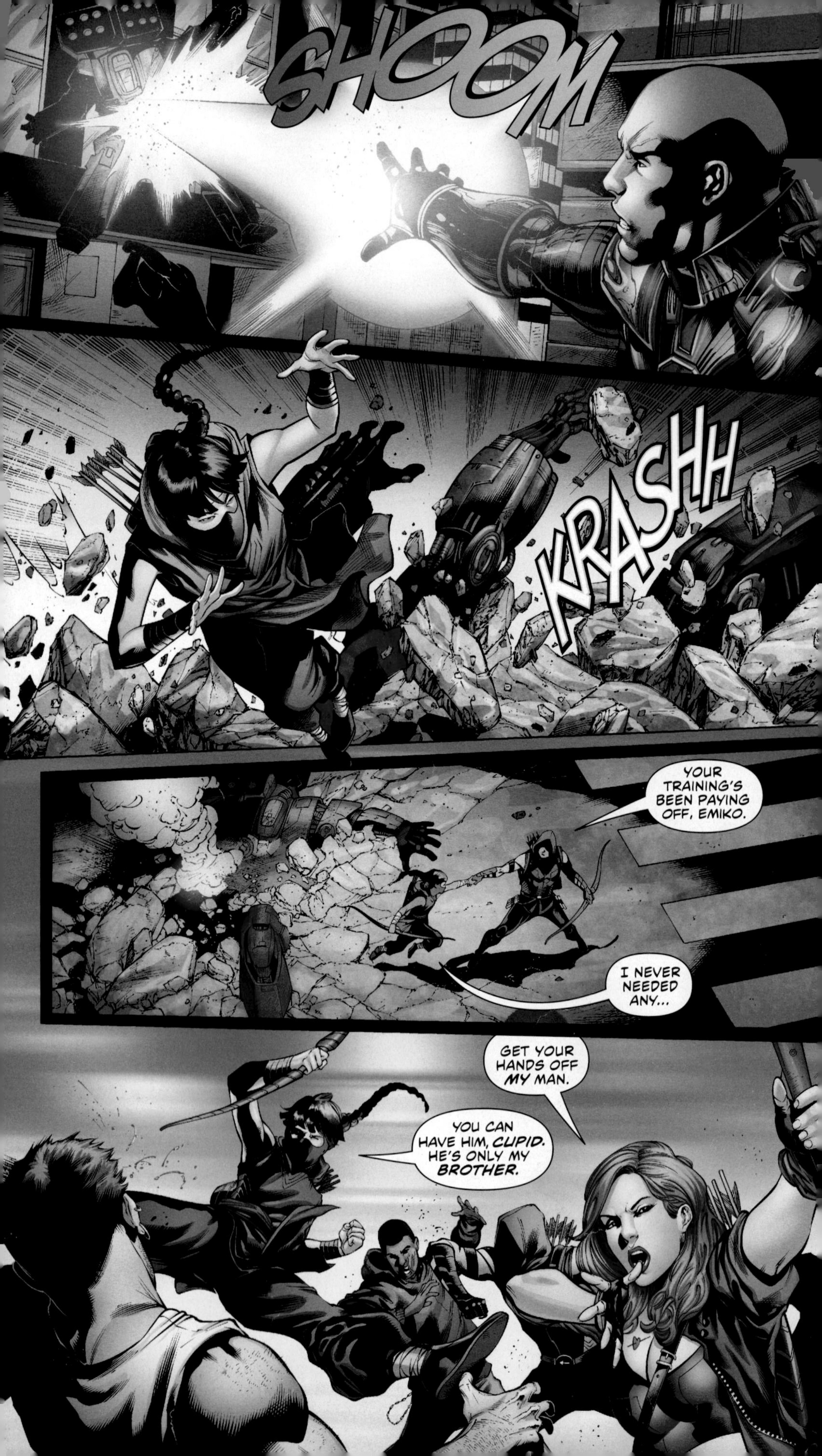
SHOOM
KRASHH
YOUR TRAINING'S BEEN PAYING OFF, EMIKO.
I NEVER NEEDED ANY...
GET YOUR HANDS OFF *MY* MAN.
YOU CAN HAVE HIM, *CUPID*. HE'S ONLY MY *BROTHER*.

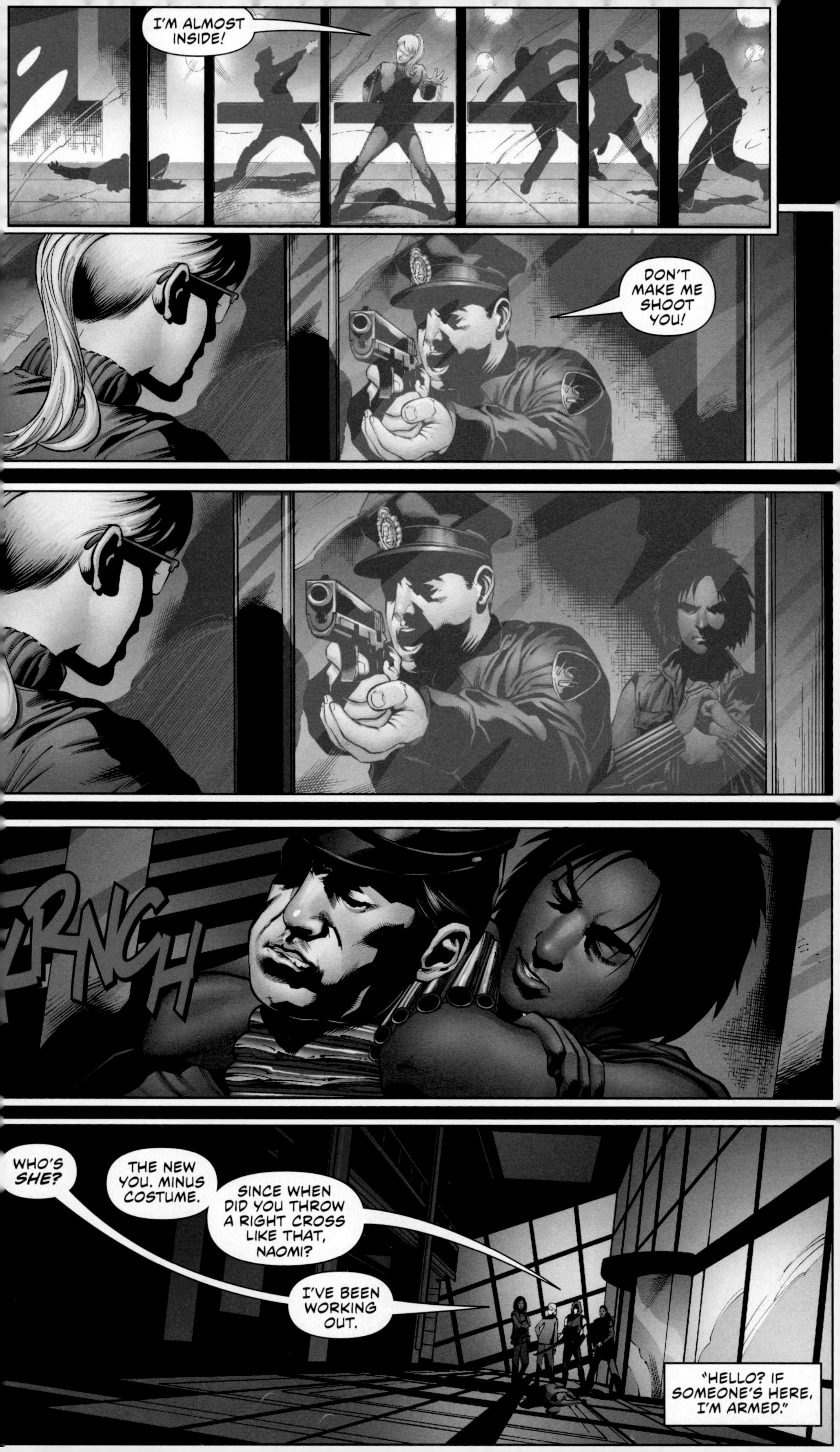
I'M ALMOST INSIDE!
DON'T MAKE ME SHOOT YOU!
KRNCH
WHO'S SHE?
THE NEW YOU. MINUS COSTUME.
SINCE WHEN DID YOU THROW A RIGHT CROSS LIKE THAT, NAOMI?
I'VE BEEN WORKING OUT.
"HELLO? IF SOMEONE'S HERE, I'M ARMED."

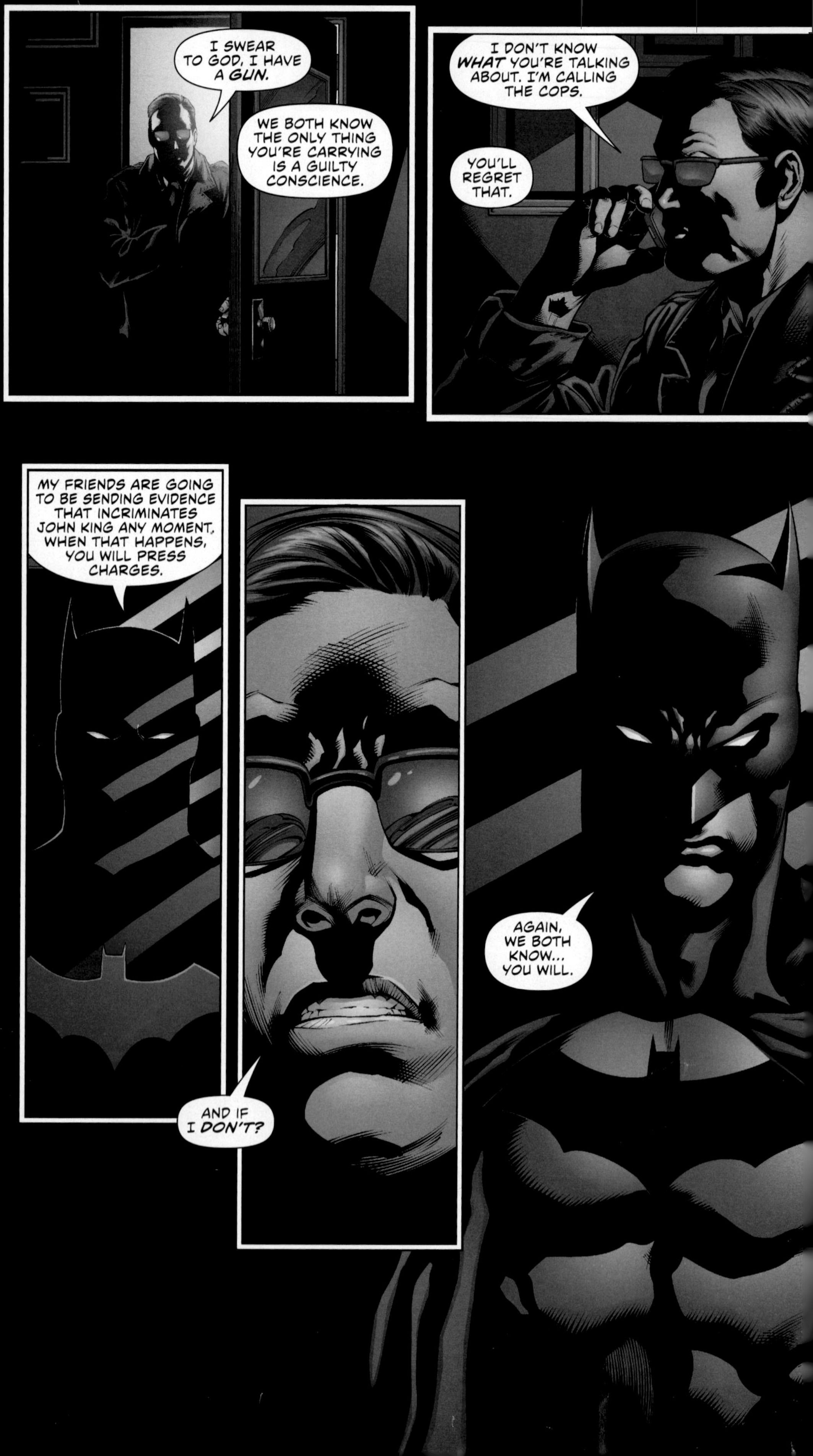
I SWEAR TO GOD, I HAVE A GUN.
WE BOTH KNOW THE ONLY THING YOU'RE CARRYING IS A GUILTY CONSCIENCE.
I DON'T KNOW WHAT YOU'RE TALKING ABOUT. I'M CALLING THE COPS.
YOU'LL REGRET THAT.
MY FRIENDS ARE GOING TO BE SENDING EVIDENCE THAT INCRIMINATES JOHN KING ANY MOMENT. WHEN THAT HAPPENS, YOU WILL PRESS CHARGES.
AND IF I DON'T?
AGAIN, WE BOTH KNOW... YOU WILL.

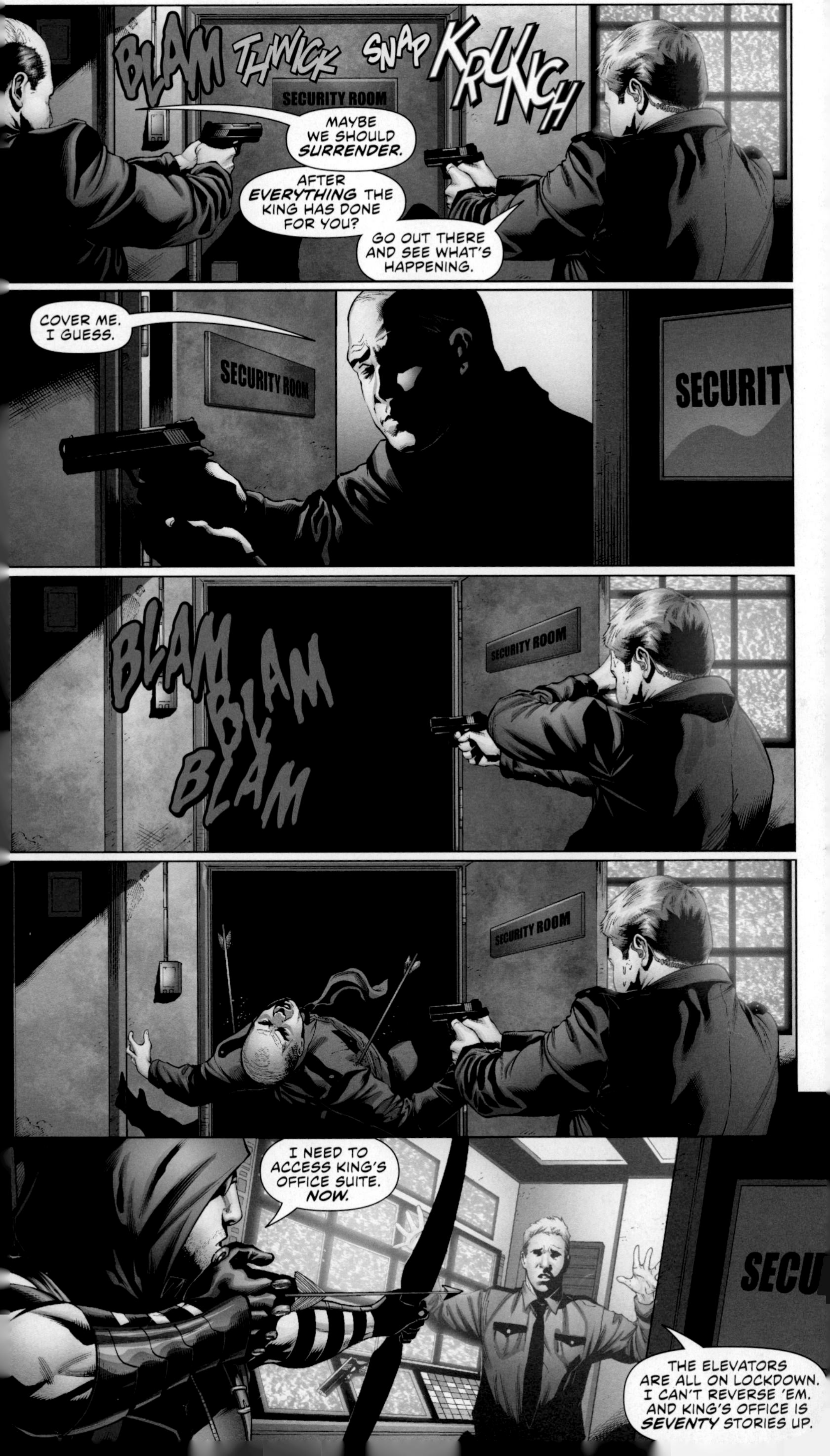
BLAM THWICK SNAP KRUNCH
SECURITY ROOM
MAYBE WE SHOULD SURRENDER.
AFTER EVERYTHING THE KING HAS DONE FOR YOU?
GO OUT THERE AND SEE WHAT'S HAPPENING.
COVER ME. I GUESS.
SECURITY ROOM
SECURITY
BLAM BLAM BLAM BLAM
SECURITY ROOM
SECURITY ROOM
I NEED TO ACCESS KING'S OFFICE SUITE. NOW.
THE ELEVATORS ARE ALL ON LOCKDOWN. I CAN'T REVERSE 'EM. AND KING'S OFFICE IS SEVENTY STORIES UP.

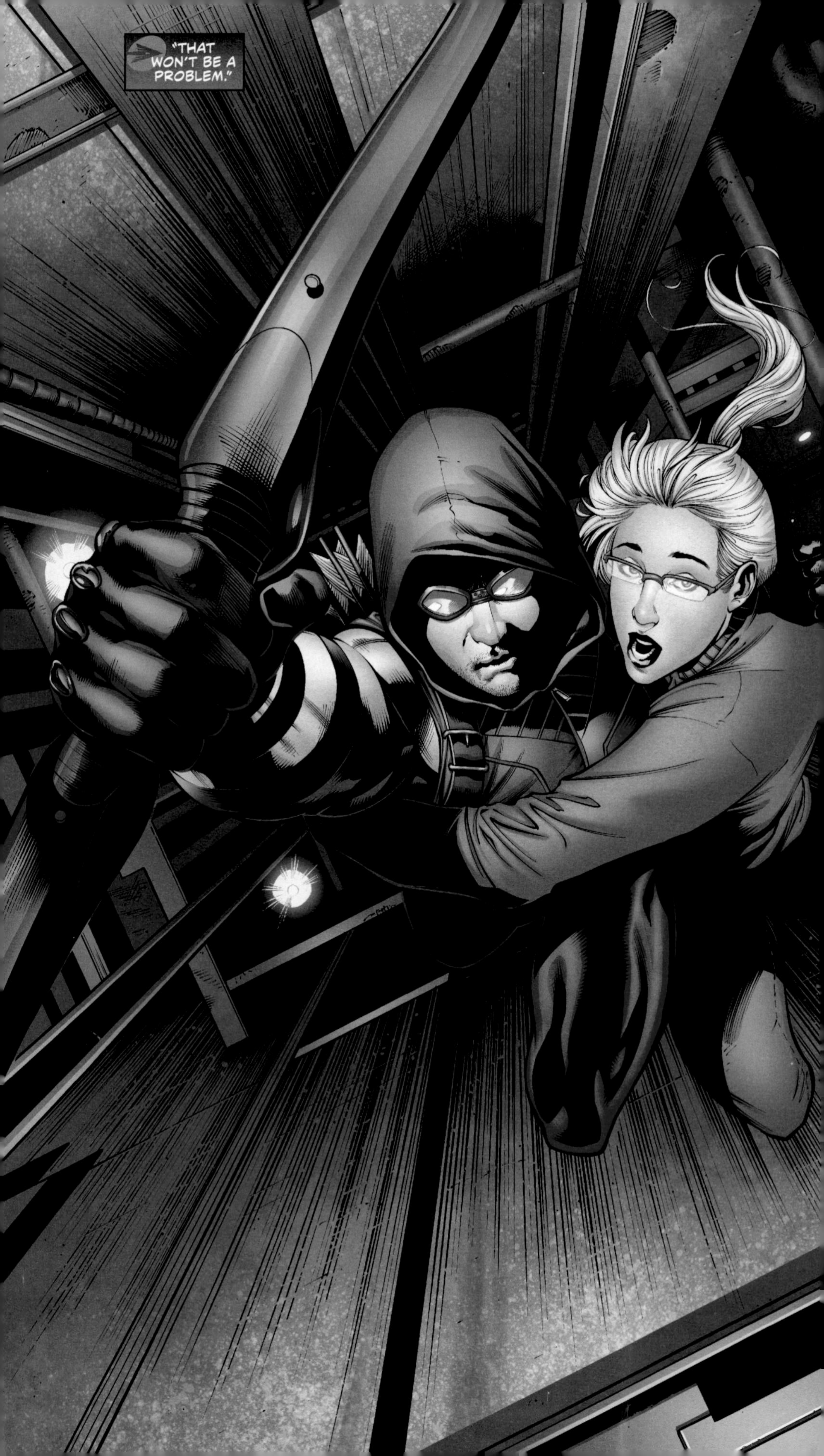
"THAT WON'T BE A PROBLEM."

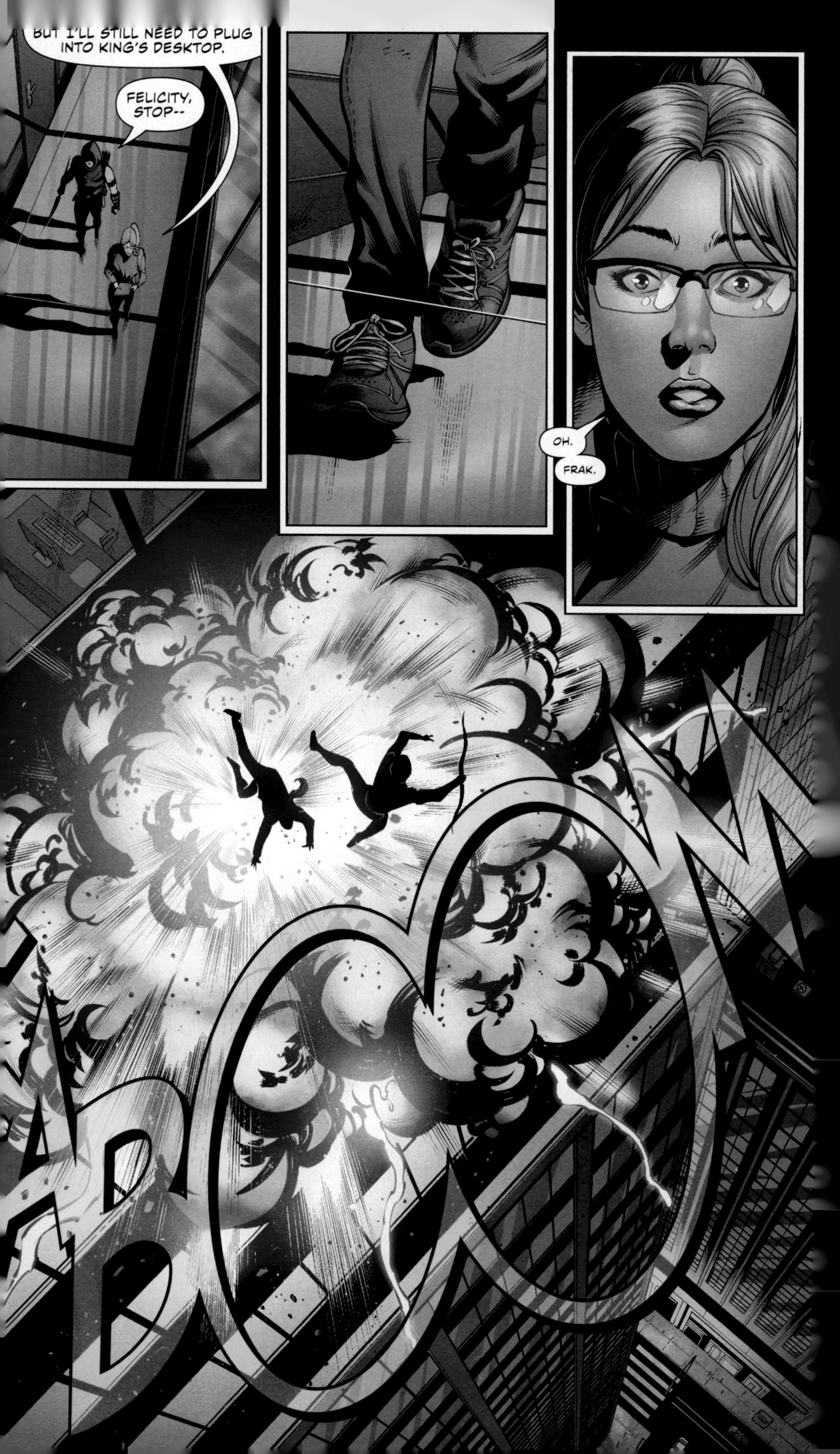
BUT I'LL STILL NEED TO PLUG INTO KING'S DESKTOP.
FELICITY, STOP--
OH.
FRAK.
BOOM

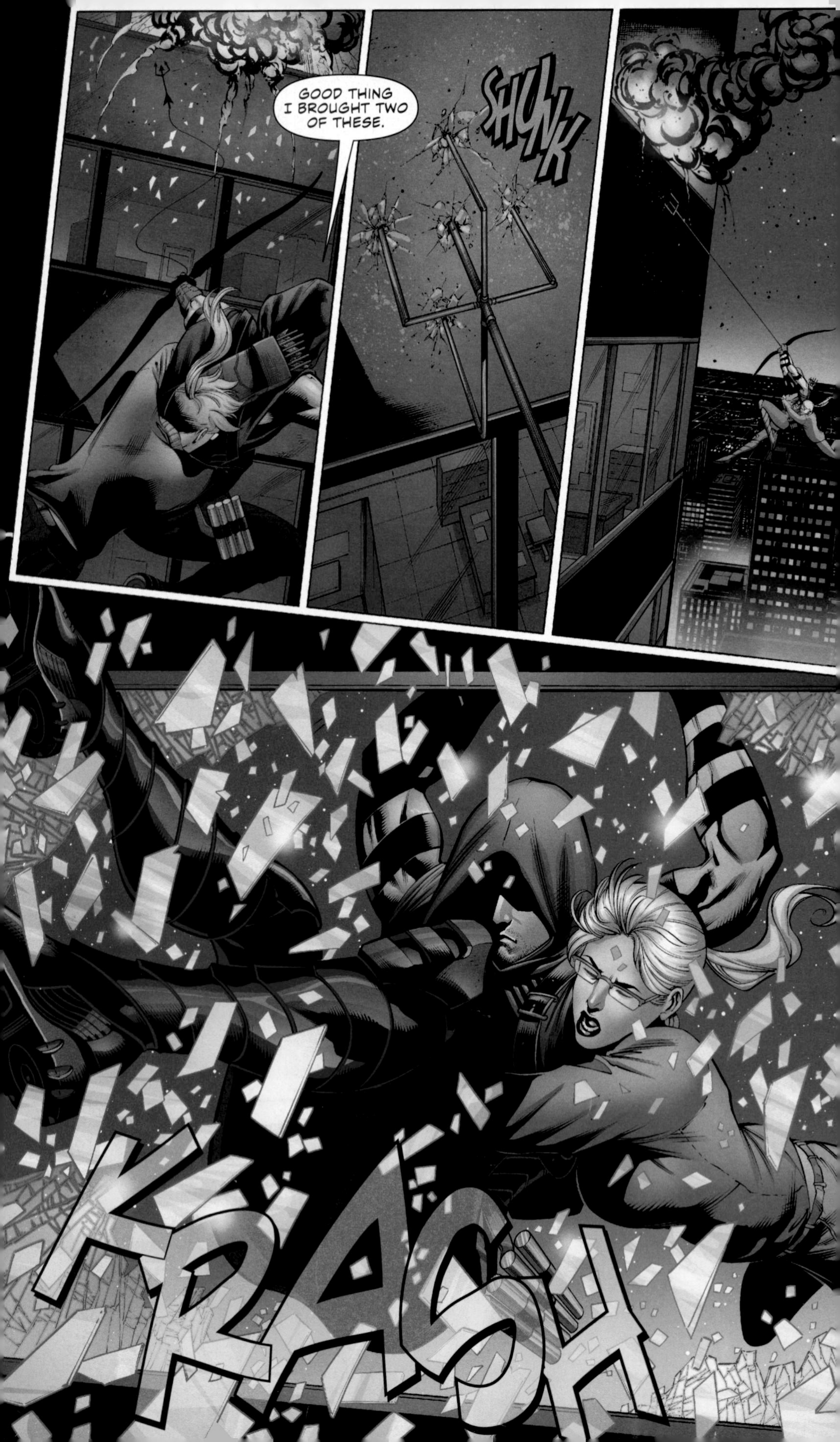
GOOD THING I BROUGHT TWO OF THESE.
SHUNK
KRASH

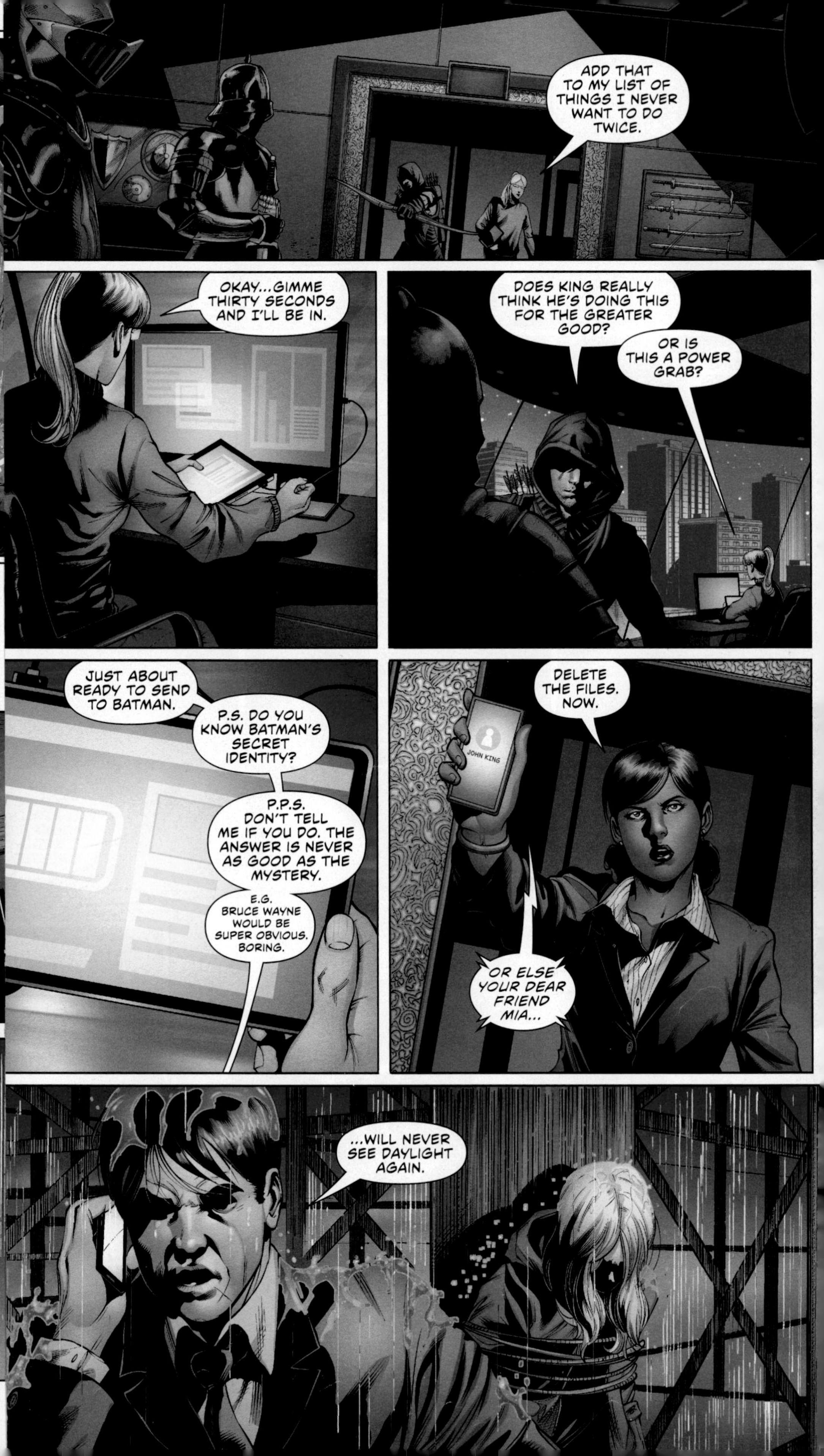
ADD THAT TO MY LIST OF THINGS I NEVER WANT TO DO TWICE.
OKAY...GIMME THIRTY SECONDS AND I'LL BE IN.
DOES KING REALLY THINK HE'S DOING THIS FOR THE GREATER GOOD?
OR IS THIS A POWER GRAB?
JUST ABOUT READY TO SEND TO BATMAN.
P.S. DO YOU KNOW BATMAN'S SECRET IDENTITY?
P.P.S. DON'T TELL ME IF YOU DO. THE ANSWER IS NEVER AS GOOD AS THE MYSTERY.
E.G. BRUCE WAYNE WOULD BE SUPER OBVIOUS. BORING.
JOHN KING
DELETE THE FILES. NOW.
OR ELSE YOUR DEAR FRIEND MIA...
...WILL NEVER SEE DAYLIGHT AGAIN.

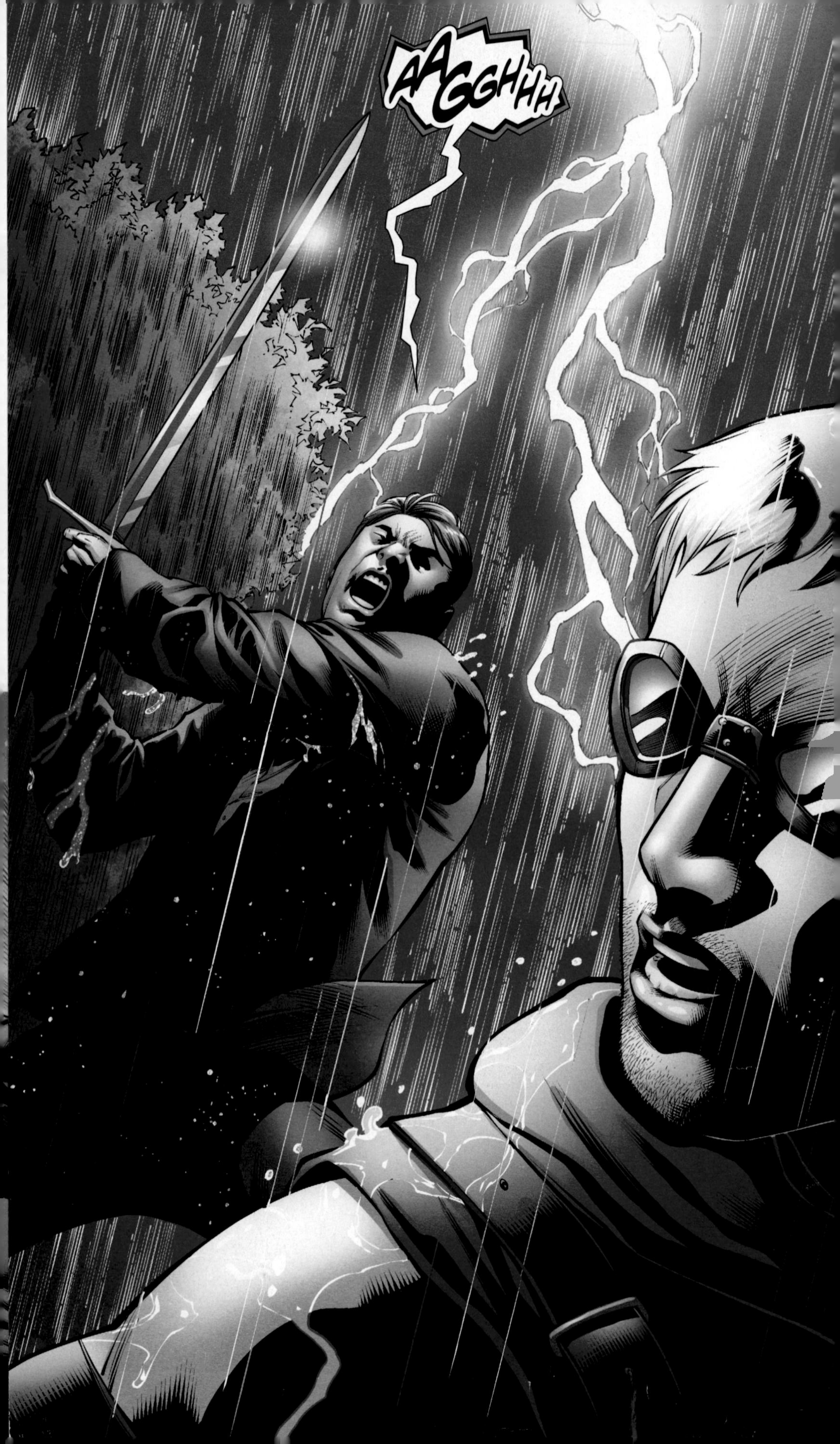
AAGGHHH

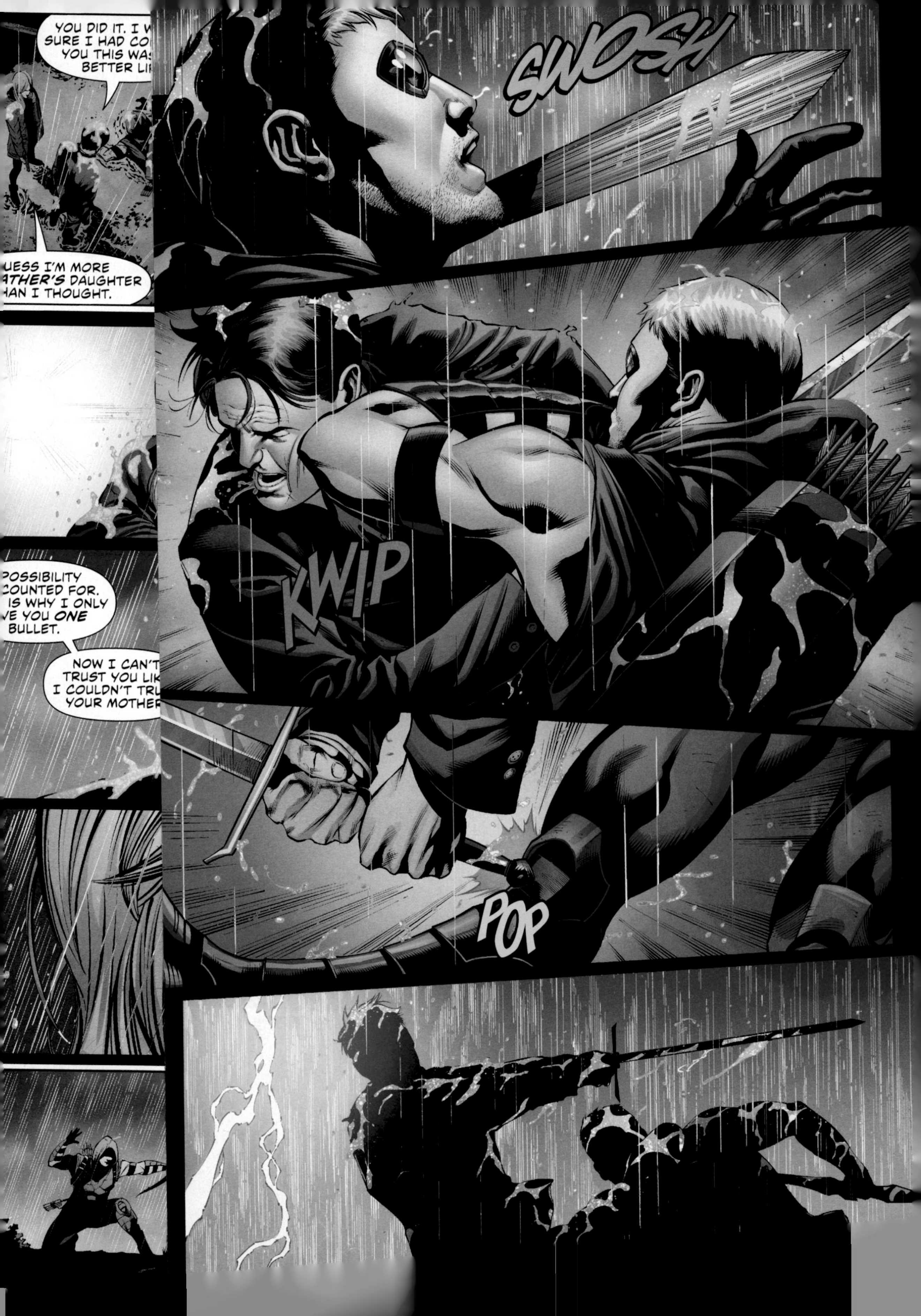
YOU DID IT. I W
SURE I HAD CO
YOU THIS WAS
BETTER LI
UESS I'M MORE
ATHER'S DAUGHTER
HAN I THOUGHT.
POSSIBILITY
COUNTED FOR.
IS WHY I ONLY
VE YOU ONE
BULLET.
NOW I CAN'T
TRUST YOU LI
I COULDN'T TRU
YOUR MOTHER
SWOSH
KWIP
POP

"SOME SAID JOHN KING WAS THE REAL SAVIOR OF OUR CITY...

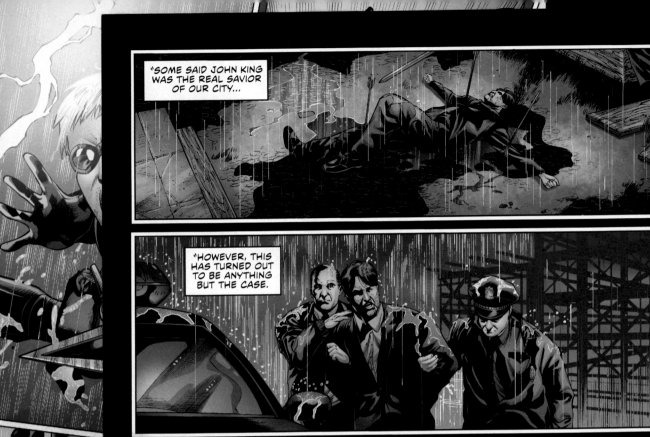

"HOWEVER, THIS HAS TURNED OUT TO BE ANYTHING BUT THE CASE.

"THE POLICE FOUND KING GIFTWRAPPED FROM THE GREEN ARROW, WHOM KING HAD SUCCESSFULLY VILIFIED.

YET THIS MORNING, EVIDENCE WAS DISCOVE LINKING KING TO *THOUS* OF BRIBES TO CITY OFFIC ACROSS THE COUNTRY, TO MENTION *SEVERA* COUNTS OF *MURDER*.

EVERYONE HAS A *PRICE*.

HUNDREDS OF HIS "SUBJECTS," THE MEN SECRETL' WORKING FOR HIM, HAVE *FLEC* THEIR CITY POSTS. IT WILL TAK A LONG TIME TO UNRAVEL JUS' HOW VAST KING'S GRASP *TRULY* REACHED.

JOHN KING ARRES

CHANNEL 52
BREAKING NEWS

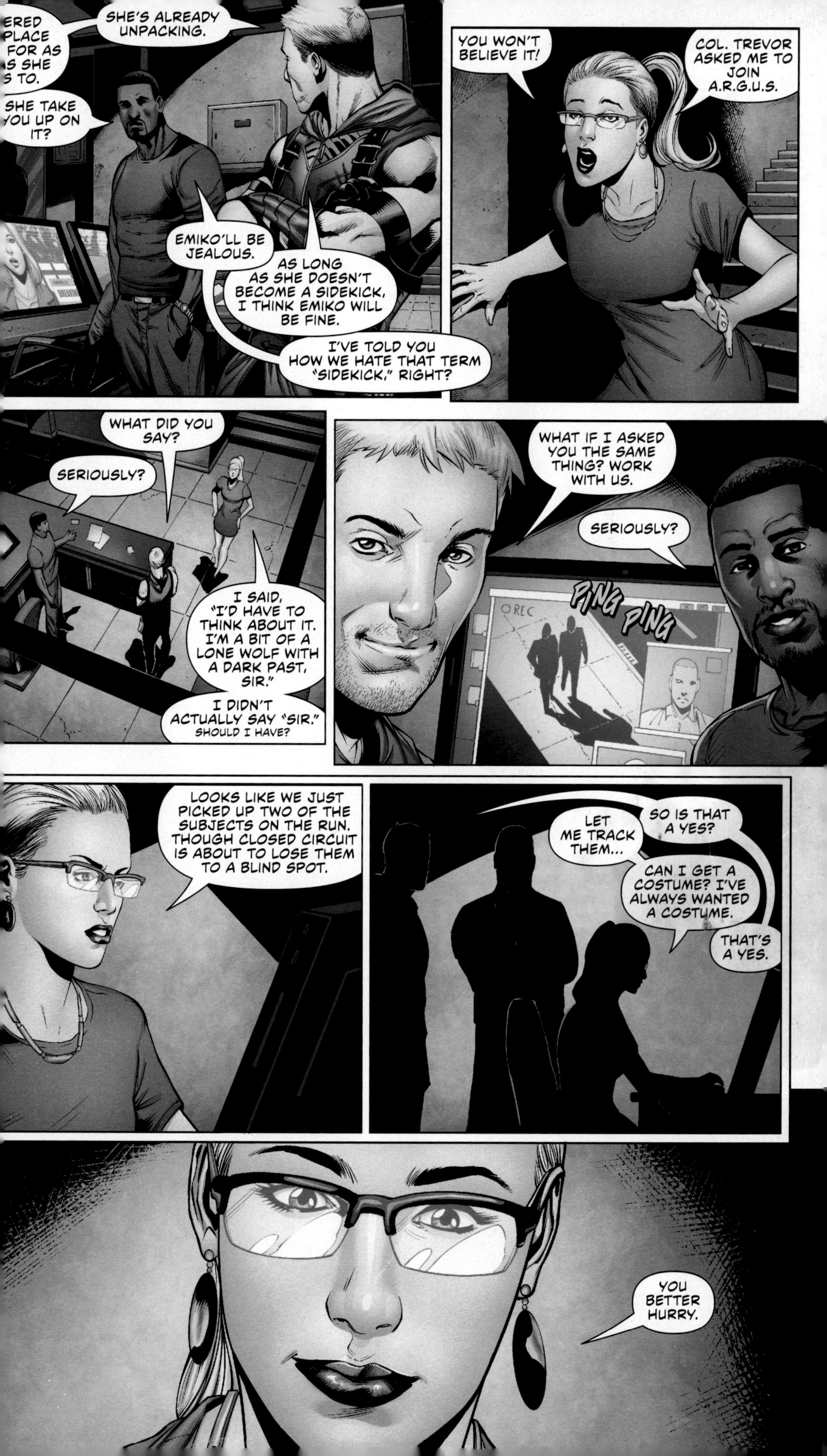

ERED
PLACE
FOR AS
S SHE
S TO.
SHE'S ALREADY UNPACKING.
SHE TAKE YOU UP ON IT?
EMIKO'LL BE JEALOUS.
AS LONG AS SHE DOESN'T BECOME A SIDEKICK, I THINK EMIKO WILL BE FINE.
I'VE TOLD YOU HOW WE HATE THAT TERM "SIDEKICK," RIGHT?
YOU WON'T BELIEVE IT!
COL. TREVOR ASKED ME TO JOIN A.R.G.U.S.
WHAT DID YOU SAY?
SERIOUSLY?
I SAID, "I'D HAVE TO THINK ABOUT IT. I'M A BIT OF A LONE WOLF WITH A DARK PAST, SIR."
I DIDN'T ACTUALLY SAY "SIR." SHOULD I HAVE?
WHAT IF I ASKED YOU THE SAME THING? WORK WITH US.
SERIOUSLY?
PING PING
REC
LOOKS LIKE WE JUST PICKED UP TWO OF THE SUBJECTS ON THE RUN. THOUGH CLOSED CIRCUIT IS ABOUT TO LOSE THEM TO A BLIND SPOT.
LET ME TRACK THEM...
SO IS THAT A YES?
CAN I GET A COSTUME? I'VE ALWAYS WANTED A COSTUME.
THAT'S A YES.
YOU BETTER HURRY.

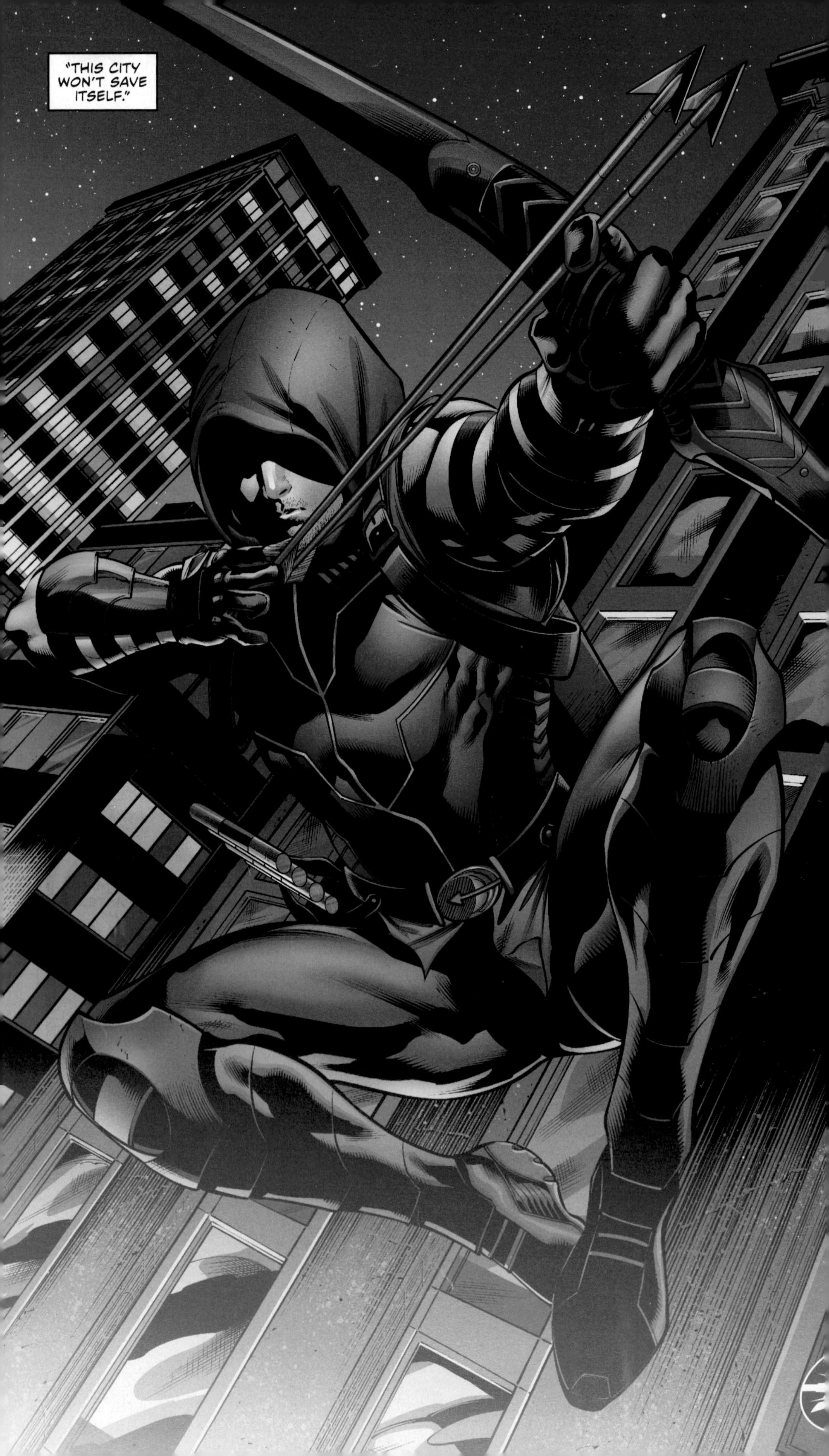
"THIS CITY WON'T SAVE ITSELF."

CHARACTER SKETCHES BY
DANIEL SAMPERE

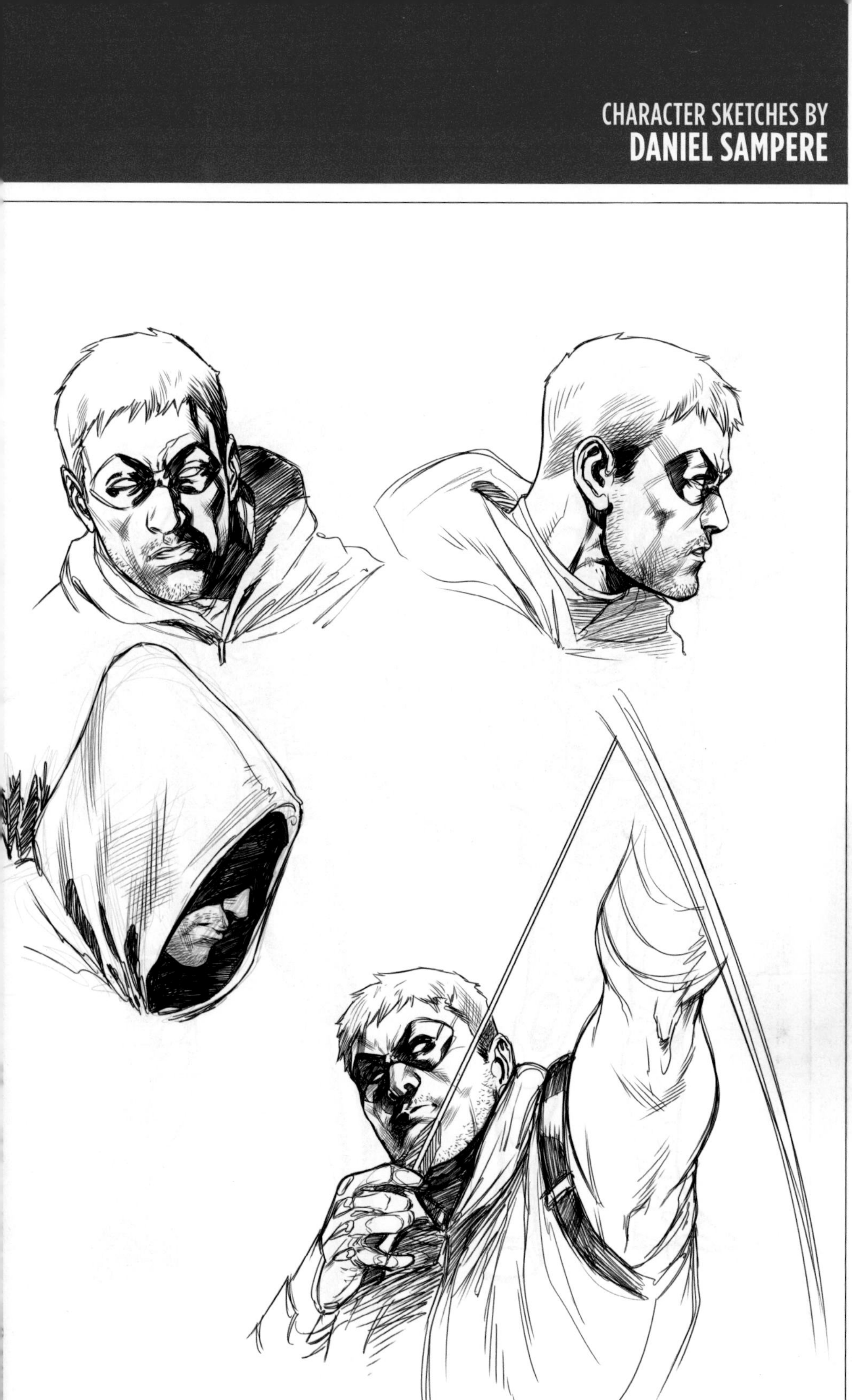

GREEN ARROW #39 unused cover by **BRYAN HITCH**

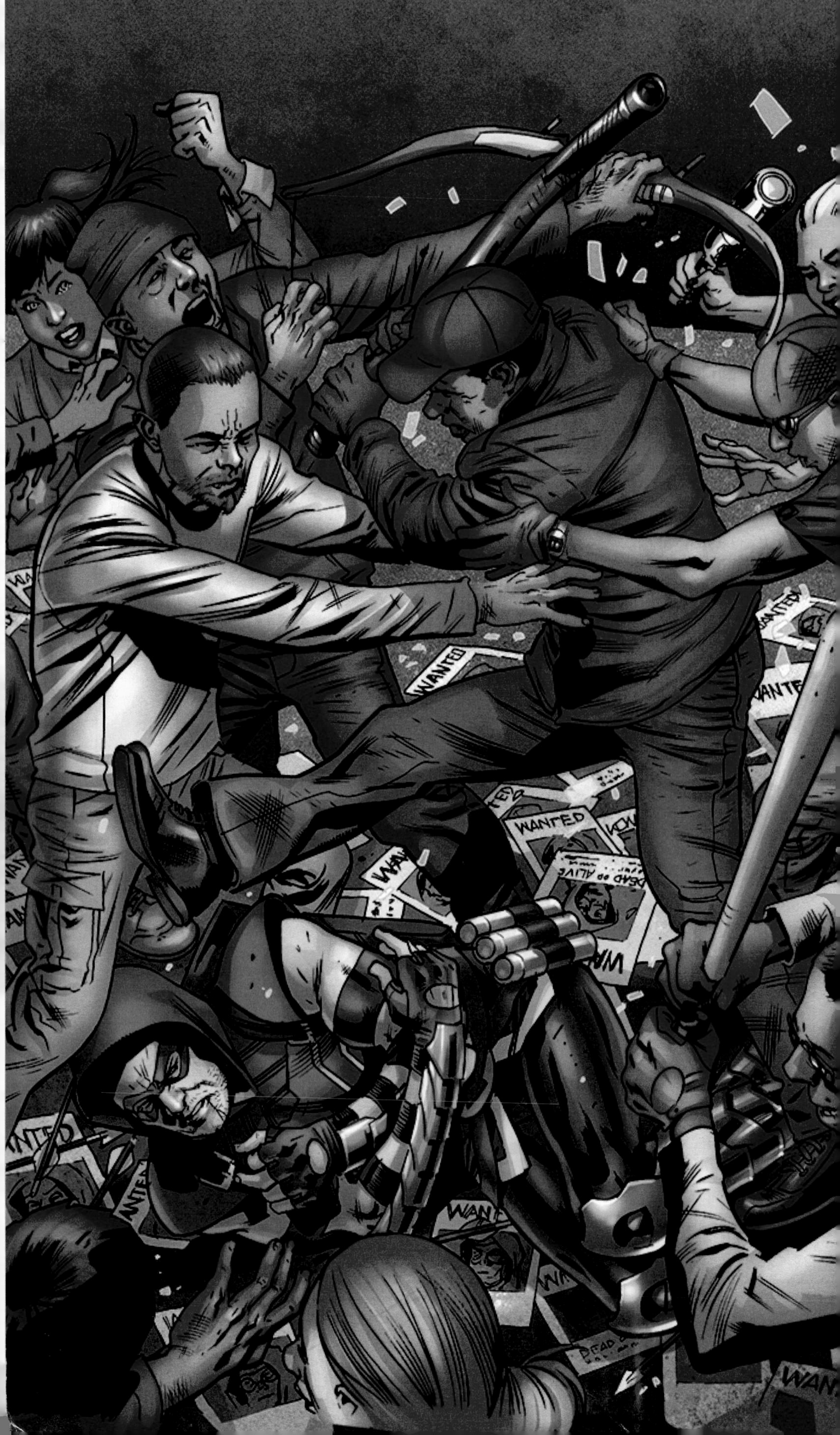
WANTED
WANTED
WANTED

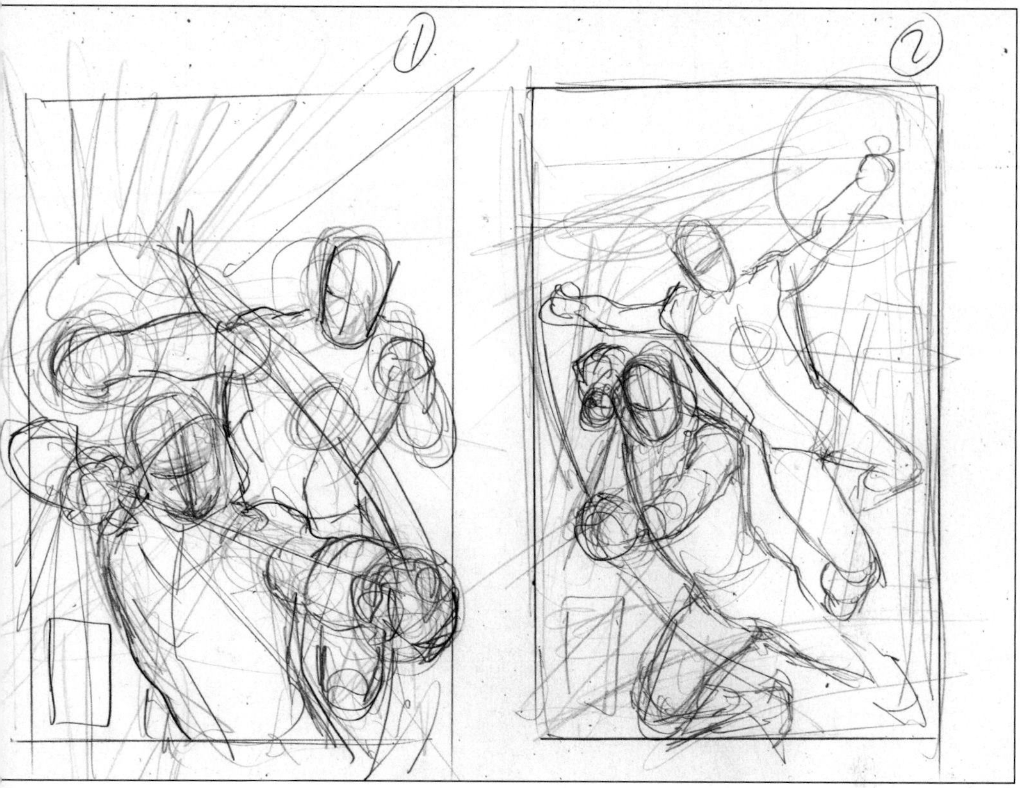
1
2

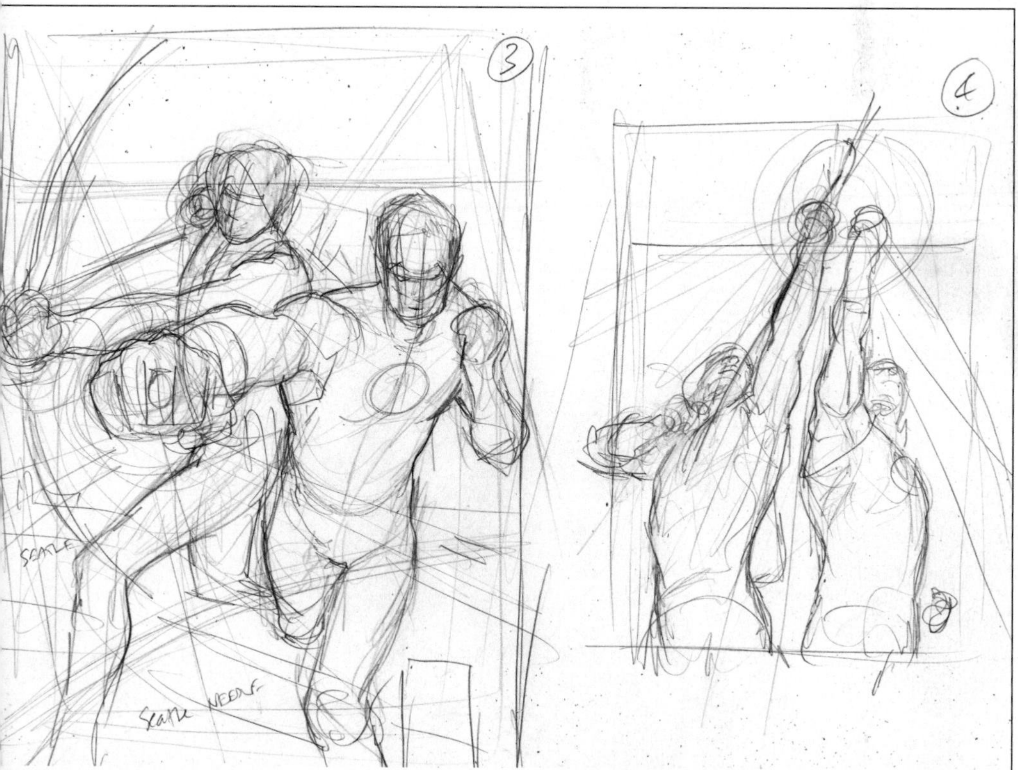
3
4

5

6
Some background shit.

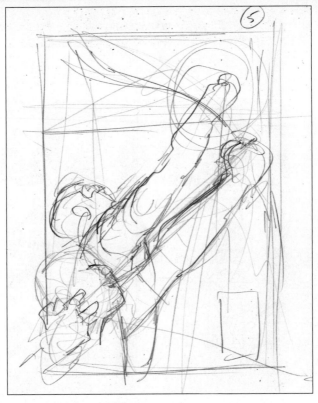

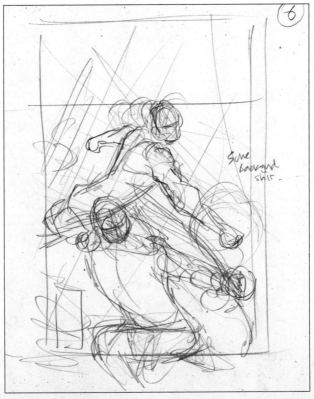

FROM THE WRITER OF *JUSTICE LEAGUE UNITED* AND *ANIMAL MAN*

GREEN ARROW
VOLUME 4: THE KILL MACHINE

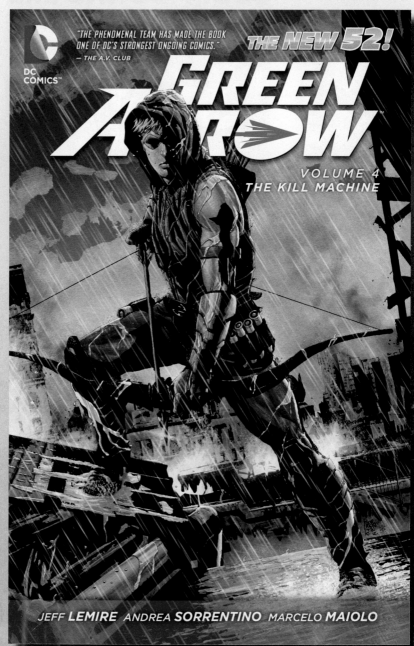

N ARROW VOL. 1:
MIDAS TOUCH

EITH GIFFEN, DAN
ENS, J.T. KRUL, and
EORGE PÉREZ

N ARROW VOL. 2:
RIPLE THREAT

NOCENTI HARVEY TOLIBAO

ANN NOCENTI and
RVEY TOLIBAO

ARROW VOL. 3:
HARROW

NOCENTI FREDDIE WILLIAMS II

ANN NOCENTI and
DIE WILLIAMS III

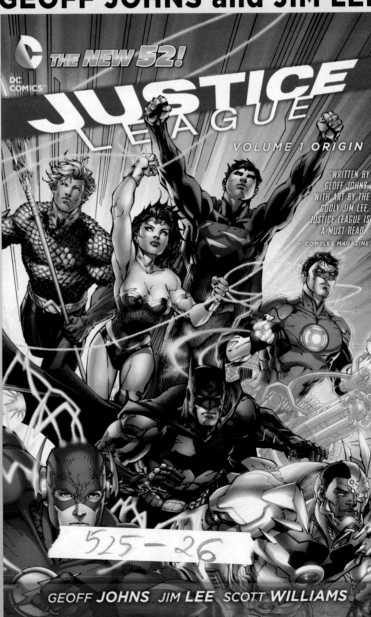